*Building credibility,
the foundation for
fundraising*

FUNDRAISING CLOSE TO HOME|1

Building credibility, the foundation for fundraising

Elizabeth Westman Wilson

KIT PUBLISHERS
ITDG PUBLISHING

Royal Tropical Institute
KIT Publishers
PO Box 95001, 1090 HA Amsterdam
The Netherlands
Telephone: 31 20 5688272
Telefax: 31 20 5688286
E-mail: publishers@kit.nl
Web site: www.kit.nl

The Royal Tropical Institute is committed to the development of ways to increase the real participation of farmers and other local stakeholders in rural development, and to increase the potential for governments, donors and the broad variety of other "development workers" to make a meaningful contribution.

ITDG Publishing
103–105 Southampton Row
London WC1B 4HL, U.K.
Telephone: 44 20 7436 9761
Telefax: 44 20 7436 2013
E-mail: itpubs@itpubs.org.uk
Web site: www.itdgpublishing.org.ku

ITDG Publishing is the publishing arm of the Intermediate Technology Development Group. Its mission is to build the skills and capacity of people in developing countries through the dissemination of information in all forms, enabling them to improve the quality of their lives and that of future generations.

© Elizabeth Wilson and KIT Publishers 2001
Design: Willem Hart Art & Design Inc., Toronto, Ontario, Canada
DTP: C&B creation, Zwolle, The Netherlands
Illustrations: Willem Hart, Chronicle of Philanthropy (cartoons, with permission), Gerard Vroon (permission KIT Publishers), Philip Street
Printing: Giethoorn Ten Brink, Meppel, The Netherlands
ISBN: 90-6832-132-3 (KIT Publishers)
ISBN: 1-85339-533-1 (ITDG Publishing)
NUGI: 686

Fundraising close to home
Book 1: **Building credibility, the foundation for fundraising**
Credibility is an essential component of successful fundraising. Organizations can learn to build on existing strengths and increase their appeal to potential donors. Staff, boards of directors, and volunteers too play important roles in building a widely respected organization. Specific steps to achieve a credible long-range plan and an easy to understand financial plan are described in detail.

Book 2: **Building structures and skills for fundraising**
Part one paves the way for fundraising campaigns, including the role of the leader, the board, volunteers, overcoming fear of fundraising, and building strategic alliances. Part two outlines the practical essentials of effective communications programs: how to make the spoken word, printed materials, media coverage, audiovisual materials, public relations events, and the Internet work for you.

Book 3: **Building fundraising programs to attract community support**
Fundraising events, income-generating businesses, donation boxes, mail and telephone campaigns, electronic fundraising, applying for local grants, and many other approaches can be used to attract support from the community. Planning effective programs is emphasized, with a special focus on techniques for face-to-face appeals and ways to engage the business community.

Please send your comments and any suggestions you have for other users to Elizabeth Wilson at KIT Publishers (address above).

Contents

Introduction-Raising the money you need when you need it   *VII*

1 Getting started in fundraising   *1*

2 The importance of credibility   *9*

3 Building credibility   *17*

4 Rating yourself: nine sources of strength   *34*

5 Rating yourself: eighteen areas to strengthen   *39*

6 Rating yourself: asking others   *50*

7 The board of directors   *63*

8 The value of volunteers   *74*

9 Building credibility by finding allies   *88*

10 Building strategic alliances   *97*

11 Writing a long-range plan   *110*

12 Writing a plan: an example   *119*

13 Financial credibility   *133*

Suggested reading and Web sites   *163*

List of Topics   *170*

Acknowledgements   *180*

About the author   *182*

Introduction
Raising the money you need when you need it

This series of books is for leaders of organizations who want to increase their financial independence at a time when grants from foreign agencies are shifting or shrinking. They want to raise funds from people and organizations in their own communities, as well as from overseas. They want to work locally to raise a portion of the money they need, at the lowest possible cost. To get all that they must build a varied, sustained, local fundraising program.

Organizations also want to show northern donors that they have the support and good will of their own people. They want to see themselves as more than the recipients of grants from the North. They want to see themselves as enterprises able to generate their own funds. They are trying to undo a generation or more of dependency. (Villagers in Uganda, who survived on their own resources for centuries, recently complained to a local organization that they are handicapped because they "don't have their own NGO" looking after their development.) The process will take time. Foreign grants will be essential for a long time, but it will take more effort to obtain them. They will still be available, however, at least for agencies that show they serve poor people's needs effectively and can also show that they have their own community's support.

Not many development NGOs are doing systematic fundraising. We don't have a tradition of philanthropy. Family giving has not translated into philanthropy. Traditional funding is drying up. And donor money is tied to varying degrees.

Right now we have two sources of money that are not the traditional sources. One is the marketplace. It is reliable. And there is fundraising. If you do it well, it can be reliable.

HORACIO "BOY" MORALES, PHILIPPINE RURAL RECONSTRUCTION MOVEMENT

Too many organizations, too little money
Against this background, development organizations are being forced to take a hard, honest look at what they are doing and how they do it. They are looking at how they relate to other organizations and to potential funders. They are asking themselves how they will meet their country's needs as foreign aid decreases.

These organizations have the same goal – to improve the community, especially the lives of its poorest members. They may be working in social welfare – perhaps in health care or women's rights. They may be battling unemployment or working for economic development. They may be involved in rural or urban improvement, or in preserving and improving the physical or cultural environment. They may also be becoming deeply involved in research, public education, and advocacy.

Because of the growth in needs and the explosive growth in the number of voluntary agencies, there will not be enough money to go around. Voluntary organizations will be forced to ask for more than cash. They will need in-kind donations and other kinds of contributions if they are going to stay in business. They may also have to start businesses and charge fees to support their core services. This will be true for agencies that have depended for their growth on foreign aid. It will also be true for grassroots groups that rely on local donors to sustain them, either totally or as the base on which to build elsewhere. Even so, some kinds of organizations – social service agencies, especially – will never be able to pay their own way completely, though local fundraising and entrepreneurship will bring a measure of independence. They will depend on foreign aid until the day comes when their national governments agree to support the work they are doing.

I am not suggesting that local fundraising replace foreign aid, but that organizations attempt to find at least a small portion of their budget from local donors. Gradually, dependence on foreign aid can be reduced.

This series does not tell everything there is to know about fundraising. It is mostly about getting ready to raise funds, with some information about actual techniques. No books by themselves can train fundraisers to be successful. They can only suggest how good fundraisers think and the questions they ask. Many of the words in these books will be questions for staff and volunteers to ask about their organization's specific conditions and plans. Knowing *why* you want to raise money, what purpose it will serve, is as important as knowing how to raise it.

In the future, organizations will thrive financially only if they know themselves, if they plan carefully both for their program and for their fundraising, if they are credible to the community they serve, if they are governed and managed effectively, if they are financially responsible, and if they communicate well. These books concentrate on those activities. They talk about *how* more than about *why* and *what for*.

A successful fundraising program is well managed; it gathers support from many different people and groups; it becomes stronger over a number of years. These books present the components of that kind of program. They are designed to help organizations that want to go beyond their existing, often traditional, small-scale fundraising practices, which should be respected and continued, and begin serious fundraising with groups and individuals to whom they may never have appealed before. The books will also help mature organizations whose leaders recognize that the fundraising climate changes constantly, who know their regular activities need a boost, and who are looking for new ways to finance their work.

There is no one way to fundraise. Clever, original ways are being tried all over the world. An Indian organization gives families small clay banks to hold the coins they will donate. Big NGOs in Ethiopia are raising money through telethons; these give people the chance to pledge donations by phone during special, promotional television programs. Hungarians can ensure that some of the income tax they pay goes to their favourite charity. An NGO in Thailand gathers paper to sell for recycling.

An organization conducting local fundraising programs may be anywhere – in Africa, Asia, Latin America, the Pacific, Central and Eastern Europe, or the states of the former Soviet Union. It may be called a voluntary organization, an intermediary organization, a civil society organization, a non-governmental organization, or a private voluntary organization. It could be called a project, as in India, a grassroots organization, a community-based organization, a primary organization, or a people's, peasant, or rural organization. In a few countries grassroots organizations are called NGOs. In other countries, the two names mean quite different things: NGOs are generally intermediary organizations with no community base and grassroots organizations have only a community base. All of these are civil society organizations, a loose term that can cover almost any private, non-profit organization, good or bad.

I have used the general term "organization" more than any other, often attaching the word "voluntary." Such an organization is typically governed by unpaid volunteers – usually a board of directors – and often depends on volunteers for help with fundraising and other activities. It does not mean the organization has no paid staff and depends entirely on volunteers, though that may be the case.

Even the word "fundraising," the subject of this series, can be confusing. To some people it may have one meaning only – asking people for donations. But it can be much broader. Bringing in the money (or people or equipment or training) that you need can also be called "resource mobilization," "income generation," and "achieving financial independence." I use the word "fundraising" in these books. That word seems to be winning out over "philanthropy," a more American usage. Fifty-four per cent of people surveyed by the Mexican Center for Philanthropy did not know in 1995 what that term meant. (Even many Americans think it has to do with stamp collecting, which is "philately.") Philanthropy is really the better word, however, because it describes what a donor thinks and does. The word means "love of humanity" or "practical benevolence." Quite correctly, it puts the donor and the donor's action, not the organization and its needs, at the centre of fundraising.

In *Community participation and financial sustainability*, James Taylor and his co-authors describe the stages of growth of voluntary organizations. Most start off as purely voluntary. One person or a group of people sees a deep social need – protection of civil rights, the cleaning of a polluted river; or a problem – perhaps a crop failure – that demands immediate relief. They use whatever resources they can gather to get the job done. To pay for what they do, they raise a modest amount of money locally. Because the needs are small and met locally, expenses are tightly controlled, and the work is usually effective and sustainable. The workers, who may be volunteers, rely mostly on low-key, indigenous fundraising techniques. These are successful because they are appropriate and well tested, and therefore less risky. Grassroots organizations can be remarkably effective – and enduring. As the head of an NGO coalition in the Philippines said, "People's organizations have a better chance to survive than NGOs. They can do garbage collection, or health care or child care." Sam Ugochukwu, of Ugo Farm and Allied Consultancy in Imo State in Nigeria, says, "Despite the contributions of NGOs and government in funding developmental projects, their impact is little felt, as some areas are wholly neglected in terms of funding. It can be said that rural fundraising is made up of the people themselves, not the government and NGOs. The rural populace raises about 70 per cent of the funds while 20 per cent comes from the government and 10 per cent from the NGOs."

At the second stage, the demands of the activities begin to outstrip the capacities of the volunteers to sustain them. Costs rise. The original volunteers cannot keep up with the needs. Someone is needed full-time. That person starts getting a salary, needs transportation. Whereas, in the first phase, the challenge was to support the volunteer effort, finding the money to keep going now becomes the challenge. Fundraising must go beyond the little events and collections that sustained the organization in the past. Intensified, broader, local fundraising at this stage may produce some revenue because the organization is still close and credible to its community. It will allow the organization to have a small measure of independence. But generally the effort goes elsewhere. Organizations at this stage start looking for foreign donors, perhaps through intermediary groups. Growth is still relatively easy, if not sustainable.

In the third phase, the burden of administration increases because the programs require it. The whole organization becomes more complex and more expensive. It works hard to bring in as much foreign aid as possible and starts approaching local corporations and individuals.

Finally, in the fourth phase, the organization becomes nationally known. It increases its revenue from foreign aid, moves closer to the government, and/or starts significant businesses and high profile, large-scale fundraising.

Some of the fundraising techniques in these books will be useful to grassroots movements. All the techniques here will be useful to organizations at the later stages of development.

Finding new money

For voluntary organizations, the need for new money will mean new ways of operating. There are many paths to explore.

Some organizations sell their services and products for fees. Some arrange to receive in-kind contributions – office space or technical help, for example. Others operate shops and other enterprises that help pay general operating expenses and return a profit that can be used to help the community. Some put a value on the free time they receive from volunteers and ask donor agencies to match that value in money.

More and more, organizations will raise money locally from individuals, local foundations, businesses. As they do now, many will approach intermediary groups who have found local sources. Together with international donors, some voluntary organizations are forming new kinds of umbrella associations and community foundations that will allocate aid money to voluntary organizations in their country. Other associations bring voluntary agencies together to seek funds jointly. Many organizations are finding new ways to cover their general operating expenses (what accountants call "overhead"). One way is to share office expenses with one or more similar organizations. Another is to persuade more donor agencies to recognize it is not enough to give financial support to projects – that help is needed as well to pay the costs of staff, rent, equipment, and other office expenses. Some are persuading donors to give them the training to develop new ways of raising money and, equally important, to give endowments, in one form or another, to sustain them until the new sources of funds are established.

The desire for financial independence can create problems and unconscious conflicts. Most northern funders have no product. They supervise work elsewhere, raise money, advise, record, report, and encourage. But it is their southern "partners" who do the work. Most northern organizations are managed by people with some development experience overseas, but few of their managers have any communications or fundraising training or experience. Consciously or unconsciously, the leaders of these organizations want to hold on to power. They could help their southern "partners" become self-sufficient by giving training when it is asked for. If they let go, however, they would have to find a new reason to exist. "The funding community needs us and we need poor people," says Zandisile Kanisa of the Surplus People Project in South Africa, "If someone says they can be independent, it is threatening." Northern organizations could also open northern doors. Instead, they are often seen by their southern colleagues as blocking access to northern funds. "This is our territory. You can't look for money here," they say.

Only a few aid donors so far are considering "exit strategies," that is, giving training and/or some other form of on-going assistance to ease the transition to self-financing.

Does the small agency have a future?

Not long ago, there was little organized, professionally-conducted fundraising though there has, of course, always been fundraising for local needs. Then big organizations such as universities, which have international connections and relatively large resources, launched regular programs to raise money. Major northern development agencies followed, setting up southern branches. Now southern voluntary organizations are fundraising themselves. If they have not already, they will soon face competition from other organizations in their country. In a few years, almost every voluntary organization will be fundraising and staff members will become more professional. They will also become more mobile, moving from smaller to larger agencies.

Competition will come from abroad as well as from home. Huge international agencies such as the Red Cross and UNICEF are aggressively raising funds all over the world. In Brazil, UNICEF organized a television program in which local organizations described what UNICEF support had meant to them; 900,000 people telephoned pledges in response. In Argentina, Greenpeace ran a sophisticated telephone campaign, in which anyone who called a certain number automatically had a sum of money added to their phone bill. All the money went to Greenpeace's international work to conserve wildlife. Greenpeace was also able to add the names and addresses of 50,000 callers to its list of people to ask for donations again. The money raised in such large-scale campaigns may be spent anywhere, not necessarily in the country where it was given.

The competition will only increase unless southern organizations work together even more than they are doing now. International development agencies in the North have so far shown little interest in forming alliances for programs or for fundraising, and the competition among them for support has intensified. Organizations in the South may prove to be wiser.

It is easy to foresee a day when many countries may have only a few dozen big voluntary organizations and many small agencies that have found a special niche, which allows them to garner modest support. This is happening in Canada. If the small agencies do not work together, they may die. No one may have set this out as a desirable goal. It may just happen.

Meeting the competition

To raise money efficiently, organizations need to be large enough to have the time and money to reach international NGOs, corporations, and foundations. Even if those bodies have local offices in the country where the money is needed, it takes a great deal of time to research their interests and prepare the necessary presentations. If the approach must be made to a distant office, it takes even more effort. It will take time and money for voluntary organizations to form coalitions and partnerships to approach donors, but the need for such an investment seems compelling. Donors pay more attention to organizations that have come together and created a coordinated plan to deal with a need such as better irrigation or preventing HIV/AIDS. Such groups of organizations can have a much greater reach and impact than any individual organization. But working together requires each organization to give up some of its individual identity, and few agencies anywhere seem to be prepared to do that. The good news is that many northern donor agencies understand the need for changes in development support. Some are making large investments in showing that new types of fundraising will work in the South. The techniques may first be tried by large agencies, but, once they have proved successful, many can then be adopted by smaller organizations. International agencies are also offering professional training to local fundraisers. But there is no quick answer. Esperanza Simon, a professor of business in the Philippines, says, "Fundraising is new in the Philippines. People thought money would come easily just by attending a workshop. It is not that way."

While the competition is likely to be fierce and the ground is relatively unbroken, the need and opportunities for fundraising in the South are great.

Where will the money come from?

No matter where you are and what you are doing, your major sources of income will likely be one or more of:

- aid from agencies that have their head offices outside your country

- money from local people and organizations who support your goals
- offerings directed to you from local religious organizations
- grants from your national or local government
- membership fees
- traditional fundraising activities such as festivals, auctions, etc.
- in-kind donations

Other money may come from:
- consulting fees
- selling services
- commercial activities
- income from cash balances and investments
- other activities

However, not every source of money is open to everyone who needs it. Nor is every technique suitable to every agency. You will want to select what looks useful for your own organization and fits within your culture.

First steps

This is the first book in a series of three. The others are listed below. This one suggests the steps to take before asking anyone for more than an opinion. It differs from many fundraising texts because it looks in detail at the background against which successful fundraising happens. It also deals with achieving credibility, the single biggest challenge development organizations everywhere have told me they face. Without credibility, long-term fundraising will not happen.

Do we know what government, business and society think of our sector? Do we want to work with business or against it? We need to know who we are.

MANUEL ARANGO, FOUNDER, MEXICAN CENTER FOR PHILANTHROPY

The benefits of successful fundraising are more than money in the bank. In asking for money, you will be telling a lot of people about the needs of your community and how your organization is meeting those needs. That good publicity will result in new donations, offers of volunteer time, and new friends for your organization.

Here are some of the questions we will look at in this first book.
- What characteristics does your organization have in common with thousands of other voluntary organizations around the world? What does that mean for your planning? How do these characteristics help or hurt fundraising? Our actions are influenced by beliefs we may not even know we have.
- What do people think of your organization? What are you doing well? Do people value your services? Do they need your services enough to pay for them? Learning what concerns people, both inside and outside your organization, will help you plan the future of the organization.
- What role does your board see for itself? Is the board giving leadership? How can you arrange for the volunteer help you need? Do the staff support your goals? (Fundraising may create difficulties and tensions in an organization. It is best to be aware of them early on.)
- How can you strengthen your organization by forming alliances with other organizations?

The answers to these and other basic questions will give you the information you need to:

- Write a long-term plan. The plan will state your goals, your strategies, and the programs you want to conduct to reach those goals. It will make clear what you need money for. You will have the information to persuade potential donors. "Fundraising must reinforce strategy, not lead it," Jon Bennett and Sara Gibbs say in *NGO funding strategies*.
- Build a credible budget for current and future operations. This budget will help your organization manage its day-to-day activities, attract support, ensure that planning is careful.
- Ensure that governance of the organization includes responsibility for fundraising. Carefully chosen board members and other volunteers will be able to meet potential donors on an equal footing.
- Increase credibility by having a budget that will tell you how much money you need to operate the organization and all its programs, good financial records, and clear accountability. You will be able to show donors why you need the sums of money you are seeking.

Book 2, *Building structures and skills for fundraising*, covers:
- studying the ground before the campaign
- setting up the campaign headquarters
- looking at what other organizations are doing
- the role of the manager in fundraising
- the role of the board in fundraising
- reinforcing the board
- conquering fear of fundraising
- the role of volunteers in fundraising
- establishing your credibility with strong, positive communications programs to create a climate where raising money will be possible

Book 3, *Building fundraising programs to attract community support*, examines ways to diversify your funding on the path to becoming financially self-sufficient. Most of these activities will be essential to your fundraising success in the future. Subjects to be covered will include:
- the environment of giving
- setting out the reasons donors should support your organization
- planning and conducting fundraising projects
- raising money from individuals through direct mail and face-to-face
- obtaining major personal donations
- organizing events
- starting business activities
- securing the support of businesses
- using the Internet for fundraising
- arranging professional help
- applying for grants
- sustainability and endowments
- evaluating fundraising programs
- planning for the future

A short list of useful books and web sites is given at the end of each book.

An example of what can be done

When I first met Amin Fahim in 1997, he asked me a question. "How do I raise money for something that can never be self-sustaining?" Amin Fahim is the president of the Association of Upper Egypt for Education and Development. Upper Egypt is in the southern part of the country. In 1966, he gave up law and became a full-time volunteer for the Association. One year later, he became president. He is doing his best to answer his own question by building a diverse portfolio of fundraising activities.

Seventy centres of the Association work in health, youth leadership, the advancement of women, literacy, cultural development, and vocational training. To support these activities, the centres run income generating projects. The Association also owns and runs 37 free primary schools that serve 11,200 children, both Moslem and Christian, from very poor families. Much of the Association's work involves children outside school. They may fill in puddles, burn garbage, and perform plays about health concerns for the whole village. Amin Fahim says, "Children can transform a village. The children with more can give knowledge to the children with less. They make sure people take their babies for vaccinations. After a one-day course in nutrition, the children told their mothers what they learned. Each child gained an average of three kilograms in three months."

Mr. Fahim says he is gradually realizing that, when people in his organization talk to potential donors, they are transmitting not a project but a message. He told me:

Very often, to get more money for their projects, NGOs give a picture of the beneficiaries that is aimed at provoking pity. The Association of Upper Egypt for Education and Development refuses to do this. It has discovered day after day the human richness of poor people, their dignity, their generosity, their sense of humour. If they live in poor conditions, it is because of bad circumstances and injustice and we want to help them get out of it. This is the image and message the Association wants to communicate. We are ambassadors of people with dignity. These people want to be respected but they have nothing but their standing up. We try to show the reality of the dignity of poor people and how people can evolve.

We have tried local fundraising. We started by asking for money from the shops and offices around our office. Ninety per cent are in the car parts business. They did not give. People will give for mosques or churches – these are tickets to heaven – or to a beggar or a person in trouble. The public is not yet educated to give money for building a human being.

Our main source locally is people we identify. In 1941 a group of enthusiastic volunteers was formed. It started with the friends and family of the founders. Now we have 120 volunteers. The young ones are attractive to people but they are not good for fundraising except for short assignments of, say, one week. For Rotary Clubs or the Lions Clubs, we use older volunteers. Every year the number of volunteers, as well as donors, is growing. The name of the donor and the sums paid are filed, together with the name of the volunteer who approached each donor.

A great number of our volunteers have been helping for a number of years

The public is not yet educated to give money for building a human being.

AMIN FAHIM,
PRESIDENT,
ASSOCIATION OF
UPPER EGYPT FOR
EDUCATION AND
DEVELOPMENT

and have reached a certain age. At the same time, there is a drawback to this type of volunteer: most of their donors come from personal contacts – family and friends. When those volunteers stop helping, through death or departure, it is very difficult to pick up their list. We are trying more and more to attract young volunteers. The best among them are those who have been educated in religious schools. They can be mobilized. The qualities we are looking for are openness, good relations with all kinds of people, dynamism, and initiative.

We talk to children in Catholic schools. We go to collect money, and also to let these children discover the world of the poor, arouse their sense of solidarity and motivate them. We give talks or project slides; they ask questions. Very often the children renounce something they want to buy, or offer some possession. We collect from 56 schools, which can be as much as 900 kilometres away. We give a letter to each child to take home. It is addressed to the parents and contains a little pamphlet for them. Each letter also has a little joke or a small game for the children. We also send young people to visit our schools. They come back and tell their classmates.

Local volunteers, mostly teachers in our schools, also collect money for our schools. They are doing heroic work, going from house to house in their village or in a nearby town, adding one small amount of money to another small amount. One retired teacher is working on collection as if it were her everyday job.

The collections in the churches started in 1941 when the first group of volunteers was formed. We get permission from the parishes to come one Sunday every year to all the masses. That is usually during Lent, so parishioners can express solidarity with the poor at that time of year. We collect from 49 churches in Cairo and Alexandria. In about 15 of these churches, someone from the Association talks during the mass. Otherwise, the priest himself says a word.

It is possible to have difficult donors. Some wealthy people are just not willing to give. We know that, when we visit businesses, we may have to go back three or four times to a possible donor. After the first donation, we send a letter the next year to the business. We may have to visits or telephone some of them before we receive a donation. Volunteers help with that.

Recently, we are using fax to try to reach businesspeople who are unknown to us, but whose names are listed in a business directory. So far, it has not brought much result, as the Association is not much known to businesses. We are pursuing this campaign with the secretaries in the businesses.

Each donor has special requirements. Donors want to know what is done with the money. Or they ask if you have a video. I am not a supermarket. But we will have a video in 1999.

Locally, the Association mobilizes public interest through a famous display of art embroidery. In the centre of Akhmim, women have learnt to produce fine embroidery and weaving, in Coptic and Islamic motifs. These works are exhibited and sold at a yearly exhibition in Cairo, along with the woodwork products of young men in another of our centres, Hagaza. The exhibits have been very successful. All the proceeds of the sale go to those who have worked. The Association earns nothing from it. On the contrary, it pays the fees of the exhibit. But it gains a lot of moral support, public relations, and publicity.

The Association raises some 88 per cent of its budget from overseas, from debt swaps and from overseas agencies operating in Egypt such as embassies. Its major funding is from agencies in Germany. Every three years we have to send an application asking for renewal of the grant. There is no guarantee of everlasting support. Money also comes from our own organizations in Belgium, Switzerland, France, Canada, and the United States. They do not ask for money from businesses. These overseas groups give access to government agencies and to people who can help the Association. They exist primarily to act as relay stations for information.

Twenty-eight years ago, on my initiative, a group of Egyptians in Montreal set up a registered Canadian corporation that can give official tax receipts for donations. The members wanted a link to Egypt by giving concrete help. They have been successful in getting grants for us from the Canadian government (CIDA). We visit once a year when there is a ball held. The representative also gives media interviews, which the Montreal group arranges.

The Belgian group was started by an Egyptian emigrant and his Belgian wife in a small village. They wrote wanting to help Egypt. He enlisted the local lawyer and the local baker. After eight years, the group was registered with the government. It puts on displays and expositions at centres for women, among other activities. Its 150 members are all Belgian. In France, the members are all French people who visited Egypt and wanted to help. In the United States, it was one Egyptian emigrant who started the association.

These partner associations each find a way to collect money that suits the local culture. They address their members and friends through a pamphlet or a bulletin, taking as a priority one of our projects. Besides asking for individual donations, each of the groups organizes one event or more each year to recruit new donors. For example, the collection last year in Paris was through a concert played by an internationally known pianist. This year, it will be an exhibition of arts and crafts from two of our centres. In Canada, there is an annual ball."

I don't rely on any foreign donors to increase their donations. It is urgent to find new ways to raise big, big money. I must find new sources. Sometimes we don't know if we can pay the salaries of our 1,400 staff members.

AMIN FAHIM

These three books are partially financed by *The Chronicle of Philanthropy*, Washington DC, USA. Corbin Gwaltney and Malcolm Scully deserve special thanks.

Many people are quoted in this series. Many others contributed ideas and information. I hope I have done them all justice. I am grateful for the support given to me by the Ford Foundation and by dozens of organizations and individuals who are listed at the end of this book and others whom I may have inadvertently omitted. Many thanks to them all.

I thank the cartoonists who gave permission to use their cartoons originally published in *The Chronicle of Philanthropy*.

Ian Montagnes gave excellent editorial comment and advice throughout the writing of these books. Willem Hart brought his usual commitment and imagination to the designof the series. My thanks to both of them.

Elizabeth W. Wilson
Port Hope, Canada
March, 2001

1 Getting started in fundraising

Many people tell me that people will give to family and religion but not to secular causes. Giving to family is simple to understand. Most of us cannot ignore family needs. People will also give to support or build mosques or churches – these are tickets to heaven. All major world religions proclaim the value of contributing to helping others. Buddhism in Thailand is a good example. Travelling monks count on being given food every day. Buddhist temples count on generous donations. But some Thais complain that too much goes to temples, when there are immediate social needs. In Thailand, Professor Amara Pongsapich said, "We are attempting to shift donations from temples to social services. We are trying to say, 'No more temples. Instead, give to a hospital or build a hospital in a rural area.'"

Development organizations that are dependent on foreign funding will disappear. Organizations must be anchored in the grassroots. They must have a solid community base.

JALAL ABDEL-LATIF, INTER-AFRICA GROUP, ETHIOPIA

Look not for the behavior of having, but the behavior of giving.

KIM KLEIN, CONSULTANT, UNITED STATES

Giving as a habit
Why do so many people give to religious institutions and not to secular, voluntary organizations? Not entirely from conviction, many people believe, but because they have been asked to do so frequently, regularly, and for generations. They have been trained in the habit of giving. This is true all over the world. In the United States and Canada more than half of all known charitable giving is to religious organizations. The average donation is twice the size of donations to non-religious organizations. There is another factor. Since in these two countries most people describe themselves as religious or spiritual, it is likely that much of their secular giving is also motivated by religious or spiritual beliefs.

The percentage of secular giving in developing countries is lower than in the North, no doubt. But that may only be because secular organizations have not been asking for support as long or as continuously as religious organizations. To increase giving to secular causes is not denying faith, only adding a new habit.

Here is the first door to success: build the habit of giving to secular causes. You will not change your culture all alone but when you, and hundreds of other organizations, begin intensive local fundraising, new habits of giving will gradually develop. People have to be asked to give regularly before they get into the habit.

To encourage this change, it is necessary to appeal to a sense of social responsibility. One way to do this is to find ways to relate your work to religion. Many voluntary organizations don't want to appear to be related to religion. But why not? Throughout history, churches have dispensed offerings to the needy. Why can't people of all religions be asked to practise their belief by supporting community needs through secular means?

Where to start looking

To raise the money they need, voluntary organizations will have to appeal to everyone in their own communities. The obvious primary target is the middle class. Historically, most northern agencies started with that kind of support. This is a good place to start fundraising, but the job may prove more difficult than expected. While the middle class is growing in many countries of the South, in most it is still relatively small, perhaps 15 per cent of the population. That is not negligible. In India, it is said that the middle class is almost as large as the whole population of the United States, about 250 million. Yet there are still not enough people with enough money to support community agencies, which are growing faster than the middle class as the need for them increases.

Fundraising is easier when you are already well connected. Many voluntary organizations are made up of members of the middle class. Many community-based organizations are controlled by middle class people. But many other middle class people may feel little responsibility for their community. They may think, perhaps, that they have delegated their social responsibilities to their government, and to their religion. They may prefer to spend their money on themselves, on their families, or their religious institutions. They may satisfy their sense of social responsibility by meeting a one-time, immediate need – a person begging, or the effects of an earthquake or bad storm. Too often, those who do have a social conscience and money to give don't know how or where best to send donations, where they will do the most good.

In most countries, few voluntary organizations are well known and established. Many are suspect. Their credibility may be questioned because they are new and have no track record of success. They may be unable to demonstrate community support. They may appear to have come out of nowhere; possibly they were formed, even by government, only to funnel foreign aid or government money to powerful interests, be they business people, politicians, or government people themselves. Some so-called voluntary organizations conduct only token social programs to mask their efforts to undercut social reforms that would reduce the privileged positions of their sponsors. Sometimes people start "ego" or "briefcase" NGOs, ones they can control but that have no legitimacy.

Reaching the middle class will take a planned effort. The people you will ask for money may not be making donations or making investments in your kind of organization each year in a deliberate, organized way. And your organization may not have been raising money in a deliberate, organized way. But now you are thinking about new ways of becoming self-sustaining. Now you want many more people to care about your organization and to give you money or some other form of support. In setting up your local program, you will not be begging, you will be asking donors to turn their occasional charity, however small, into a regular investment in their community.

Develop many sources of support
It is a serious mistake to think support can come only from the middle or upper class. You may get money from rich people but unless you can meet them face-to-face they are not your most likely donors. During your first steps towards independence, you are more likely to find support, surprising as it may seem, from people who are less well off. In my own country, in many years the poorest province, with 40 per cent unemployment in some places, reported the highest level of giving per person to charities. Look first to the people you know, whatever their class or their resources. It will always be harder to raise money from strangers. Recognizing that fact is the second door to success.

The best way to encourage local giving is to ask people to give. Amelia Jones of the Community Chest in Cape Town, South Africa quotes an old saying, "If my purse is always open, there will always be money in it." Not everyone feels that way, of course. Gavin Andersson, of The Development Resource Centre in South Africa, puts it another way: "Fundraising success will come when people realize you have to give something to get something. People think if they are poor and give nothing, then they will get. They have the classic idea that development starts with dollars from outside."

"If my purse is always open, there will always be money in it."

Nowadays, financial security for an organization like yours means more than just obtaining grants or donations, either cash or in-kind. It means having a number of different ways to raise money. Some may be traditional – sales of donated goods, for example. Others may be newer – providing professional advice for a fee for services to other voluntary agencies, government, or private enterprise. It means working with others in joint appeals. It means learning to work with the new agencies that are forming to decide how international and local aid money will be used. It means using imagination, developing patience and persistence, investing time and money, and, above all, overcoming fear.

Fundraising is more than luck
In fundraising, you may be lucky once in a while but you can't count on luck to keep you going. The difference between occasional luck and sustained success is careful planning. Good planning is based on knowing what the trends are in your field, locally and internationally, and on detailed knowledge of your agency and its place in your community.

Planning is so important that it takes up much of this book. Many chapters in the two books that follow talk about planning specific communications and fundraising programs. There is also one chapter (Book 2, Chapter 7) as well as many references that refer to the fear of fundraising that gives people a pain in the stomach, an urge to run away, a desire to laugh nervously. This malady strikes many people when they are asked to ask other people for money or other kinds of support. It can be alleviated with planning, training, honesty, and good humour.

Start carefully
It may be tempting to decide one afternoon to charge fees for your services or to ask a local corporation for money – the next day. Many books on fundraising let you think that is the way to start. "Just ask," they say. They suggest you start your fundraising program by finding a person who will persuade people to give money, or collect fees for services, or build a retail business. They urge you to get on immediately with the business of bringing in money. This may be necessary in a financial crisis to give some breathing room, but it is not the route to long-term growth. It would be wonderful if fundraising were that simple and easy. It is neither simple nor easy.

Specific fundraising techniques are like the leaves on top of a tree. Even when they look green, the tree may be poorly nourished. It is the soundness of the root system under the soil that really matters in the long run. Without that, the tree will not flourish. In fundraising, many organizations do not take the time to develop the root system. Some may simply not have the time. They need money now: they have no time for preliminaries. Because they did not need to build a community base when they could still rely on foreign funding, they could be out of business before they can establish the credibility, let alone the relationships needed for successful fundraising. "If the reality is that there is no time, organizations must face that they are out of control. It's too late," says Barry Smith of INTERFUND, South Africa: "It is important for an organization to understand that it should wind down because it is inevitable or logical. That is just as important as a decision to carry on. The recognition can take the pressure off. It can be a relief, a release from misery." The alternative is to start nourishing the root system now, before it is too late.

Get team support
Before you can attract new supporters you must be sure your current ones will support any new plans you have for fundraising. You may think your current supporters will automatically want to help with anything that will strengthen your organization. But you may be surprised. You will be suggesting change, and change makes people nervous. You will need to reassure them. The best way to do that is to have a clear vision of where you want the organization to go. You must also get everyone to share your enthusiasm for that vision and the changes needed to realize it.

To begin with, you will have to identify some key people in your organization who are willing to help make the changes you want to make, and gain their support. Eventually, you will want to inspire everyone involved. This will take time. Resistance will surely appear for, in one way or another, everyone will be affected. This is true whether you are going to look for corporate money or open a shop. Resistance may come from the board, especially if you want to make new demands on it. Or it could come from staff or volunteers you thought you could count on for support.

People will pretend they welcome change and challenge, but often they are deeply fearful. Will some people be given new responsibilities and authority? Will an alliance with three other agencies force us to change our program? Will our name disappear? What will happen to our reputation? Change is especially threatening if new people will be joining the organization. Will new people be given power – or salaries – that staff have not had up to now? Will some volunteers lose status because of the newcomers? It is also threatening if the way money is allocated within the organization is going to change. Will some programs get less money because more money will be spent on fundraising?

It is wise be cautious in proposing change. Just because you have been thinking about future programs and about new fundraising for months does not mean anyone else has. Selling your vision will always be at least twice as hard and take at least twice as long as you think it should. This means that, while you are doing the research and making plans, you must already be working to get everyone on your side. You want them to share your sense of urgency and to commit to making the plan succeed. An important part of building support is learning how others feel about your organization and its services. This process is covered in Chapter 6.

Time, patience, and some early successes may overcome much of the resistance you will meet. But some may remain no matter how much care you take to get everyone together. It can be destructive, especially since it may be hidden. So be on the lookout. If you must deal with it, try to be reassuring but don't let it put you off doing what you know is right.

Get people talking

Fortunately, there is another side to the story. Small agencies may not be out of luck if they start fundraising in a small way and have a long perspective. If you can get their attention and then their support, people will feel a special involvement and interest in your work that they will never feel for a large, impersonal organization. Once you can get regular support from even a small group of committed donors, you can feel some confidence of more financial support in the future. As you go on to ask more and more people for support of many different kinds, you will raise more money. You can get publicity too – if you want it. In many countries, publicity can mean unwanted scrutiny, and possibly interference, especially by the government. Be sure beforehand that you want publicity. It may be wiser to keep a lower public profile with an active, but less visible, communications program.

Let us assume for the moment that publicity would help your cause. Why? Because being in the media means being on people's agendas. People will talk together about what they hear on the radio, see on television, on posters and wall papers, or read in newspapers and magazines. Many people form their opinions as a result of these conversations. We listen to other people and decide what is good or bad, what we believe and what we suspect, who we will support and who we won't.

Many types of media may be used to make sure people are talking about your organization and its achievements. You may decide to start a newsletter, issue press releases, organize speaking engagements, or arrange an interview on the radio. Getting publicity in this way can take a lot of time that could have been spent in direct fundraising, but it is important for credibility. Credibility creates an environment in which you can ask for money with some chance of success.

People not only want to give to success, they want to be part of a success story. As people hear of your success, you will attract more volunteers, with more skills. Those volunteers can fill many roles in your organization. They can help extend your fundraising. They can help ask other people for money. They can add new strength to your board. They can assist the staff. They can keep records and write thank you letters and receipts for donations.

Success will follow success

People like to give to success: success builds on itself. The organizations that have the most success in raising money are the organizations that already have a reputation for conducting successful programs. And for raising money. Visible successes on both fronts are what donors want to see. People do not want to give to organizations that are teetering on the edge of collapse or staggering from one financial crisis to another. They want to be able to say to themselves: "I am confident that my money will be spent sensibly," or "I helped make something good happen."

Supporters, whether big or small, like to feel in good company. Farmers in a village want to know their neighbours are also contributing to buying a biogas plant. Before they buy tickets to a fundraising dinner, business people ask who else will be there.

Of course, this means small agencies like the one I was part of (the Developing Countries Farm Radio Network) have an uphill fight to establish themselves as credible and deserving. Prominent people were reluctant to lend their names to our cause or to join our board of directors. They hesitated to make big donations without knowing who else had done the same. We were worried that people would not even bother to open a letter from us because they did not recognize the name. UNICEF or Care or Oxfam get attention right away because people have known of those organizations for years. It was too expensive for us to try to attract international money. When we asked foundations for grants, they sent us information about their procedures, but often did not answer our later inquiries. We had to demonstrate our success before they took us seriously.

Establishing credibility is the hardest part of fundraising. It took many years for us to overcome even a few of the obstacles that confronted us.

Fundraising develops independence

Your financial goal should be a measure of self-sufficiency for your organization. Success in fundraising will mean having enough money from a variety of sources to conduct your programs without always worrying about the bills you have to pay.

Local fundraising will be one part of your funding. It will certainly not meet all your needs. In fact, it may play only a small part; in the first few years, it may produce 5 to 10 per cent of the budget. But, unlike most foreign funds, this money has no strings attached. It may be spent any way you want. As Paul Themba Nyathi of the Zimbabwe Project Trust says, "If we raise 15 per cent, we have 15 per cent leeway, 15 per cent autonomy to think what we want to do."

Having enough money means peace of mind, a sense of security. Nothing is harder on an organization's staff than financial insecurity. Leaders who have to spend most of their time trying to find the money to pay the bills cannot concentrate on programs. Pressure drains their energy and imagination. Programs suffer. Leaders get burned out. Staff members suffer too. They worry that, if their projects are reduced or cancelled, they may lose their jobs. They start to think small, making economies that often cost more in time than the money they save. They say things like:

> We can't afford to buy that book you need about preventing tuberculosis in your village. You will just have to try to borrow a copy or go to the library in the city.

Thinking small can mean lost opportunities.

> I know you would meet people who might support us but we just can't afford to send you to the conference next month.

The staff may become accustomed to working within a program budget that is too small. They may keep working even if it is reduced further. But what will be the result? A program that was not meeting the full needs of the community in the first place is cut still further. Staff continue to work at low wages. Their morale drops, and so does their pride in what they are doing. The ambitions of the organization shrink.

When I was executive director of an international development agency in Canada, our chairman boasted at four consecutive annual meetings that, once again, we had ended the year without a deficit. The staff thought his pride was misplaced. We believed he was missing the point. To us, breaking even was not a source of pride. It was a source of frustration. We knew that, to meet the actual need, our program should have been at least four times bigger. Instead of praising our financial management, we wished our chairman had been leading a fundraising campaign to enlarge the program. Then we would have felt truly proud.

Success in increasing financial resources means enjoying work during the day and sleeping well at night. A financially secure organization is able to chart its own course. It is not subject to every new priority (or reporting demand) of every major donor, especially its own government. It doesn't have to run after every grant it hears about, whether it is part of its mandate or not, just because it needs the money.

Straying from the mandate is a very real danger; it can creep up on you without being noticed. You may have a run of success at getting foundation grants, for instance, because you have carefully matched your requests to the foundations' interests, not your own. But all of a sudden, you find your original, well-focused program has become a collection of projects with little relationship to each other or, more important, to the original mission – or the skills – of your organization. This happened to a foundation that exists to publish books about social action and democratic principles. Because it needed the money, it accepted a grant to publish books about good forestry practices. Once the grant ran out, the foundation published no more books on that subject. Meanwhile, its small staff had become distracted from its original purpose.

Having some financial independence means you can get up off your knees. You can stick to doing what you do best. You can conduct the program in a way that satisfies your high standards. You can serve more people, and serve them better. That is the best reward for the effort required to raise funds.

Fundraising has its own special satisfaction

The value of what we do in voluntary organizations cannot always be measured easily because the benefits of our programs are often intangible. We often have to defend a project we believe has been successful, although we don't have the facts we need to support our claim. We may say:

> *Are crop yields larger since we sponsored the training programs about planting trees to protect crops? We think they are but we can't say by exactly how much.*

Often we can't afford to measure results. We can only say:

> *We believe fewer people are malnourished than in the past.*

Or the projects we work on take time to show results. We cannot immediately answer questions our donors ask:

> *In what ways can you demonstrate that the lives of women in your town have improved because of the new community centre?*

In fundraising it is always possible to be more precise. The results of fundraising can be seen and measured. This gives a special satisfaction. There is a thrill in setting a goal and reaching it on schedule.

> *We wanted to raise the money to give milk to 1,000 children every school day this year. We have raised the money we need.*
>
> *We sold 400 baskets this week. That was double what we expected to sell.*

There are few thrills to compare with the call from a foundation saying you have received a grant, the arrival of several cash donations, the sale of every ticket to a special event, the success of your latest fundraising project. Think of the excitement in the group the last time you had such good news.

Even failure can be valuable, because in fundraising you can learn from your mistakes quickly. If you don't reach your target, you can sit down and analyse what you did. What worked? What didn't? You will be asking for money again and it will probably be soon. In a well-organized campaign, for example, you may decide to reach out to a different group of possible donors every three months. It will be possible each time to improve your appeal. There are plenty of chances to improve your fundraising skills and test new techniques. Fundraising represents a continuing challenge, with fast results. And, when it works, there is good reason for satisfaction.

We wanted to raise the money to give milk to 1,000 children every school day this year. We have raised the money we need.

2 The importance of credibility

Credibility can be increased but it takes work and time. A high public profile may be helpful in getting foreign grants but is not essential. It is more important that your organization have a record of accomplishment and a good reputation among granting agencies. In attracting support from individuals and corporations at home, all three – high profile, good record, and good reputation – are essential. Together they give the organization credibility. People in voluntary agencies around the world have told me repeatedly that the biggest hurdle they faced in local fundraising was their lack of credibility within their own community. Local poverty was mentioned only once.

Having credibility means being seen as entirely trustworthy. Without credibility, fundraising is next to impossible. People and organizations don't want to give money to groups they don't know or are not sure they can trust. Only with local credibility do you have a chance to raise local money. But credibility cannot be built overnight. Many organizations simply will not be able to build credibility fast enough to enable them to attract more than a small portion of the local financial support they may need right away. They will likely fail. And would probably have failed no matter what they did.

The techniques of fundraising are easy to learn and to begin to apply, once credibility has been established. One reason is that credibility creates confidence. Your organization will become more confident in what it is trying to do: others will be more confident about its work.

The NGOs in Chile acquired a very bad image during the dictatorial regime. We have to restore credibility in the sense of demonstrating that NGOs are there to work in the service of people and not simply for their own survival. During the dictatorship, we had external aid, mainly from Europe. But now that external agencies have an image of Chile as a developed country, aid has fallen. That is a big problem.

CICELIA DOCKENDORF, CHILE, CIVICUS MEETING, 1997

Goals on the path to credibility

In later chapters we will look at the questions you need to ask before writing a plan for your organization and its fundraising efforts. The answers to these questions will give you a good deal of information about what current and potential supporters think of you and how these opinions will affect fundraising.

Any organization that wants to raise local money must set goals. Techniques to achieve these goals will be discussed in the following chapters.

Possibly you will set one or more of the following goals:
- Potential supporters need to know about your organization.

- Even if potential supporters know about your organization they need good reasons to want to give you money.
- Even if people are ready to give support, you must overcome your fear of asking for it.
- Once all else is in place, you must secure access to people who want to build your community.

Let us examine each of these goals.

Potential supporters need to know about your organization

Small community-based or grassroots organizations have a special problem. Some are not known except to the communities they serve. Others have an international reputation but are relatively unknown in their own country. All of them may have depended on foreign funding in the past. Many may still depend on it. They may get grants by applying directly to foreign agencies. Or they may receive international funding indirectly, through grants given to their government or to an intermediary agency. Even large intermediary agencies may be little known. These organizations may have big budgets and may arrange funding for dozens of smaller organizations serving millions of people. They may have an excellent reputation among their peers, with their government, and with overseas donors on whom they have depended. But the media, and the financial and business communities in their own country, may scarcely have heard of them.

Until recently, there has been no pressure on most voluntary organizations to cease being invisible, to strengthen their public image at home. As a result, they are not known to or trusted by the people they are going to have to ask for help in the future. But now foreign funds are shrinking. Small and large organizations will have to look to a public they have had almost no need to cultivate in the past.

One problem they must face is a historical division between people in development and people in business. Each group is sceptical about the values of the other, so they have rarely talked to one another. That will have to change. The change may not be as difficult as many people in development fear. The head of a large NGO in the Philippines told me about going to his first meeting with business people. He felt nervous beforehand, but by the end of the meeting the business people were talking about protecting the environment and he was talking about foreign investment. He had learned a good lesson. Useful and productive conversation with business people is possible: it can be done.

Being accountable, building a reputation for achievement and trustworthiness, takes effort and time, but it too can be done. The big question is

---

In the United States, only a tenth of charitable giving goes to the poor. The rich simply don't know who to trust with their money. What the world needs badly is a system for rating the world's charities. The existence of a reputable guide ... would pry a lot of money from the nervous hands of would-be philanthropists.

A poll shows that the [Canadian] public is concerned with the spending and management practices of charities. Almost half those polled agreed with the statements, "Many charities and other non-profit organizations are run by disorganized amateurs" and "I have heard so many stories about corruption among charitable organizations that I am reluctant to give to any organization."

GLOBE AND MAIL, TORONTO, 1997

why to raise funds, not just how. It is a question of reaching out to people, to give them an opportunity to build society.

The people who can make a difference to your organization will likely have known for years about large international organizations with a long history and a high profile. Think of UNICEF, WWF, Oxfam, CARE or other agencies that work to help the poor. Many of your potential supporters may not know exactly what services these organizations offer but they will have a vague idea of what the organizations do and likely believe it is worthwhile. They will likely know, for instance, that UNICEF works to improve the health of children. They are also likely to know about the successful marketing programs of some of these organizations, such as the UNICEF greeting cards that are sold all over the world. From successes like these, people get a mental picture of an organization that is worth supporting.

Think also of the voluntary organizations in your own country that are well known. They are most likely to be charities that work in cities. That is because cities have large populations and most of the mass media. These organizations are also likely to have a long record of achievement, a good reputation, and social and corporate connections. The late Mother Teresa established such an organization in India. Her Missionaries of Charity earned such a good reputation and high profile that it had no trouble attracting support from people and organizations in India, and later from donors and volunteers in many other countries. It now operates schools, hospitals, orphanages, and food centres in more than 25 countries.

One senior trade diplomat argues that NGOs often display none of the transparency they seek in others, hide the sources of their funding, and represent only narrow special interests, not the wider public. Some of the more aggressive NGOs are more interested in confrontation than consensus, and are out to kill rational debate through biased, if not erroneous scaremongering. Their holier-than-thou tactics are often clearly undemocratic.

REGINALD HALE, INTERNATIONAL HERALD TRIBUNE, MARCH 1996

Nevertheless, scepticism runs deep. The executive director of an NGO in South Africa said to me that he hesitated about supporting St. John Ambulance, an internationally-known organization, because he did not know whether it did useful work. Scepticism about such an agency shows the difficulty of establishing and keeping credibility.

Even if potential supporters know about your organization they need good reasons to want to give you money

The "good reasons" for supporting you are the value of your mission, your organization's accomplishments, and what you will do to achieve your objectives in the future. (Building a long-range plan is discussed in later chapters of this book.) But "reasons" alone are not enough. You have to have the skills to interest potential donors in the first place, then to convince them of the worthiness of your case, in itself and in competition with other good causes. (These communications skills are discussed in Book 2.)

Businesses, governments, and individuals may be more than uncomfortable when they are approached by people they have not met before or programs that are unfamiliar. They may have fixed ideas, difficult to change, about organizations like yours. Potential donors may think you are unbusinesslike or inexperienced. You must overcome such suspicions. In the next chapter, we will look at ways you can do this.

Potential donors are also likely to sense if you are suspicious of their motives for giving. That is happening in the Philippines, where many large corporations belong to an organization called Philippine Business for Social Progress. Some people in development in that country suspect that the organization uses its support of voluntary programs as a way to give its members early knowledge of business opportunities.

Potential donors may even be openly antagonistic. Your work may be seen as a threat to the rich and powerful. In many cases, it is. Social changes, social reforms are threatening. Members of the elite ask: Why should we give people money to criticize us and to work to change policies that have given us our power and wealth? Land reform is perhaps the most threatening issue of all. Why should landowners help people to try to break up their land holdings? In many countries, voluntary organizations have been and continue to be seen as the enemy of established power, as leftists, if not outright communists.

Many corporations and individuals recognize the need for social change and for serving the poor. They also want to improve their communities and they want to be seen to be doing it. But when they give money they want to be certain it will be used to their liking. They give money mainly to people or organizations they know already and feel comfortable with. Or they set up their own personal or corporate foundations to pay for projects; then they can be sure how the money will be used and that they will get full recognition for their gifts. Magic Eyes, a well-known environmental agency in Bangkok, is an example. The name has several meanings. Magic Eyes will follow you if you do something wrong like dropping paper on the street. Magic Eyes can also make magic by cleaning up litter. The organization was started by the family that owns the large Bangkok Bank and is affiliated with the bank. In 1997, it had 36 corporate members.

Some people simply don't trust development organizations. They have heard stories about organizations that have apparently worthy goals but don't deliver what they promise. They may have heard, for example, about an organization that claimed to benefit farmers' groups, except that none of the farmers' groups knew about the organization that was supposed to be helping them. In fact, the organization had no constituency. No one wanted the service it claimed to provide. Or they may have heard of another group that was formed just to receive foreign funding. Little of the money it received actually was spent to benefit the rural poor. Most went for "administration" and into the pockets of the founders.

Stories like that circulate in many countries. There are few frauds in the development community, but there are some. However, most mistakes in development, as in all organizations, are the result of incompetence. Nonetheless, they harm the reputation of development organizations. Voluntary organizations have to work extra hard to overcome these suspicions.

Sometimes people like the ideas set forth by a voluntary organization but don't know enough about the people who are responsible for its program and finances or about the way it runs its organization. They may see a list of names, most of them unfamiliar. When this happens, they are likely to think:

- Who are these people anyway? How do I know they are responsible and honest? I don't. Finding out would take a lot of time and effort, and could I trust the results?
- Supposing I do take a closer look. The budget they sent me does not look businesslike. I cannot see any money set aside for training, for instance. Aren't they doing any? And they are talking about improving the lives of marginal farmers but they don't include facts to prove that they really have done that. So why should I help them?
- They already get money from overseas. And they don't seem short of money. After all, their office is in that large house downtown. Do they really need my support?
- If I want to give money away, I will give it to people I know something about. It is much easier. And I can trust those people to do the job.

You must expect these questions. It is best to answer them before they are asked. That can be done by making sure, when you ask for money, that your presentation is complete. This will be discussed in Book 3.

Because voluntary organizations tend to be sceptical about the way the commercial world operates, they too often refuse to adopt sound commercial practices and compete for attention in the marketplace. Also, they are often:

1 afraid of business people. This makes them nervous when they approach corporations and business people for grants or other help.

2 blocked by a personal dislike for business. This makes them reluctant to approach business people, or unattractive when they do make an approach.

3 unfamiliar with the way the marketplace works and the words used there.

As a result, they don't communicate their past achievements and their plans for the future effectively. They have trouble calling their service a product. They don't like talking about marketing; they talk about resource development. They don't talk about conducting a public relations program; they talk about building awareness. As a result, the people they are trying to convince don't understand them.

Limited technical capacities and relatively small resource bases may characterize some NGOs. NGOs sometimes may have limited strategic perspectives and weak linkages with other actors in development. NGOs may have limited managerial and organizational capacities. In some countries, the relationship between NGOs and government may involve political, legal, ideological, and administrative constraints. Because of their voluntary nature, there may be questions regarding the legitimacy, accountability, and credibility of NGOs and their claims as to mandate and constituencies represented. Questions sometimes arise concerning the motivations and objectives of NGOs, and the degree of accountability NGOs accept for the ultimate impact of the policies and positions they advocate.

ASIAN DEVELOPMENT BANK NGO POLICY DOCUMENT, COOPERATION BETWEEN THE ASIAN DEVELOPMENT BANK AND NON-GOVERNMENT ORGANIZATIONS, 1998

Even if people are ready to give support, you must overcome your fear of asking

A Canadian development agency recently celebrated its 20th year. At a board meeting, the president proclaimed, almost defiantly: "This is not a fundraising board. We give direction to the organization. We do not raise money." She did not mean to, but in saying that she showed a fear of fundraising.

There are several reasons people like this chairwoman are reluctant to ask for the funds they need for causes they know are good. The first is that many people feel that asking for money is begging. But asking a donor agency for a grant to help develop your community is not begging.

Begging helps the beggar survive, and may make the donor feel charitable, but it builds nothing lasting. All it does is make it possible for the beggar, and perhaps the beggar's family, to live for another day. In contrast, a grant for community development is an investment made by the donor in your organization and your community. It is people investing in people.

We can easily accept foreign grants as an investment made by one country in another. Foreign aid agencies make their investments in the belief that there will be a return on the investment. They expect that a prosperous economy in the receiving country will help bring security and an improved economy, and will eventually give the donor country new markets for its products.

Raising money through local grants and donations is the same. It is not charity. Asking a friend or a business to strengthen a local organization is not begging. It is a legitimate part of your organization's work towards greater security, health, prosperity or other improvements in your community. Donations are investments made by people to improve their own communities. Your organization is the engine that drives that change.

The second reason people hesitate to ask for money is because they are frightened by economic and social barriers. In many countries, 80 per cent of the wealth is owned by 20 per cent of the people. An extreme example occurred in Nicaragua, during the 1970s, when the Somoza family owned 75 per cent of the land. How easy would it have been to approach a family member for support? When most of the wealth of a country is controlled by a small group, it is hard for outsiders to think of themselves as anything other than powerless beggars.

Another kind of barrier is faced by women in development organizations. Women have been conditioned not to ask for money. Their salaries are lower than men's salaries and they find it hard to ask for equity. It is to men's advantage to keep women's salaries low. It increases their power. These kinds of cultural attitudes make it extremely difficult to ask for what is socially and economically right. They need to be rejected and replaced with a less hierarchical view of society.

The third reason people won't ask for donations is because they are afraid of failure – of being rejected. There is only one way to overcome this fear. It is to keep trying. Eventually, if you have a good cause and present it well, you will have a few small successes. You are more likely to succeed if you do not begin too ambitiously. This is one reason to start small.

Finally, people are reluctant to assume what could turn into an obligation. They may fear that, at some time, the donor may ask for something in return that they will be unwilling to give. But that is exactly how much important fundraising is achieved in countries of the North. People give to

> *Charity separates people. It confirms social divisions between givers and receivers by the very act of giving. Community erases barriers; we do what we do for ourselves as much as for others.*
>
> RICK SALUTIN, SOCIAL COMMENTATOR, GLOBE AND MAIL, TORONTO

each other's organizations because they are friends and they know both causes deserve support.

Once all else is in place, you must secure access to people who want to build your community

Many organizations work in one or more small communities and are well known to the people they serve, either directly or indirectly. They may also be well known to overseas donors and to the intermediary organizations that secure the overseas funding. It is the local support, however, that gives these organizations their strength, legitimacy, and capacity for growth.

Your organization may already be trusted by many local organizations and people. But those organizations may depend on foreign funds to help you, and the local people you serve probably have little money of their own. If overseas funding declines or if your program expands, you will need local support from people who don't yet know you or trust you. You will have to find ways to raise money from them.

To gain new financial support, you can follow several strategies. Here are some of the most common:

1 Build on the credibility you already have with people you serve. Use it to establish credibility in your broader community, moving outward gradually but deliberately. Start small, relying at first on your own community for financial support.
- *Advantages:* This approach promises long-term stability and independence.
- *Disadvantages:* It requires skills your organization is not likely to have now. It is slow; it may take years before you see any major increase in funding.

2 Gain further credibility by getting under the wing of an intermediary group that knows the right people and has the skills to raise money from local sources.
- *Advantages:* This approach ensures adequate funding in the short term and without a big effort.
- *Disadvantages:* Dependency on the larger organization is likely to continue. Your own organization will not need to develop its own capacities, but in time it may come to resent the power of the intermediary and the fact that the intermediary retains a portion of money it finds, to help pay its own expenses.

3 Use the credibility you have already earned to start income-generating projects. For example, you might sell handicrafts or greeting cards, farm produce, or a special bread. Your staff might offer training courses or take short-term consulting assignments. You might rent out your office in the evenings. All these methods of generating income have worked for other organizations.
- *Advantages:* A small business can make a sustained, but perhaps modest, contribution to income.
- *Disadvantages:* It requires business skills your organization may not have now. Most ventures fail.

At this point you may be asking "To become credible, will I have to change so much that I will risk losing sight of my mission of serving the poor?" The simple answer is "No, you won't." Realizing these goals is possible if you have a long-range plan that sets out the missions, goals, objectives of both the core program and fundraising – and if you stick to it.

For a more complete answer, in the next chapter we will examine the assets your organization already has that make it credible. These are the underlying strengths that will make all future efforts successful.

3 Building credibility

You may feel that the cause for which you work makes your organization credible – that everyone should want to support it. The previous chapter suggests some of the reasons why, no matter how worthy you believe your work is, you may still have great difficulty raising money for it. But do not be discouraged. Your organization already has many of the assets you need to build credibility with potential donors. Take advantage of those assets! You may also find that you lack other assets: those you must develop.

The assets that will make your organization credible to even the most sceptical potential donor are:
1. your intelligence, energy, focus, and determination
2. your public image
3. a record of accomplishment
4. the necessary legal status
5. clear, accountable financial management and organizational structure
6. the personal reputation of your staff members
7. the high regard of your supporters/funders, new and old
8. an appropriate name, used carefully
9. the quality and commitment of your board members and patrons
10. a corps of valuable volunteers
11. a carefully prepared long-range plan
12. your membership in strong, supportive networks
13. your carefully prepared financial documents
14. an effective communications program

The first eight of these assets are discussed in this chapter. Chapters 4, 5, and 6 describe ways to rate your own organization in these areas. The board is discussed further in Chapter 7, volunteers in Chapter 8, finding allies in Chapter 9, building strategic alliances in Chapter 10, long-range planning in Chapters 11 and 12, and preparing credible financial documents in Chapter 13. Communications programs are covered in Book 2. These include presenting the value of your organization clearly and in an interesting, persuasive way; promoting your organization's newsworthy activities; and arranging media coverage.

Most civil society organizations are proud of themselves. They don't know that they are not credible.

KATALIN CZIPPAN, GÖNCÖL FOUNDATION, HUNGARY

Credibility is what you have achieved, not what you have tried.

ALAN FOWLER, CONSULTANT, ETHIOPIA

Intelligence, energy, focus, and determination
Building credibility will require action on several fronts at once, plus some good luck, but it can be done. The base for all your action will be your knowledge of the areas where you are strong already and the areas where you could be stronger. Recognizing these areas is so important that it is the subject of the next three chapters.

Obviously, it is impossible to develop every asset at once. It is important to decide priorities. Start with the most important, and do not be distracted from achieving the goals you set for yourself. Staying focused is essential. So is investing time – lots of time.

The success of many organizations depends on a single person having intelligence, focus, determination, and energy. That is a weakness. The leader may become dispirited, exhausted or sick, may lose enthusiasm, or may leave for another job. Then the very existence of the organization is threatened. The energetic leader – paid or volunteer – must be supported by a number of committed, enthusiastic board members, who also have the qualities of good leadership, and an equally committed and enthusiastic staff or group of volunteers.

The public image
Hur Camporendondo, of the LAWIG Foundation in the Philippines, says he has no trouble establishing credibility with overseas donors because the needs met by his organization are so clear. What his organization is doing is simple to explain, he believes. LAWIG strengthens cooperatives on Samal Island – at first, 17 of them, and later 28. The cooperatives contribute to community development all over the island. They have improved the lives of many people on an island with a subsistence economy.

If the work of the organization springs from the needs of the people and if the project is sensible, then the rightness will be clear. That does not mean it will be instantly marketable. Good causes do not always attract money. They must be made to appear attractive. Your work must interest the people you are going to approach.

In the study of your strengths, you will identify whether or not your work is in an area that is popular with local donors at the moment. If it is not in a popular area, can you link it to another subject that is more popular? For example, if you are working in sustainable agriculture, your research may tell you that potential supporters are not giving priority to that subject at the moment. You may find that protecting the environment is more popular. Then it would make sense to think how you can focus, in presentations to prospective donors, on the environmental benefits of your work in sustainable agriculture. Or you may find a keen interest in organic products because people are becoming concerned about pesticides on vegetables. You know that your work in sustainable agriculture is reducing the amount of pesticide that farmers must use. Take advantage of this concern and frame your message around it.

Many people are touched by a story of a child in need and, even more, by a story about how the life of that child has been or can be made better.

They recognize a cause that is worthwhile, and they may be glad to give money to a child. If you are working on improving health in rural areas, it may help your cause to emphasize how it improves the health of small children.

This method of selective emphasis is perfectly legitimate, provided it does not distort the image of your program or the program itself. You need to be honest with yourself. Don't try to cram your work into a mould that it does not really fit.

A record of accomplishment

Nothing contributes to credibility like having been in operation long enough to build a good reputation. When I was executive director of a development organization, people sometimes sounded cautious when I called them for the first time. They had never heard of my organization. Usually they would sound friendlier the moment I said the organization had been around for nearly twenty years. That gave it considerable credibility.

Many voluntary organizations are not that old. Many have been formed in the last ten years. They must base their credibility on their more recent performance. That *is* their history.

Presenting a record of achievement requires skill in communications. It also requires planning and organization. The first step is to be sure that you have a record to draw upon. Organizations need to be able to talk about their achievements; this means they need good records.

"So then the alien stepped out of the U.F.O. and said he was a fund raiser from another planet, which was quite novel, I thought."

Is each project well documented? Do you have concrete evidence of what you have accomplished?

As each project has been completed, you have probably had to report to a donor. Even if no report is required, prepare one anyway. A summary of this report, or the report itself if it is short, could be put in a binder for easy display or reference. Keep a record of the results in detail, including all specific measures of success – especially results that can be expressed in actual numbers. If you have too much material to fit in a binder, put it a box. Include a pictorial record in photographs, slides, or videotapes. Also include testimonials – in writing or on audiotapes or videotapes – from the people you served, telling how they benefited. Try to get this material while the project is under way, or soon after the project is completed and while it is still fresh in people's minds. As these summaries accumulate, you will develop an impressive record of your performance.

Do you keep a scrapbook with clippings, photographs, and other important material about your organization and everyone who plays a part in it?
A book like this is useful to show to visitors and to take with you when you

want to introduce your organization to prospective donors. It is also useful in orienting new board members, volunteers, and staff. Take the book to every board meeting to bring members up to date and to make them proud. When the book gets too heavy to carry or to open out flat easily, start another. Even if you don't want to carry a heavy book to board meetings, do take along any interesting letters or other communications. This will give your board members a sense of the benefits that come from their support.

Are you asking for letters of endorsement from everyone whose good opinion of you could help – politicians, bureaucrats, business people, educators, religious leaders?
People will often compliment your organization in person, but it doesn't often occur to them to write down their opinion for the record. They will usually be happy to do so if you ask them. In asking, you may suggest something you would especially like them to emphasize. You may also get letters you did not ask for. You can put them all in your scrapbook, or frame them and hang them on the wall. Whenever possible, show originals. They are far more appealing than photocopies because they often are in colour, and have an emotional impact that copies lack. Keep copies in your files. Don't make copies on fax paper, because they are likely to fade over time.

Be sure your files are so well organized that you can find what you want fast. Nothing can make you look sillier than being unable to locate a file when a visitor – perhaps from a potential donor agency – comes to your office.

Are your plans for the future laid out clearly?
You should be able to show your long-range plan to anyone. If it is well done, it will inspire confidence and attract support. (See Chapters 11, 12, and 13.)

The necessary legal status
People who want to help people are often impatient with legal details. They just want to get to work. They don't want to spend time with lawyers or pay their fees. But some of the credibility of an organization depends on its legal status. Legal documents help to introduce the organization and to convince people that support it (staff, volunteers, board members, donors, governments, and media) that the organization is well established and meets all legal requirements. An organization may also need these documents to obtain charitable status from the government. In addition, few major donors will give money to an organization that is not a legal entity, properly registered in the country.

Do you have a book containing minutes of all your board meetings?
This may be a legal requirement for organizations in your country. Even if it is not, a book of minutes is a necessary tool at board meetings for quick reference about previous discussions and decisions. It is useful to give to new board members to read as an introduction to their responsibilities. It can also be used to show almost anyone how your organization works, and the concerns of its people. Minutes are the only accurate, permanent record of the actions of an organization.

Have you considered incorporating your organization?
Incorporation creates a legal entity with a life of its own. It ensures that an organization has:
- people designated to act on behalf of the organization
- the legal right to own and transfer assets such as real estate
- a continuing existence even if the people running it now don't continue, assuming others want to keep it going

Incorporation also safeguards the directors and staff from personal financial responsibility for actions taken by the organization. A prudent person, when asked to serve on a board of directors, will ensure that such a safeguard is in place.

Do you have a constitution that describes your aims?
Anyone who might support you – staff, volunteers, board members, donors, governments, the media – will want to know the purpose of your organization, the qualifications for membership, the number and responsibilities of the officers, and the length of time you have been operating. The constitution should also set out what is required to change the structure and purpose of the organization. Supporters may need this information to convince others (for example, the board of a corporation) that you are well-established and meet all legal requirements.

Do you have by-laws? Are they adequate? Up-to-date? Has everyone read them?
By-laws govern the day-to-day procedures and practices of an organization and (unlike most constitutions) can be changed easily to meet changing conditions. Well-written by-laws contribute to good management by spelling out carefully who is responsible for every aspect of an organization's operations and who is supposed to decide what, when, and how. They set out the board's composition, election procedures, terms of office, appointment of auditors, size of quorum, management of assets, rules for closing the organization and other matters. By-laws describe the relationships of board and staff – who the executive director reports to, for instance.

By-laws need to be reviewed from time to time to make sure they are still appropriate. Your organization may have grown greatly since the by-laws were written. It may have enlarged its board or added new officers who are not mentioned in the by-laws. It may have added new purposes and abandoned others. The by-laws also need to be consolidated in one version every few years. No one should have to look in four different places to learn what the by-laws say about terms of office because changes were made but not consolidated into one version.

By-laws are also of no use if they are hidden away in a file. If they are going to be useful, they must be available to everyone. And everyone should be familiar with them – or, at least, know they are available to be readwhen needed.

In some countries, by-laws must be filed with the government. If that is true in your country, be sure to send in any changes in by-laws as soon as they are made.

Have you applied for all necessary registrations with government agencies? If you haven't, are there good reasons for this decision? If you have, has the government accepted the registration?

Strangers interested in your organization will be concerned if you have not met all legal requirements for operating in your own country. They may assume you are operating illegally – perhaps in active opposition to the government. They will hesitate to support an organization that may reflect badly on them, which might even get them into trouble with the authorities.

They may be satisfied if you can prove to them that there is nothing illegal about your work, but that there are convincing reasons explaining why you did not meet all the regulations.

Do you have charitable status so that (if the laws of your country permit) supporters of your organization can get credit for their donations when they pay their income tax?

In many countries, citizens can deduct donations (or a percentage of donations) from their income when they calculate their income tax. Understandably, they are much more likely to give money to organizations if they can get a tax benefit.

If your country has such an arrangement, have you registered so that your donors will benefit from it? Normally tax exemption is allowed only for donations to registered organizations.

If you have not registered, or are waiting for your registration to be processed, can you join another agency that is already registered and will act as an intermediary for donations to your organization? If this is legal, which it is not in many countries, that is often the quickest way to finance your work while awaiting government permissions or if you have chosen not to register.

If you intend to sell a product to raise income, do you have the necessary licences?
Starting a business will likely require a new set of applications to government, different from those for operating a voluntary service or receiving donations. Many municipalities require a retail licence before anyone begins selling products to individual buyers.

Clear, accountable financial management and organizational structure

The administrative structure of your organization will determine its efficiency and effectiveness. It will also affect its credibility, because donors can usually tell when an organization is poorly managed. If they have trouble understanding who is in charge, or have trouble getting answers to their questions, they will be unlikely to give their support.

There are many books on organizational structure and management. Our concern in this chapter is only on how the structure of an organization affects credibility – with outsiders, with staff, and with volunteers.

Transparency is a word that is much used nowadays. Organizations are urged to be transparent in their operations. That means they are being asked to be open, honest, and easy to understand.

Financial management
The most significant area in which voluntary organizations lack transparency is financial management. Lack of transparency does not mean the management is corrupt, although that does happen. It is more likely that the people who are managing the finances, including the bookkeeping, lack the necessary training. Voluntary organizations often begin with simple financial systems and then outgrow them. The operations become more complex; that means the accounts also grow more complex. When this happens, unfortunately, loyalty or inertia may leave financial management in the hands of people who were there at the beginning. Often they simply go on using the old systems even when the organization needs more sophisticated financial information. They simply don't have the ability to present financial information so that it is clear to everyone, inside and outside the organization, who needs to understand and use it. They don't know how to present it in a form that matches standard business practice and is thus acceptable to people in business or government.

A large environmental education organization in South Africa suffered from this weakness in financial management. The founding director had no interest in the details of the finances. She left managing the money in the hands of a person who did not know the basic principles of accounting. When the Canadian government gave the organization a large grant for a two-year program, there were constant problems. Statements were altered constantly as errors were discovered and corrected. Printouts of monthly statements were pages long because of the endless changes that had to be recorded. Moreover, the staff member managing the two-year program was not allowed to see the monthly printouts; as a result she had no way of knowing how much money had been spent, how much was left, or whether the charges to the project account were accurate. No reason was given for refusing to give her the statements. Money that should have been spent within a certain time to meet the program schedule went unspent. The executive director refused to get involved. What was the result? Suspicion and irritation on the part of the project manager and, of course, even more on the part of the donor. Was the grant likely to be renewed? You decide.

Supporters want to know clearly who within the organization is responsible for the good, or bad, financial management. The line of authority must be written down carefully. Too many people responsible can cause just as many problems as too few. In a university where I worked in the Philippines, every payment authorization had to be signed by six people. That procedure was intended to stop corruption. What it did was slow everything down. Also, if too many people are involved at every step, it becomes too easy to blame mistakes on someone else.

Clear accountability does more than build donor confidence. It reduces the likelihood of unpleasant surprises. No one likes to find out nine months into the financial year that there will be a deficit, when the budget forecast was for a small reserve. How did the deficit develop? If the bookkeeping responsibility is spread too thinly, it may be impossible to find out.

Bookkeepers need appropriate training at a local educational institution, perhaps a business college. Bookkeeping skills can also be acquired through correspondence courses offered by some technical colleges and universities. Without training, it is difficult to manage the finances of even a small organization. It is also highly desirable, if not essential, to have at least one person on the board of directors who is a trained accountant or financial manager. This person, who is likely to be elected the treasurer, can be invaluable in keeping a close eye on the volunteer or staff member who is keeping the books.

Sound administration
Once a prospective donor – especially a businessperson or organization, or a major donor agency – is convinced of the worthiness of your work, financial management is likely to be the most important factor in your credibility. But that is not the only place where there must be clear lines of accountability. If you have staff members, you should be able to show or explain clearly the lines of staff authority and reporting.

In addition, there should be a clear description of every position in your organization, outlining the duties and responsibilities of the job in enough detail to guide the person who holds the position. A clear description is valuable for every new employee. It also makes it possible for the manager to evaluate each employee's performance fairly and consistently. This contributes to staff morale and to the credibility of the leadership. Clear job descriptions are also useful for board members and, with the organization chart, are a demonstration of efficiency to any prospective donor.

It is not enough to make sure that staff members understand the expectations of the organization. Volunteers, no matter what their role, also have a right to know what is expected of them before they agree to help you. This is discussed in detail in Chapter 8 and in Book 2, Chapter 8. Briefly, volunteers want to feel useful, and to know exactly how the work they do assists the organization. They also want reassurance that they are not wasting their time by being involved in a sloppily run organization. They want to talk with pride about the organization and the contribution they are making. You too want this important contribution to your credibility.

The personal reputation of your staff
Staff members are any organization's front line. They represent the organization to the public on a day-to-day basis. It is essential that they do this part of their job enthusiastically and effectively.

The board and the executive director should be able to speak about the staff with pride. Staff members should feel that way about each other, too. This requires staff policies that create good morale; it also requires some further organization and planning. Some questions to ask yourself follow.

Do our records include carefully prepared, up-to-date biographical information about all the key players in our organization?

Even if the organization is new, your staff, board members, and volunteers were doing something previously. It may have been something that can help you now. You won't know if you don't ask.

You should have well-prepared, current information about everyone who matters to your organization, especially staff. The chairman, the executive director, and senior managers should be able to talk easily and knowledgeably about the staff.

It is helpful to have that information at your fingertips. When I was an executive director, I was once asked about the experience and expertise of a writer who had been on staff a long time. I was taken by surprise and hesitated. Did she have a degree in agricultural economics? Was it a graduate degree? How many years' research experience had she had? I could not remember. I hadn't looked at her record for several years. I did my best but I was wrong. Her education and experience were much more impressive than I recalled. As a result, the questioner did not give her work the respect it deserved. The same would have been true if I had been asked and could not answer knowledgeably about board members. The reputations and credentials of the volunteers in your organization are equally important.

There are many names for biographical data. In some countries these records are called résumés (the word I will use), in others curricula vitae, in others biodata. A good résumé can take two weeks to put together. That does not mean two weeks of continuous work, but two weeks to give the writer time to think about how it can be improved and whether everything important is included.

Do the résumés of our staff give the right impression?

Fashions in résumés come and go, but there are a few basic rules to follow. Use them in preparing your own résumé and as a form for your colleagues to follow. For your own résumé, begin with a list of the jobs you have held and the time spent in each position. Start with the current job and work backwards. A skeleton list of your titles is not enough. Describe briefly the work of each organization where you have been employed and outline your responsibilities. Describe your specific, measurable accomplishments in each position. Don't overdo the list of accomplishments; make sure they are credible. After that, list other activities that might be relevant to your current work – volunteer activities, interests, professional organizations to which you belong, publications. State your educational qualifications. Personal details such as marital status, age, citizenship, and religion may be added if desired.

In my experience, résumés are rarely proofread carefully. People almost always make spelling mistakes. Since I have usually been hiring people for their writing skills, résumés with even small spelling mistakes go in the wastebasket immediately. Especially if it is going to a donor, a résumé must be attractive, clean, and accurate. Be sure to get several people to check that it gives the right impression and is error-free.

Do we use résumés when we are trying to establish credibility?
People like to know the background of anyone they may work with. Don't be too modest about accomplishments. Use résumés to create confidence. Anyone who is giving a speech on behalf of the organization, for example, should provide the people in charge with a copy of his or her résumé. Résumés of senior staff members, volunteers, and board members can be sent to media people and to anyone else whom you want to interest or impress.

For this purpose, résumés must be accurate. For many purposes, one-page summaries are preferable to the long documents described above. Include either kind in grant proposals, as appropriate. Have them available as handouts. Send them regularly to your major donors with material about your organization. Give them to board members occasionally. Over time, board members are apt forget an employee's past experience, just as I did, and in any case the board should be aware of new experience and achievements.

Have we looked for every interest and every possible accomplishment of our staff that could influence people if it were known?
Look beyond résumés. When you hire new people, ask about their additional experiences and abilities. Do they write for pleasure – a skill that you could put to use? Have they had success in sports, in theatre, music, or in their education? How could these successes help the organization? With employees of the organization, it is appropriate to ask them more about themselves. Do they have relatives in important positions? Could these people be useful? Did they go to school with people who have become well known? Have the same conversation with volunteers, board members, and anyone else who becomes connected to your work.

Do our staff members know what is going on in the organization?
All new members of staff should receive an orientation package, which may include:
- the history of the organization
- its by-laws
- past and recent annual reports
- recent financial statements
- current brochures and newsletters about the work of the organization
- major policy documents, such as a three-year plan
- a list of current staff members with positions, and information about how they may be reached day or night
- position descriptions for each staff member

Staff members should also have regular briefings by the executive director or, in large organizations, their manager. Since managers are usually very busy, it is often difficult to remember to pass on news to staff. I found that, even with seven people, I had a hard time ensuring that everyone knew everything. Some staff were part-time. One or two were often travelling. Different volunteers came and went each day. If they weren't in the office on a day when there was a lot to talk about, it might take days before we realized that we had not told them the news.

There are various ways to keep people informed. Here are a few that have been proven in many organizations.

- Establish a regular time for meetings when everyone can be there. At the meeting, ask everyone, especially the managers, to describe what has been achieved in their area, what problems have been overcome. Try to meet every two weeks.
- If your office is large, try circulating incoming mail and copies of outgoing mail (including faxes and e-mail messages if you use them) to everyone regularly, perhaps several times a week.
- If the office is small, leave mail for 24 hours on a table where people can read it.
- Make less important mail, magazines, leaflets, and anything else of general interest but no urgency available too. These materials can be put in a box or a big envelope and circulated weekly, or left out in the main office for a week before they are filed or discarded.

The high regard of supporters and donors, new and old

The respect you want will have to be earned over a long time. There are a number of steps you can take to quicken the process and to increase your support in the community.

Gather evidence

One of the best ways to build confidence in your organization is to demonstrate that other people have confidence in it. Compliments from donors are a good way to do this. At the end of a project or program, ask donors for letters expressing satisfaction with the results of the work. Ask beneficiaries of your programs for their comments, written or oral, about the services you provide. Include all these statements in the records of each project. You will use them in publications, displays, and fundraising materials. Keep them ready to show to people at any time.

Expand your network

- Introduce your organization to new people. Send them your publications. Invite them to open houses. Arrange tours of projects for them.

Start small. Local people can be helpful at a local level where you may need them most. Others may be helpful at the national level if that is where you need assistance. Decide the kind of help you need, and then choose the right approach to the right people.

- Find names of people to invite by having a brainstorming session with the members of the board, asking them who they know who can help in any possible way. By themselves, people are not good at making the connection between their acquaintances and their organization. They are much more likely to come up with names in a group where everyone makes suggestions. One suggestion leads to another and then a third and fourth. (A dictionary describes "brainstorming" as "a concerted intellectual treatment of a problem by discussing spontaneous ideas about it.")

Ask them to suggest people they know at all political levels – the village, the town, the city, the region, the province or state, the nation – and in different categories. Do they know business people? merchants? politicians? teachers? workers in newspapers, magazines, radio, television? professional people such as lawyers, accountants, and doctors? Find out what talents, experience, or influence are available through the board. Look for people who have done more than talk about improving their community. Look for people who have made important contributions, either in their jobs or as volunteers.

Once the people you invite have shown some interest, think of them as potential supporters, board members, volunteers, staff. Do another round of brainstorming with the board to get everyone thinking about how these people can be of most help to your organization.

Communicate regularly

- Make a list of all the people who need to know about your work. Make another list of people you want to know about your work. These may be people that no one in your organization has had a chance to meet. They may be recently elected politicians, managers of a new factory, or a new editor at the local paper. Send them material regularly. Better still, visit them, or invite them to see your work at first hand.

- Write and report regularly to all donors – local and overseas – about the progress your organization is making and about its plans for the future. Be careful to include all financial information that will reassure supporters about your stability and add to your credibility.

Part of building credibility is building good personal relationships. Write to the donors and friends of your organization (and talk to them when there is an opportunity) in a friendly and personal way. If you are writing a letter that will go to many different people, think of a typical recipient. Then write in a way that will interest that person. If you are in fact writing to only one person, think about that person when you are writing. Don't write as an organization writing to another organization. People like personal letters. They don't like form letters that could have come from a computer.

In any such letter, talk about what the organization has accomplished and what it will do in the future. Don't be too chatty. Don't talk too much about staff members, unless the person you are writing to has had a very close connection with a staff member. Staff news can be boring to outsiders.

- Consider whether you need a regular newsletter for your friends and supporters. Consider this question carefully: if you answer "yes," it will involve both time and money. Many organizations publish a newsletter without really analysing whether or not it is a good investment. They think that they need a newsletter to look important. A newsletter doesn't automatically make an organization important. A bad newsletter does just the opposite. Newsletters are effective only if they are well produced and only if the right people read them.

Most of the people you want to reach already see more printed material in a day than they have time to read in a week. As a result, each separate piece must battle for attention. People make up their minds in two or three seconds whether or not to read something. Articles in a newsletter or newspaper compete with other articles in the same publication. Publications compete with other publications. They compete as well with radio, television, videos, and other forms of information and entertainment. And all these media compete with other demands on their intended audience: telephone calls, correspondence, meetings, social events, sports, not to speak of family, friends, noise, sickness, and the need to sleep.

Huge amounts of money are wasted printing and distributing unwanted, unread publications. Some experts say that people read only the publications they have to pay for. Even then, I find that magazines I pay for go unread for months at a time.

Be absolutely sure you have good reasons for publishing a newsletter if you decide to proceed. You should have something important to say and an audience that really *wants* to hear your message. The key word in that sentence is "wants." Organizations often say they should publish a newsletter because people "need" to know what they are doing. Most of the time, that's not true. The only information people really "need" to know is about their health, their family, their security, their financial situation. They don't "need" to know about the work of another voluntary organization that does not help them directly: they are not waiting for your newsletter or annual report. To make them read about your work, the information must be so interesting and so attractively presented that people want to read it. If you cannot do that, then forget publishing a newsletter! (This question is discussed in greater detail in Book 2, Chapter 20.)

- Say thank you to all supporters in a systematic and appropriate way. The sooner you say thank you, the better. Be sure to set deadlines for this. You should be saying thanks for any support – moral, political, media, and volunteer support as well as financial support. Most people would agree with that. Just how to say it is another question.

The world seems divided on what is appropriate. The British have one style. They tend to say thank you graciously and do it only once. Perhaps as a result of colonization by the British, people in many other countries follow this practice. Nevertheless Americans believe people love to be thanked for supporting a cause. They say thank you endlessly, over and over. But in the Philippines, a former American colony, people almost never say thank you. There the American style of saying thank you would be quite inappropriate. Unless, of course, they were thanking an American, when effusive thanks would be in order.

Volunteers need special thanks. One Philippine women's group gives services instead of direct expressions of gratitude. It runs a lending program for its volunteers. They can get loans easily or in an emergency. Or they can get technical help; for example, a technician will immunize their baby piglets. This group also recognizes the need for volunteers to have fun: they sing after meetings.

When deciding what is the right style, think about what is appropriate in your country. Think too if the style is changing and if you could benefit from changing your own practices.

Be sure also to answer all questions and concerns expressed by supporters. That is one way to show that your appreciate their interest. Ignoring their questions and concerns does just the opposite. Here too, set a deadline for responses.

- Share good news! Take a scrapbook of projects and achievements to conferences, meetings, or visits where you want to provide evidence of your worth as an organization. Take it to every board meeting to show the members evidence of your success. Send copies of good letters to board members in between meetings, if you can afford the postage. Call the chairman any time there is good news that you should share. Encourage the chairman to tell other board members. Tell the media.

Make a good impression

- Train the staff in good telephone manners. People who call you on the telephone should not have to ask if they have the right number. The office of a voluntary organization is a business office. The staff should treat it as such. When they answer the telephone, they should tell the caller right away the name of the organization or a large part of the name – not just a set of initials. They can follow that up with a pleasant but businesslike greeting as simple as, "Good morning." People using cell phones for work should also answer with their name and the name of the organization. They should not just say hello.

After that, they should deal with the caller in a gracious, helpful, efficient way. They should do their best to answer questions. They should not sound impatient or too busy to talk. If they can't answer a question right away, they should offer to find the answer and phone the caller back. Or, if necessary, they should refer the caller to someone else who will know. Check messages daily and return all calls.

Good telephone manners build credibility. Bad telephone manners destroy it. They can also cost money. Callers who are treated rudely do not donate.

- Answer all letters and messages, especially from donors. Pay particular attention to complaints. People who complain often just want attention. If you give it to them, they may be happy.
- Remind your supporters at every opportunity that they are welcome in your office at any time. Some organizations include an invitation in every letter. Issue invitations whenever you see an opportunity to gain an ally. People should be able to see what you do for themselves.
- Develop a system, including assigned responsibilities, for dealing with visitors. It is disconcerting to visit an office and feel as though you are intruding, even if you have an appointment. Think of the times you have stood awkwardly, waiting for someone to notice you have arrived, then waiting while someone goes off to see if the person you want is in the office. Have someone who is friendly near the entrance to your office to greet visitors.

Give visitors a place to sit down. Give them material about your organization to read and, perhaps, to take away. If the person a visitor wants to see is temporarily busy, tell the visitor quickly how long he or she may have to wait.
- Build a display about your organization in the place in your office where visitors wait. It need not be large. Display any products you have for sale. Have brochures, newsletters, annual reports, research reports available for visitors to look at or take away with them. Then they will have something to do while they wait.

Many visitors may not know much about your work. This is an ideal way to educate them. What they read in your office and what they take away to read later will reinforce the impressions from their visit. Put your mission statement on a big poster or banner so everyone can see it.

Recognize donors and grant makers, board members, and volunteers in such a way that every visitor can see who is helping you now and how much you value your supporters. Hang an up-to-date list of them (written in large letters) on the wall. Put up their pictures. Write names on a blackboard.

Post a wish list of anything the organization needs right now and of anything the organization dreams of having.
- Ask visitors to sign a guest book, giving their address. Most people are flattered to add their name to a book, especially if other names in it are well known. People who sign are always interested in who else has visited. This is an excellent way for you to gather names and addresses of potential supporters. Put the book in a prominent place where it can't be forgotten.
- Keep a tidy office. Piles of paper, uneaten food, and litter on the floor create a bad impression. I ask myself if I really want to work with an organization that cannot keep its offices in good order and does not provide a pleasant working space for the staff. I ask myself if the staff can be efficient if their working space is a mess.
- Decorate your office. Hang attractive pictures or posters on the walls. Recognize that even paint colour sends a message. Customs differ between countries, but the example tells what one American expert had to say about painted walls.

> **What colour to paint your clinic ... Or, looking really poor and needy through colour**
> *It is time to paint your clinic. Given that all colours cost roughly the same ... consider the psychological message that colours transmit.*
> Beige: *We're too poor and humble to be bright, but we're so drab that we must be doing wonderful work for the poor.*
> White: *Clean. Very clean. Professional, sterile, and pure. No parties here. No time for fun ....*
> Yellow: *Bright. Sunny. We're cheerful and we like children.*
> Institutional green: *We are so cost-efficient that we took the leftover paint from the prison.*
>
> P. BURKE KEEGAN,
> FUNDRAISING FOR NON-PROFITS

An appropriate name, used carefully

Do you have a name that describes what you do, that paints a picture? The imaginary organizations used in this book – WaterLink, BookLink, BestHealth – are examples of names that paint little pictures of what an organization does.

Many organizations have long names that describe their work very well. Here are some examples:

Centro de Agricultura Sostenible con Tecnologia Apropriada (Centre for Sustainable Agriculture with Appropriate Technology)
Chitungwiza Integrated Youth Survival Alternative Project
Philippine Partnership for the Development of Human Resources in Rural Areas

But the people who work for those organizations find it cumbersome to use the whole name every time. They use initials instead – CASTRA, CHIYSAP, PHILDHRRA. Sometimes a set of initials, like CASTRA, is easy to say. However some, like PHILDHRRA, are difficult to write. In either case, initials rarely tell people what the organization does. They do not give a sense of the spirit of the organization. Initials only identify. They pack no emotional punch. CUSO, a Canadian international development organization, was founded 35 years ago. It was then called Canadian University Service Overseas. In 1981 the university connection was less important and it changed its name officially to just CUSO. In 1997, it ran an unsuccessful contest to find a new meaning for its acronym. It has yet to find a good one.

Here is one of my favourite examples of this failing in initials. Members of some Christian faiths often refer to the BVM. What do those letters convey? Not much. Is that the name of a car? A BMW? Well, no. The full name is much richer in meaning – Blessed Virgin Mary.

Some initials hide their own failings. We talk of NGOs, and in doing so we define them by what they are not – non-government organizations. It is much more positive to say what NGOs *are* – voluntary organizations, development organizations, people helping people.

Sets of initials do not stir people's hearts or guide their hands to their pockets. A few organizations have overcome this problem. UNICEF is so well known by its initials that most people probably don't know what they stand for. CARE formed a word that expressed its mission. A few organizations have come up with a set of initials or a word that does paint a picture, though it does not tell the whole story. An organization in Zimbabwe called CAMPFIRE is a good example. It stands for Communal Areas Management Program for Indigenous Resources. How much more appealing than CHIYSAP, another organization in Zimbabwe? Others too have found short names that tell immediately why they are worthy of support. These include ACTIONAID, Mobile Creches, and Greenpeace.

Even when the full name expresses the spirit of the organization, it may not be used well. Near me in Canada there is an international development NGO that calls itself "Horizons" on its letterhead. That name could describe a travel agency, an art school, or a surveying company. There is nothing that says the organization helps people. The organization's full name is Horizons of Friendship. How much more appealing that is! At the same time, think how dreadful it would be to use only that organization's initials. Imagine hearing someone say, "I am calling on behalf of HOF." It sounds as if the person has a cold.

Even a name that is descriptive may not be the most appropriate. On Samal Island in the Philippines there is an organization usually called the LAWIG Foundation. "LAWIG" does not mean anything in the local language. It stands for Learned Assistance for the Welfare of the Island Grassroots.

You can see why people use the initials. The full name is not easy to understand, but it is acceptable to use with overseas donors, most of whom are fluent in English. Is it the best possible name when the Foundation is seeking grassroots support from people who don't speak English or don't understand it well?

Have you worked at finding your organization a name for everyday use that is easy to use and understand, and is not a set of initials? How many business people, possible new donors, or government agencies are going to know the meaning of the name you use now? How many will understand from your name exactly what you do?

If your name will present difficulties, change it sooner rather than later, when the confusion would be worse. But change it only to a name that paints an accurate picture. Foster Parent's Plan changed its name to Plan International which, to the extent that it conveys anything at all, sounds like a multinational corporation.

The quality and commitment of your board members

At the head of most organizational structures is a board of directors made up of volunteers. The membership and authority of this board is so important in building credibility that it is discussed in a separate chapter.

The board may need to be reinforced with other groups of supporters. Patrons are people who allow you to use their names to increase the credibility of your organization. You may call them patrons, or honorary board members. Or you may set up a separate committee of such persons and call it an Advisory Council.

The criteria for selecting board members, and ways of encouraging them to be active in fundraising, are discussed in Chapter 7 in this book and in Book 2, Chapters 5 and 6. Patrons and other ways of reinforcing the board are discussed in Book 2, Chapter 6.

4 Rating yourself: nine sources of strength

An organization is not a problem to be solved. Affirm strengths and values to keep the organization alive.

JAMES GREGORY LORD, CONSULTANT, UNITED STATES

Most voluntary development organizations share certain ideas about themselves and certain attitudes to the world around them. Some of these ideas help them in fundraising. For example, donors may be attracted by a selfless commitment to helping other people improve their lives. Other ideas can damage even the best fundraising efforts. For example, an organization that displays its suspicion of business or government cannot expect to build partnerships with corporations or government agencies.

While your cause may be good and the need great, there is no point in setting up or expanding a fundraising program until you know what kind of organization you are, what your goals are, and how you relate to your community. This analysis is not a one-time event: every organization must look at itself this way from time to time.

If we don't examine ourselves, we go on playing the same old tune while the audience grows smaller and smaller. If we do a careful examination, we can learn how our often-unconscious beliefs influence our work. The point of the exercise in Chapters 4, 5, and 6 is to create a framework for fundraising. What does your organization value? What is its potential?

This chapter is about the strengths of voluntary agencies everywhere. It is those strengths, not the weaknesses, that make them what they are. The next chapter will talk about the weaknesses that often affect such agencies. The questions will give you a chance to decide how much these two sets of characteristics apply to your own organization. You can do this exercise by yourself or you can involve colleagues. Once having noted the weaknesses, you can set about turning them to strengths.

Spending time now answering the questions will save you time later on. Your answers will fit right into your long-term planning. They will also help you build your case for financial support.

Believing in what we do

Voluntary organizations work for good causes. They want to improve their community and the lives of the people in it. The people who work in them know their work is valuable and they are proud of what they do. Most of the people I know in voluntary organizations work long hours, often with great intensity, often for low pay because they believe passionately in the mission and feel rewarded by their service. Maintaining a commitment to

these values is essential. These organizations are driven not by desire for power or money but by their shared beliefs. As a result, they can undertake programs that businesses won't touch because they would lose money.
Why was your organization founded?
How have its goals changed over the years?
What goals are important to your organization now?
Are these goals supported by everyone?
If not, what other goals do staff and volunteers have?

Providing inspiration
Charities set a wonderful example in our communities. They show what people with courage and initiative and a desire to help can do, often in the face of great difficulties. Thousands of people, for example, have left good jobs in cities to go to rural areas to work with poor farmers. One I have met was an engineer in Calcutta, India, who saw there were no schools for children in isolated villages in the first range of the Himalayas. He left his job and moved to a mountain village with his wife to open a school. Another is the head of a social welfare agency in Peru who has turned down many offers of high-paying jobs from foreign businesses. They both wanted to do something good in the world. Such people are inspiring. They attract other people to help them.
What people like that do you have in your organization?
How does your organization inspire others to do good work?

Being close to the people we want to help
Voluntary organizations know from experience what the people they serve need to help them learn to read, grow more food, have better health, earn more money, and in other ways improve their lives. Community development agencies are important because they keep other people aware of the social changes required to meet these needs. Because service is their motive, not profit, they may be listened to with respect.

Governments are distant. For example, the Ministry of Education of Bangladesh may decide, with an international bank, that a village needs a new school. The villagers know they also need a trained and dedicated teacher. The government may borrow money from the bank to build the school, but there are not enough trained teachers to work in it. The government is also getting money from the bank to train thousands of teachers, but that will take time; there is no guarantee when the village will get a trained teacher. The building alone is not enough. Instead of waiting for the government to act, the villagers raise the money to bring in a good teacher.

In New Delhi, the government tried to improve life for people living in slums. They began by giving men a small piece of land. The government thought that if the men owned the land, they would improve their property. Too often, the men sold the land and spent the money, sometimes on gambling. No improvements were made. Pressure from social welfare groups led the government to change its policy. The social welfare groups knew that women are the ones who have to stay at home. They don't want to lose their

land. The government began giving land jointly to wives and husbands. Now land stays in the family. Gradually improvements are being made.
What are the real needs of the people you serve?
How are you helping your community to meet those needs?
Are there are other needs you could help them meet?
How does your organization work for social change?
What examples of your success can you recall?

Responding quickly
Governments react slowly because they are large and distant from the people. They must think always of politics and the national good. Voluntary organizations are located in the communities they serve. And, because they are smaller they can respond quickly and flexibly to new problems. When a typhoon damages communities in the Philippines, local agencies are rebuilding houses well before government people are on the job.
Has your organization responded to social needs quickly and imaginatively? Were the responses successful? Why did they succeed? If they did not succeed, why did they fail?

Adopting new ideas easily
Governments are often slow to experiment with new ideas because they have large bureaucracies and must please many interest groups. Non-profit organizations have fewer restrictions and usually are more open to experiments. They can try out new ideas more easily than government. Because they are close to the people, they can also get things done quickly. They may also come up with more innovative solutions because they are small enough to be flexible and are not subject to the political constraints that hamper government action. For example, they began teaching farmers how to use organic gardening techniques while governments were still debating whether it was a good idea to reduce reliance on chemicals.

The government of India promoted one model of smokeless stove for a long time but it did not become popular. A women's group recognized there needed to be many models of stoves to meet different needs. Some women want stoves that use very little firewood. Others want large stoves in which they can bake bread. The women's group has helped design and build several models of improved stoves – 300,000 of them across India. It succeeded where government failed because it understood what women need. Now many women are healthier because they are breathing less smoke. And, because the stoves burn more efficiently, the women are making fewer trips to the forest for firewood.
What research have you done about new techniques you should consider?
What experiments have you conducted in the last year or two?
What did they achieve?
Have you continued these programs?

Tackling problems together
A government or a business may have no incentive to fix a local problem –

for instance, to clean garbage and other debris from a stream or drainage channel. They may think it would cost too much. Or they may not even know about the problem. But the people close to the garbage know. By banding together they can achieve what they could never achieve alone. They can clean up the waterway. Voluntary organizations can get poor people involved in their own development to a degree unmatched by government or business. Usually they can do it for less money than if it was done by government or business.
What services has your organization provided?
What did you accomplish?
Has this become a regular program?

Safe investment in progress
When people see a job that needs to be done, and money has to be raised to do it, they often prefer to give their money to a voluntary organization. They think an organization committed to helping people will use most of the money to solve the problem at hand. They believe a commercial organization would be more interested in profit. They are concerned that a government might be corrupt or inefficient. They believe a voluntary organization is the best way to invest their money in community progress.
Do people in your community think this way?
How has your organization benefited?

Volunteers are one of the greatest strengths any organization can have.

Using volunteers
Voluntary organizations can make use of low-cost volunteer energy. Neither governments nor private enterprise know how to do this. Volunteers are one of the greatest strengths any organization can have. It is not only that they work without pay. They bring enthusiasm and a commitment to the job. They also tell their friends about what they are doing. They are good ambassadors.
How many unpaid volunteers help your organization? What do they do?
How are you encouraging more people to volunteer to help you?

Scaling up
Voluntary organizations can constantly expand their base of support by enlisting new volunteers and by serving new kinds of needs. In this way, many organizations that began as small groups of villagers or city dwellers continue to grow after achieving their first goals. With growth they become more effective and may become stronger financially.

The pattern is similar around the world. Here is how it works.

Stage 1 A group starts with local, small-scale projects. When those projects succeed, the group expands geographically and starts similar projects in other communities.

Stage 2 The group starts projects in new but related areas. Maybe it began by advising farm women how to grow better kitchen gardens. From there it may expand into health clinics for rural families and schools for farmers' children.

Stage 3 As the group becomes larger, its members begin to look at the reasons people need help. They decide that the way to improve conditions in the long term is by changing public policy. They add social policy to the work they are doing already. An organization that provides farmers with seed for crops starts campaigning to change national policy on seed distribution. Some groups may decide to devote themselves entirely to policy change.

Academics and development experts call this evolution "scaling up."
At which stage is your organization?
What stage will it be at in five years? In ten years?

Other questions
What other strengths does your organization have?
How do they benefit your work?
What attitudes do you most want to preserve?

5 Rating yourself: eighteen areas to strengthen

Relationships with government
Voluntary agencies are only as strong as the government under which they operate. In countries such as Somalia and Liberia, which for a long time have had almost no government or a government in turmoil, voluntary organizations have been weakened. They cannot operate efficiently or effectively without political stability.

Voluntary organizations can also suffer from too much government. They need some freedom from government interference. When they are subject to too much regulation, they may spend almost as much time filling out forms as they do getting their real job done. And their voices may be stilled. MWENGO, the NGO coordinating body for Eastern and Southern Africa in Zimbabwe, noted in July 1998 that, "In some countries the state has begun to monitor their activities or attempted to control NGOs through elaborate registration or coordination requirements. NGOs want to maintain their autonomy while establishing a constructive relationship with the state."

The head of a corporate foundation in Bangkok said, "If you want foreign money, you are supposed to register with the government but agencies don't want to register because the government thinks agencies are opposed to it. You must be approved by the security police. If an organization participates in protests, then the organization is not approved. Organizations cannot be political. The government can come in any time. But the government has no money. So now organizations go under a registered organization that is eligible for foreign money. Some funding agencies care, others don't." Such problems are widespread.
If your agency has been affected by government suspicion, how can you overcome this problem?

Some organizations are almost entirely dependent on governments. Some run programs financed from outside the country by international development agencies, but the money is given to the national government and reaches the voluntary organization through a ministry. Others receive money directly from their government and may in fact be acting as agents of the government, supplementing its activities. However, they may not think of themselves that way. Often the money from government pays more than the costs of a program. It also helps to pay the organization's general expenses for office and staff.

Dependence on government makes an organization vulnerable to government control. Even if the government does not interfere, the organization must always be concerned that a change in public policy, or in the bureaucracy, will affect their finances, their programs, and their long-term survival.

If you receive money from your government, has it affected your independence? How?
What can you do to reduce dependence on government support?

Revising the vision

Voluntary organizations are usually built on the enterprise, vision, and dedication of one person or a small group of people who saw a community problem and set out to solve it. They had – and may still have – enthusiasm, vision, and dedication. Everything may go smoothly while the original, committed people are around. But when they leave, the organization may falter.

The people who join later may not have the commitment of the founders. Therefore they may be less successful at making a strong case for support. And they may not be prepared to work as hard as the founders or in the same uncomfortable conditions or make the same financial sacrifices. Even if they do have the same commitment, it may be to an outdated vision.

New leadership can change a whole organization – its mandate, program, staff, fundraising. In many organizations, the founder made all the early decisions and, even after many years, continued to dominate policy and planning. Under a new leader, decisions may be made collectively. Democratic changes of this kind can be good, but they can also be deeply disruptive. Often they pit staff loyal to the previous leadership against those who support the new regime. The situation can be made worse if the old leadership does not go away or criticizes the new leadership from outside. If the new leaders are to continue, the old leadership must be confronted and overcome.

Have you changed leadership recently? Are you likely to have a change of leadership?
If your leadership has changed, how has your organization changed?
In what ways is your organization better or worse as a result of those changes?

Responding to needs

Many organizations are started by amateurs. Often the same amateurs, or new ones, continue to run the organization for years after its founding. In the beginning they know how to do what needs to be done. But as the years pass, the complexities increase; amateur leaders often don't know how to deal with the new problems.

This often happens when an organization grows from Stage 1 into Stage 2 (see Chapter 4). More people are needed to run it. Amateur leaders may not know whether to hire professional staff, arrange to train the present staff to handle new responsibilities, or just muddle along. Many NGOs are limited to small projects simply because they don't have the technical skill needed to manage large, complex undertakings.

Technical expertise and management skills are essential for long-term success. Yet it is often difficult to persuade leadership of the need for new expertise to manage growth and achieve financial stability. Some managers are nervous about hiring people better qualified than themselves. They feel threatened by people who know more than they do. Some fear the organization will change in ways they don't like, that new people won't share their goals. While new staff or experts are not an automatic solution, failing to bring in new skills can hold the organization back.

It isn't hard to find examples of this type of weakness. An agency in Central America was involved in building tube wells to provide villagers with clean drinking water. Instead of hiring an engineer to oversee the work, it decided to save money and use its own staff to supervise the local volunteers who were doing the work. The wells have never produced the amount of water the people need. In West Africa, another organization decided it didn't need a trained bookkeeper even though the number of its projects had doubled in just two years. Its accounts were never up to date as a result, and it had no clear idea of how it was spending its money and whether the money was being used wisely.

How has your organization obtained new skills and expertise to meet its present needs?

Thinking for growth

Some people know their organizations need to invest in their future even when money is tight. They know big thinking is essential for development. That belief frightens other people who worry about even the tiniest expense, especially when money is short. People argue about how many pencils should be used in an office. Or about whether money should be spent to entertain someone who might give much more money than a meal would cost. Leaders may spend more time thinking of ways to save money than of ways to raise money or grow. They prevent growth by being unwilling to take even the smallest risks.

A study conducted in Uganda by DENIVA (Development Network of Indigenous Voluntary Associations) in the late 1990s found that many organizations attributed their difficulties in raising funds to external factors: "Organizations felt quite helpless and had a lot of self-pity and maybe got obstructed from being creative and innovative in their resource mobilization strategies."

Conflicts between leaders with imagination and others who think small can paralyse an organization. This sort of tension threatens even the smallest local service agency. It is more likely to arise when an organization begins scaling up and takes on new responsibilities. It can threaten, and often overcome, a commitment to goals that everyone thought were shared.

What signs of this type of conflict can you detect in your organization?
What might you do about any you do detect?

Keeping people

People become involved in voluntary organizations for many reasons. Some want to help people in their own community or in other countries. Others join because they see opportunities to advance themselves – to get a job, get a grant, get a car, a bicycle, or a place to live. Still others have no choice: they may have to become a member of an organization to get some of its benefits, such as low-cost food or better health care. Sometimes an organization runs into financial difficulties, or changes its policies, and isn't able to do as good a job of giving its members what they want. Members may start to fight among themselves. Others get bored with repetitive jobs, especially if they get less recognition than they feel they deserve. Many may drop out.

What attracted the staff in your organization to work with you?
What attracted the volunteers in your organization to work with you?
Do you feel the staff and volunteers of your organisation are continuing to get good value for their work? What evidence do you have?
Are you losing staff or volunteers you would like to keep? If so, why? What could you do to keep them?

Looking to local resources

Many organizations are too susceptible to foreign influences and trends and not sufficiently responsive to local pressures, local needs, and local possibilities. The result is a lack of credibility in their communities. This is inevitable as long as the money flows from the North. The DENIVA study says, "Most NGOs spend enormous amounts of time and energy identifying potential international donors and writing project proposals for resources which may well exist in their own localities. NGOs need to begin considering the resources right here in their Network. The local resources within the Network are more likely to provide socio-economic and political support, contribute to the member organization's independent thinking, and could be more sustainable in the long term."

What local resources are you drawing on?
What other resources are available that you are not using? What benefits would you get from them?

Keeping the mission in mind

Some organizations turn into businesses even though they still call themselves voluntary organizations. They change because they need to raise money to keep going, and business operations promise to bring in regular income. Running a small business may also seem more exciting than looking for grants or some other source of funds. But an organization's humanitarian purpose can shrink in importance, or even disappear, if its leaders have to devote most of their time to running a business or fighting for a share of commercial or government contracts. That has happened to one voluntary organization in Zimbabwe, where every morning the director would ask his staff, "What have you got for me today?" He was not asking, "Who has been helped and how?" He was asking, "What contracts have you brought in? What grants have come through?" Survival had become the only imperative.

Voluntary organizations should be businesslike. But if they let business thinking take over, they are in danger of losing their sense of their mission. *Has this kind of thinking shown itself in your organization? In what ways? What can you do about it?*

Listening

Every organization likes to think it is unique, if not in its program, at least in the special qualities it brings to its work. This can lead to at least one internal danger. Staff members may come to think they have the right answer to every question. They don't ask the people they intend to help how they see their own problems, what they think they need, how they think they can best be helped. The staff don't look outside their own offices and ideas. They know they are right!

As a result, the organization decides by itself what the problem is and imposes a solution. Both may be wrong. In southern Africa, an agency decided a village needed more water and built an expensive dam on a small creek a good distance from people's homes. The villagers had to walk to the reservoir and carry home water in heavy jars. There was actually plenty of water right at home. The people simply needed to catch the water off their roofs in the rainy season and save it, and reuse water whenever they could.

In this case, the organization was at fault in two ways. Not only did it not listen to its clients, it did not listen to ideas and opinions from outside the organization. This meant its solution was out-of-date and far less helpful than it might have been.

How do you arrange to listen regularly to the people you want to help?
How do you use the information you get by listening to them?
How do you keep up-to-date with developments in your area of expertise?

Accepting what we don't understand

People in voluntary organizations often fear anyone outside their own closed circle. They too often think in terms of "we" and "they." In this case "we" are doing good through our commitment to our organization. "They" are all the people we don't know well.

Being willing to join forces with other sectors of our community makes an organization stronger. But to do that, we must try to understand what people in those other sectors are thinking. Instead, too often we generalize about what we see as their failings. Consciously or subconsciously we say, "These people don't really understand us, so we don't need to listen to them." We may feel we have nothing to learn from them, that their ideas are the opposite of ours. Or we may close our minds to new ideas that could come from them because we are afraid that if we did accept their way of thinking we would have to change.

People with money are suspect. People in business and people with power are suspect. We say, "Business people are only interested in money. They are just greedy capitalists. What will they want in return for helping us?" We think, "Governments are all corrupt. Unlike us they have no real interest in the welfare of our people." Then, no matter how well we think

we are hiding our prejudices, we are apt to get a cool reception when we approach business or government.
What comments do you hear your staff and volunteers make about other organizations? How do you respond?

Building alliances

When organizations think they are special or unique, they are often reluctant to work closely with other agencies or to build alliances. They don't see any need to bring in other people. They won't cooperate with other agencies because of pride. Douglas Ramage, then director of the Asia Foundation in Indonesia, commented before the departure of President Suharto that factionalism and hatred were common, especially among human rights organizations, because those activist organizations could not come out into the open. They wanted to be on the big stage, he said, but they ended up in little organizations. So they fought. In Mexico, the members of two major groups of non-profit organizations – the Asociacion Civil (AC) and the Institucion de Asistencia Privada (IAP) – are reported to distrust each other. AC members are seen as left wing, revolutionary, with a strong political agenda sometimes masked as development work. IAP members are considered to be arms of the government or, even worse, mere excuses to get money from foreign sources, some of which they keep.

Some organizations won't cooperate with others because of fear. They know there are other agencies doing much the same work, sometimes in the same places, and doing as good a job or better. They could think of these other agencies as allies. Instead, too often, they think of them as competitors for money, for programs, for volunteers, and even for beneficiaries.

We sometimes also separate ourselves from other voluntary organizations because they are working for causes our own group could never support. We may think people who believe in those causes are ignorant, or immoral, or even dangerous. In countries where the spread of HIV/AIDS is not acknowledged or where contraception is not practised, people who work in these areas may be seen as threatening.

Frequently, all the agencies working in the same field could reduce their costs, do better work, and help still more people by working together. Outsiders – people who might give money – are not impressed when they see organizations that won't share resources and costs to improve their services.
What agencies do you feel may be "competing" with you?
In what ways do you think your organization is affected (for good or bad) by the presence of these other agencies? Have you tested your impressions to see if they are true?
How do you share ideas and work with other agencies? Are there more ways you could share ideas in the future?

Pulling together publicly

Voluntary organizations not only disagree with one another in private. They often disagree publicly. One American professor looked at all the talking that goes on and decided voluntary organizations can't even agree that the sun rises in the east. When we attack other groups, or hold ourselves apart from them, we do more than protest: we show the divisions in the voluntary sector publicly. This weakens the entire structure of voluntary development in our communities.

If they could come together to speak with one voice more often, voluntary organizations could influence, even more than they do now, the policies of their governments. They could also be more effective in fundraising. That is why, in both North and the South, many volunteer organizations have stopped appealing for money on their own. Instead, they join together, as a United Way or a community foundation, in one appeal; then they share the money it raises.

In spite of such examples, too many of us won't give up even the smallest amount of independence. Individual organizations protest, "No one else can speak for us! We must speak for ourselves!" Then a pharmaceutical company may be asked for funding by ten different organizations, all caring for AIDS patients. When that happens, the company is likely to ask, "Why don't you people get together?" The company doesn't want to deal with ten different applications for funding from organizations doing much the same thing. It would much rather receive one joint application. If agencies persist in approaching the company separately, its management may eventually become annoyed and give no money to any of them.

How does your organization work actively with networks/associations of NGOs?
Does your organization join with other organizations in public statements or in applying for funds?
If you have done this, how successful has the joint action been?
How could successful cooperation be increased?
If organizations in your community have not cooperated, how has it affected your organization?

Sharing knowledge
Voluntary agencies are geared for "action, action, action." Staff members don't like writing the detailed plans that are needed when applying for funds for the work they hope to do. And once a project is under way or finished, they don't like writing reports that are detailed enough to help other people who are trying to solve the same problems. They don't see it as their job to make sure as many people as possible learn from their experience. They rarely have any training in communications. People in granting agencies also rarely have any communications experience, therefore dissemination of information seldom finds its way into funding proposals or project agreements.

Agencies that make grants expect reports, but usually just file them as evidence of funds spent and work accomplished. As a result, the lessons learned in one place in sustainable agriculture – or health care, or literacy training, or granting small loans, or fundraising – are seldom known elsewhere.

Here is just one example: Some farmers in India have known for centuries how to make an excellent natural pesticide by boiling the leaves of the neem tree in water. Those farmers don't have to buy chemical pesticides.

Yet to this day other Indian farmers know nothing of the technique. Neem trees grow in Nigeria as well, but farmers began using this technique only a few years ago. They learned of it through an organization that is devoted to communicating the good practices known in one country to other countries around the world.

How do you communicate the results of your work?

How much have you benefited from learning from other organizations? Are there more networks, mailing lists, or organizations you could join that might provide information of value to your work?

Most NGOs ignore or do not understand the political, economic and social context in which they operate, nor recognize that the communities in which they work are part of a broader system of conflicting interests and agendas. Project-oriented activities are insufficient to effect fundamental changes in the condition of their constituencies. NGO staff require skill in policy analysis and advocacy, information in the form of persuasive arguments based on empirical evidence, and access to the political arena.

MWENGO – CENTRE FOR NGOS IN EASTERN AND SOUTHERN AFRICA, THREE YEAR PROGRAMMING FRAMEWORK 1995–1998

Spotting trends

Many people in voluntary organizations are so busy that it is hard for them to look beyond their daily problems. They don't have time to follow world news in detail. Even if they have the time, they may have only limited access to useful radio, television, and newspapers. And the media that do reach them may not tell them about important changes in their country or in the rest of the world. They have to depend on word of mouth, and it may not be accurate. So they may not know nearly enough about what is happening beyond their own community – or even within it. Yet these changes could shape their future. Ezra Mbogori of MWENGO believes its members know more about the psychology of donors than about their own social environment. This is echoed in his organization's major planning document.

An example: Several years ago Bangladeshi NGOs had to mount a defence against the accusations of Islamic fundamentalists that the NGOs were destroying rather than helping their society. The NGOs had been concerned about their track record and reputation with each other and with foreign donors, but they had neglected to build support locally. As a result, they had left themselves vulnerable. Imagine if NGOs had begun to launch fundraising campaigns before they realized how threatening they appeared to the established powerful people who were attacking them, and by extension the values of traditional Islam.

How do you keep up with the world, including the local world, beyond your organization?

What networks and/or intermediary groups do you belong to now?

Do you go to conferences and workshops that would keep you up to date with developments in your work?

Do you read about national and international policy changes?

How do you keep up with daily news?

Reducing burnout

The LAWIG Foundation (Learned Assistance for the Welfare of the Island Grassroots) began life as a theatre troupe of 16 volunteers who performed in villages on Samal Island at the southern tip of the Philippines. In the early eighties, the island was home to marginal farmers and fisherfolk. Then in 1991 the island was declared a tourist destination. Developers from Manila bought a lot of land to build hotels. People were forced off their land. Fishing is no longer an industry. There is not even enough fishing to feed the people.

The Foundation is now a facilitating organization that has been working to strengthen around 30 cooperatives. In the example, Hur Camporendondo, its founder and executive director, describes the change.

People involved in voluntary organizations work hard because they have a special commitment to the goals of the group and because they believe they are doing work of great social value. As a result, staff and volunteers often try to do far too many things at once. And long hours have a cost. There is a high risk of burnout. People get tired, or discouraged. The director of the Philippine Peasant Institute said, "NGOs [in the Philippines] were very discouraged, especially in 1992 and 1993. We have recovered, but we are still tired. We are fighting a giant. That is universal. We must be optimistic: we are doing missionary work. We need a lot of energy."

Managers wear out from the pressures of struggling to survive financially while at the same time they are expected to give daily leadership. Their expectations and ambitions shrink. They may no longer believe their community values their service enough to support it. No one promotes new fundraising ideas. So, when the group asks for money, the people speaking for it are likely to be half-hearted. They don't really expect a donation, and the result is that they don't get one.

Do you see symptoms of burnout in your organization? What do people say? What can you do about it?

Managing donors

Some organizations get more money than they can really manage, rather than too little. Perhaps they have taken on programs to satisfy an international donor agency eager to spend money at the end of its financial year, or perhaps funding for a new project was seen as a way to help cover overhead costs. The programs bring the organization money but they may not suit its goals or its capacities.

An organization may obtain so many grants that it

We decided we could be more effective if we changed from a volunteer group to a professional organization. The process took one year. It was painful and tedious. A huge headache! But it worked because we planned very carefully. We brainstormed every day almost until midnight.

I succeeded in getting a grant from Cebemo [an aid agency now called Bilance] in the Netherlands. There was one big problem, however. The grant allowed for eight staff to be hired and there were sixteen volunteers. They were all close friends. And all with a deep commitment, an ideological perspective, and a dynamism resulting from the needs of the island people. What to do? We spread the grant over the 16 people and gave ourselves six months to install a system of performance reviews. Two people left because they preferred a more informal structure.

But, since that time, the commitment has lessened. The old staff want job security. They count their hours of work. It is an awkward situation. We can't count on the commitment now. It was our strong base. It is very sad.

What is my formula for managing? Stay ahead of the staff. I was ahead for three years. But now I feel I am getting weaker. The problems are so broad – electricity, the cooperatives, the fisherfolk, the land use policy. This is the last chance for people to get equity. If they don't get it soon, the people will go back to a new era of feudalism like we had under the Spanish. LAWIG *is the best challenge of my life. I can survive.*

HUR CAMPORENDONDO, LAWIG FOUNDATION, THE PHILIPPINES

seems too prosperous. It may look more like a donor than a body that needs money. I remember looking out of an office window in a development agency in Zimbabwe and seeing seven white cars and vans parked in the courtyard, all owned by development organizations. This was in a city where most people travel for hours every day on crowded busses.

The demands of donors can seem overwhelming if you are carrying more projects than you can reasonably manage. Donors want organizations to be accountable, but often in quite different ways. They want financial reports in a wide variety of formats. Some foundations want detailed program reports. Others say: "Don't bother us with a lot of paper." This can result in administrative chaos. Professor Amara Pongsapich believes that, in Thailand at least, management is not cheating. She says, "There is just not enough competency, especially in financial management; for example, bookkeepers have no training."

Have you felt overwhelmed by the demands of supporters? How do you deal with these problems?

CARTOON: CAROLE CABLE

"Agreed. This organization's primary objective in the coming year will be the recruitment of new board members."

Strengthening governance

Voluntary organizations are called that because they are governed by boards of volunteer members. (The word "board" is used in these books to describe any group that is legally responsible for a voluntary organization.) These volunteers are often dedicated. Nevertheless, very few boards do a good job. Most simply do not know what a board should do; this is often a problem, even for large organizations. But also our organizations are not central to their lives. Their families and their careers are always more important.

Board members often have almost no idea how voluntary organizations work. They find it hard to understand that voluntary organizations try to combine two conflicting goals – to grow and serve more people, and at the same time to keep their special spirit and goals. Board members may think a volunteer organization can be managed like a business. They often disagree with the organization's managers. They are not always involved in important policy decisions and do not always receive enough information to know what is happening in the office or the field. Often they don't read the information they are given. They often trust management far too much, especially about financial matters. They sometimes make terrible decisions, especially when hiring senior people.

Do you see these problems in your organization? What has happened? What can be done to improve the board's involvement?

Reaching out

The director of an NGO coalition in the Philippines said in 1997, "NGOs get big bucks but they are not broadening their physical area, though they have expanded lately. The pioneering spirit is less now than it was ten years ago. Many voluntary organizations claim to be serving poor people but they don't want to work in isolated, rural areas. There are 20 million poor people. NGOs are reaching only 2 per cent of the poor with credit, for example. They prefer to be close to cities, to wear ties and go to offices. NGO people must be an example. They should not have fancy cars and big offices." John Gwynne of Oxfam (India) Trust believes one reason people in voluntary organizations can enjoy the urban life is that donors do not care about the real grassroots, or cannot agree on which programs to support.

How far is your organization reaching out?
Are there people it should be serving that it is not serving now?
How can it reach them more economically and efficiently?
How practical is it to consider such an expansion of service?

Support for fundraising

Many volunteer board members are unwilling to help raise local funds. They may be afraid of approaching other people and businesses for money. Or they may think asking for money is too undignified for them to do it.

This failure in leadership often starts with an organization's first board, when all the needed money comes from overseas grants. The founding leaders recruit board members who are friends, or are committed to the cause, or have a special expertise the new organization needs. Local fundraising is never mentioned. Over the years, the original board members replace themselves with people who have similar backgrounds. Again, they don't say anything to the new members about fundraising as a responsibility of the board. In fact, the idea that board members are responsible for the financial health of the organization they are agreeing to govern is rarely mentioned. Attention is focused on programs. If the organization begins to lose grant money, the board members are at a loss. They tell the manager: "Go out and raise money!" But they don't offer to help. Often they are even offended if the manager expects them to help.

How do your board members view fundraising? What has been the result?

Further questions

Do the organizations in your area have weaknesses that have not been mentioned?
Does your organization also have some of these weaknesses? Which ones?
Does your organization have other weaknesses?
How do they affect your work?
What strengths do local organizations have that you don't have?
What attitudes in your organization would you most like to change?

Many of the topics presented in this chapter will be addressed in more detail in later chapters and in Books 2 and 3.

6 Rating yourself: asking others

In the previous chapters, we looked at ways to examine your voluntary organization from the inside. In this chapter we look in detail at how others, including the community, see your organization. Asking people both inside and especially outside your organization what they think about your work is vital. All of us are too close to our own work to judge it objectively or to see how we look to the users of our service and the community in general.

In your study you may:
- ask staff and any volunteers where they think the organization should be going
- gather a group of people to talk about their experiences with your organization
- interview organizations similar to yours to see where you compete and where you could work together
- talk to other organizations to find out how your service is regarded in the community
- interview business people, granting agencies, politicians, and civil servants to learn how their opinions and plans may affect your work
- send or deliver questionnaires to other people whose opinions you value, if you have the resources

What you are doing, in effect, is similar to a rapid rural appraisal. In this case you are not looking at the situation in a village, but in an organization. With this information you will have the raw material for a plan for your organization for the next two to three years. Such a plan is essential if you are going to begin fundraising in a serious way. A long-range plan will provide a road map for you and your board. It will show what your organization will do in the next few years, why what you will do is needed, how you will do it, and how much money is required to fund it. You will use this strategic plan to put together a fundraising plan that suits the needs and style of your organization. You will also show it to potential donors. They will be reluctant to give money without evidence that you are well organized and well focused. A long-range plan is the best way to demonstrate that.

From the type of self-examination outlined in this chapter, you will know where people think you are doing well. You will also know where they think you are failing. Then you can try to include the necessary improvements in your long-range plan.

You will never feel that you have all the information you need to make the best possible plan. The challenge for managers of all organizations is to have just enough information to go ahead with some confidence. If you forget this fact, you are in danger of studying and re-studying. "Paralysis by analysis," Jim Lord calls it in *The raising of money*. It is a wonderful way to avoid getting on with the job of fundraising. At some point starting local fundraising requires an act of faith that may have to override what you don't know. You have to begin.

How to plan your research

Step 1 Decide which groups of people you need to consider. Think about all the groups of people who are already involved with your organization or who you would like to involve. Be sure to interview some typical members of each group. You do not need to talk to everybody.

Step 2 Decide the style of your research. Should it be elaborate or formal? Should it be small-scale and informal? A short list of questions asked of a limited number of people over a few days should suffice.

Step 3 Draw up a list of questions. What do you need to know about your organization? What questions do you want to ask inside the organization and what questions outside?

Step 4 Decide who will ask the questions. Will it be you? Volunteers? Board members? Local students? A consultant? Others?

Step one: deciding who to ask

Who do you need to talk to?
Begin close to home; then spread out to include representatives of the groups of people that will decide your success or failure. What groups can do you the most harm and the most good? Give them the highest priority. If your organization is made up entirely of volunteers, be sure to question members of the core group at the very least. Place geographical limits on your research. You may want to survey people around a rural community in which you are based, and also people in cities who are donors or potential donors, or who can be influential in drawing attention to your work.

How many people do you need to talk to?
You need to talk to enough people to ensure that you have representative opinions. As long as the opinions you are collecting are varied and useful, it would be good to keep going. You may need to talk to only six people in one category, say, of potential clients or individual donors. When you start hearing many repetitions of the same thoughts, you can stop questioning that group and go on to other audiences. However, you need to talk to the whole board and the entire staff.

Who should you be asking?
Here are some of the most important groups and some of the kinds of answers your questions could produce.

- Current staff are your biggest asset and your biggest investment. They can do you the greatest good but also the greatest harm. They are the people who know the most about your work. They should be the people you talk to regularly and frequently. This study is a perfect time to get them to reflect in an organized way on what you are all doing and what improvements could be made.

> *Our health program would be better if we could get more families to use oral rehydration therapy.*
>
> *Our agency is strong because communication between the leaders and the staff is good.*

- The people you serve will vary in their willingness to be honest with you. They may not want to risk losing the service they receive from you. But their satisfaction is your whole purpose. Be sure to talk with different sorts of people: women, men, young, old, and so forth.

> *The extension worker you sent to help us should tell us more about how to use natural fertilizers.*
>
> *What we really need is a credit program for women who want to start small businesses.*

- Don't forget to ask the people you no longer serve. It could be useful to find out why they drifted away.
- Potential "customers" who could or should use your service but do not use it now are important too.

> *I am glad you will be building irrigation ditches here. We need your help.*
>
> *No one ever told me that you would help me write a letter to the government.*

- Former staff members will likely have strong opinions and may be more direct and more objective than current staff in their criticism and praise.

> *I moved to another job because the organization was not doing enough to raise money. I worried I would not have a job in a few months.*
>
> *People in the community think that big water project we did has not solved their problems.*

- Board members, because of their contacts with people outside the agency, will have a broad perspective. Even if there is not a big or active board, it is important that the members be consulted as the research is being planned and as the survey is conducted. As you move on to talk about fundraising, they will be involved whether they want to be or not. Their support is essential. If it is not there, you need to know.

> *I will be chairman but I won't ask anybody for money.*
>
> *You are doing great work. There are two people in my office who might help us.*

- Volunteers often have different views than the staff. They may think highly of the organization and its staff for entirely different reasons. And they may have skills you could put to use.

> *This day care centre is really needed here. I am glad I can help.*
>
> *I have some nursing training. But here I am just doing office work. Your health clinic people could use my experience.*

- Other agencies in the same field will know whether you are seen as cooperative and supportive of their work. You will also want to learn whatever you can about their programs and hopes, to see where they complement or compete with what you are doing.

I don't really know what you do. People from your office hardly ever come to NGO meetings.

We would definitely be interested in working with you on a joint day care program.

• Other agencies in the community that are aware of your organization can add to your information about your standing in the community.

Everyone is talking about your new small loan program. We all think it is a great idea.

I heard last week you may have to close because you have not been able to get new grants.

• Media people can tell you what they hear about your programs. They can also tell you how they view your communications program. If you are just beginning a communications program, they can advise you on how to get good coverage.

Media people can tell you how to get good coverage.

You know how hard it is to get on the radio in this country. I don't think I can do anything. Your organization is just too small.

I like working with your people. Your human rights program made a good story for our paper.

• Current individual donors will tell you why they support your organization now and what you must do to ensure that they continue their support.

My daughter sings in the choir you started. As long as she is there, I will give you money.

Preventing more pollution is important. Your recycling program looks good to me.

• Potential individual donors will tell you, and quickly, whether or not you are likely to attract local donations and other kinds of support that you are not getting now.

I just don't see that you are doing what our town needs right now.

This is exactly the kind of work we want to support.

• Local businesses will also tell you quickly how they view your work, their policy on donations, if they have one, and the form in which donations might come. They will also tell you how to apply for a donation.

Your work is all in the northern part of the country. We only support agencies around here.

We might consider giving you some office furniture.

• International donors will tell you their current policies and suggest ways you might gain their support. They will also tell you what they will not support.

We are not giving directly to small NGOs any more. All our support goes through a community foundation we are just funding that will channel grants from inside the country. You should apply to it from now on.

Yes, we will start giving grants for urban agriculture next year. We are looking for new ideas. Give us a proposal.

• Politicians and civil servants can explain government regulations, current plans for your community, and the official reaction to your program.
Our tax revenue has dropped and we are likely going to have to reduce funding for clinics. You will have to manage with less money.
We want community organizations to charge fees from now on.
We are going to build a number of pipe wells and need help doing it.
• Neighbours who are not users of your service will have a good idea of how your organization is seen in the community.
You put your garbage on the street. It blocks our doorway.
We are grateful to you for giving jobs to local people.
Before starting and as you proceed through the study, ask yourself:
Must we talk to all these different kinds of people? Can we safely omit any groups?
Are there other groups of people who should be contacted?

Step two: the style of your research

Are you going to be satisfied with a relatively small-scale survey of a few people? Or are you going to undertake a larger and broader research project? The answer will depend greatly on what you hope to learn from the effort and the use you will make of the results. The answer must also be determined by practical questions. If you want to survey a very diverse group of donors, or potential donors, or those who benefit from your services, you likely will have to settle on a sample. But how large a sample? If the results are to guide you in fundraising, a smaller but representative group of people will be enough. If you want to use the results to prove the effectiveness of your program, you may need a more thorough survey of the communities and people who have benefited. If you do not have or want to build the skills and resources to conduct such a survey, and cannot find someone to help you, such large-scale research may not be possible.

What do you want to learn?
The research for a long-range plan is different from an evaluation of how well your organization is meeting the objectives of one particular program. You will want to measure the impact and effectiveness of all your work as fully as possible. Find out what makes your organization special or unique.

It is not enough, for example, to be proud of having introduced a new type of latrine in your district. You want to know how many latrines have been built and how many people are using them. Even more important, you need to know how much the health of the families using them has improved. You also want to know about any problems those families have encountered with the latrines, and whether the design of the latrines can be improved. You want to know whether people are using them every time they need a latrine, and whether more education is required in their regular use and maintenance. You want to know how many more communities in the area you serve need latrines, and how many more latrines would need to be built. You may want to explore ways communities can be encouraged to build latrines. You will want to find out whether other organizations are also working to improve village sanitation, and how your work complements other efforts to improve community health. And so on.

This kind of evaluation is far more difficult than simply counting the number of latrines and users. It takes more time and care and is less precise. The results may take years to become clear. But they will interest donors, persuade them of your abilities and credibility, and attract funds for your work.

Measuring results of this kind is always complicated, but especially so if several groups are working in the same general area. Good crop yields, better medical care, and all sorts of other factors as well as latrines may contribute to better health. If you are working for social change, measuring results is even more difficult. Most of the time it takes more than one agency's efforts to change government policy, except at the most local level.

Sometimes the people who give you money want evidence but are not willing to give you the time or money to gather it. Everywhere funders too want to show "results." They may not be looking at whether an organization they are supporting has done good work, but instead are bent on "proof" that a project was successful. This demands an evaluation of the organization's programs. Yet most evaluations are flawed. Results are often put together from a series of anecdotes because we simply don't know what is really happening, or don't have the expertise or resources to gather and analyse the necessary quantitative data.

Research of this kind should be a continuous activity, part of your everyday work. Measure whatever you can and record your findings. While the project is going on, make sure data is recorded that will show whether the objectives have been met. Also write down, as soon as you hear them, anecdotes that show the value of your work. Get the whole story. It is the details that make the story come alive for people. Anecdotes are not the same as the hard data about results that will be demanded by funders more and more. But they certainly help in fundraising when you want to stir the emotions of a donor. Facts are important. But when you can show how your program improves lives, you are more likely to convince a donor to help you.

Keep in mind that "results," if they are to mean anything, are always outside the organization, not inside. Recruiting better board members is worthwhile, of course, but it is meaningless unless it pays off in terms of results. If the beneficiaries are better served because of better management, that is what counts. That is a result.

Making people feel comfortable
There are two important rules for getting good information from a survey. First, have good questions (Step 3). Next, ask the questions in a way that will make the people being questioned feel comfortable, relaxed, and open in answering.

You may choose to ask people questions in groups or individually. The groups may consist of several different kinds of people, or may consist of only one kind (for example, people who benefit from a particular program). Choose the approach that seems most likely to gain cooperation. Otherwise people are likely to feel awkward, or may hesitate to give negative opinions. For example, you may feel that staff members will speak more freely if they are surveyed individually. On the other hand, discussions in groups often prompt ideas that would not have arisen in individual conversations. Some people respond more openly if they can answer anonymously – if they are asked to write comments without signing their names, or if the questioning is done by an independent third party who will report results without identifying who said what.

Great sensitivity is needed in planning and carrying out surveys. Interviewers need patience and the ability to listen. They should be given a written set of questions so as to ensure that all questions are asked in the same, and most effective, way.

Every reassurance must be given to the people being questioned, especially if the questioner is unknown to them. Questioners must have proper identification and information about the organization. They should begin by explaining who they are and why they are asking questions. They might say, "My name is …… and I hope you can take a few minutes to help us. I represent WaterLink, a local organization that works to improve the water supply in villages. We are looking for ways our organization can provide better service. We hope you will help us do that by answering a few questions." Without this kind of reassurance, people may be nervous or suspicious. Poor or uneducated people, for instance, may see the questioner as an intruder threatening their fragile security.

Along with consultation comes a risk. People may expect that, because you have asked for their opinion and advice, you will do what they suggest. That does not always happen, of course. It helps for the questioner to explain that many people are being asked; later a decision will be made. Leaders must have the final say, always leaving some people dissatisfied. Still, in the long run, the benefits of consultation outweigh the defects.

Planning the structure
It is helpful to have a structure to guide your investigations. You don't want to end up with a lot of information and no slots to put it in. One well-known approach is to talk about Strengths, Weaknesses, Opportunities, and Threats. This is called a "SWOT" analysis after the first letters of each word. It is as good a system as any for planning your questions and then organizing what you learn. You are already familiar with the approach since you have looked at the possible strengths and weaknesses of your kind of organization (Chapter 5).

Strengths describe what the organization does well, preferably better than other similar organizations. Is your organization older? Does it have an established reputation? Is it new and/or meeting a new need? Your service might feed more children than other agencies do, or have more effective water management programs. You can list any number of strengths, with the reasons for your choices. Try ten strengths for a start.

Weaknesses may show up in your program. Has the organization been doing the same thing every year and not trying anything new? Is it resting on its reputation? Do the staff need more experience or more training? Look at your management: is morale low? Are people depressed about the future? Are you on shaky ground financially and yet no one is enthusiastic about fundraising?

Opportunities require imagination to recognize. They may be within the organization: to start a fundraising program, to find new volunteers, to launch a new project. Or they may be outside: a respected agency wants to affiliate with you so you will both be stronger, a company is looking for a way to improve its image in your community.

Threats to success come in many forms. Do you fear losing staff to local businesses because your salaries are too low? Is a major funder leaving your country? Is drought damaging crops you have been promoting?

Step three: planning the questions
What questions do we need to ask?
The questions listed at right cover some of the topics you might want to address. You will want to add or subtract questions to suit your interests and your circumstances. In conducting a survey it is important to have carefully written questions which are asked in exactly the same words to each members of a group – or to everyone. Otherwise you cannot add the responses together in a meaningful way. Of course, this does not mean questioners cannot follow up the set questions to get more details or a clearer answer, but there must be some commonality.

Questions using SWOT can apply to the whole organization or to one part, such as an individual program. Plan your questions carefully. Whatever approach you choose:

• Be specific. Make sure questions are short and easy to understand. The first question could be, "Are you satisfied with the water supply in the village?" If the answer is no, then, "What don't you like about it?" Then maybe, "Has it changed since WaterLink put in the new wells?" "What could be done to improve it?" etc. The answers to these specific questions are themselves specific and can easily be drawn together to show clear trends.

• Test your questions. Ask them of several people unconnected with the survey to see if they are clear.

• Seek concrete answers. Whenever possible, avoid questions that can be answered "yes" or "no."

Questions to ask almost everybody
What is the first thing that comes to mind when you think of our organization?
What is the most interesting thing about us?
What do you think is the mission of our organization?
What are our greatest strengths?
Do you think our mission is relevant?
Should the mission change? If so, how?
What services do you think we provide?
How do you think we could improve the quality of each service?

Questions for staff
Before preparing questions for staff, read Chapters 4 and 5 in this book. Chapter 4 talks about the strengths of many voluntary organizations. Chapter 5 describes the challenges facing many organizations. Then consider questions like those that follow.
What do you see as the strengths of our organization?
What challenges do you see facing our organization?
Are you satisfied with our current goals?
How can we judge morale?
Is morale high in our organization?
If it is low, why?
What can we do about it?
Should we be satisfied with our current programs and services?
How could current programs be improved?
What services should we provide in the future?
What new resources would we need to be able to provide these services?
Do you think we have a consistent long-term commitment to meet specific local needs?
Or do we aim to accommodate the ever-

*changing goals of donors?
Is it possible for us to do more than we are doing now?
How could we save money?
What opportunities do you see for us to increase our revenue?
Do you support increasing our investment in fundraising? Would you think so if it means a sacrifice on your part or a reduction in your program?
If not, what would have to change before you would be enthusiastic?
How would you feel if we were to charge our clients (those we serve) a fee for the services we now provide free?
How can the commitment of the founding or previous leaders be used to advantage in fundraising?
What is your perception of the board? What do you think its role should be?*

Questions for the people you serve
*What are the best of our current services? Why?
How could we improve our program?
Do you feel we could reduce or close some of the services we now provide? Which ones? Why?
What new services should we provide in the future?
If we could no longer afford to provide a service you are now using, would you be willing to pay for it? How much would you pay?
How might it be possible for us to increase our services?
Do you feel that we care about your opinion?*

Questions for potential users of the services
*Have you heard of our organization?
Where did you hear of it?
Which of our services might interest you? Why?
What other services should we provide?*

- Be positive. If you ask: "Has the new dam improved your water supply?" The negative answer is "No, we are not better off. We still have to walk a long way." People don't like delivering bad news. Better to ask: "What other steps do we need to take to improve the water supply?" Then you may get a positive answer: "We need a pipe to the village."

- Listen for silences. Because people would prefer to make you happy if they can, they often won't say anything, rather than appear critical. Think of a way to rephrase the question so the person does not avoid answering.

- Keep the questions honest. Be careful all the time that you don't intrude your own opinions. It is tempting to design questions that tell you only what you want to hear. The question, "You do agree with me that we should first improve the water supply, don't you?" does just that. Later, this makes it easy to say, "Everyone wants more hand pumps in the village." But people said what they were led to say, not necessarily what they felt.

- Test the strength of people's opinions if necessary. One way is to ask their preference on a scale of 1 to 5. "How do you rate the water quality here? Excellent, good, adequate, poor, unsafe?" Another is to ask for comparisons: "If you had to choose between these two new programs, which would you pick? Why?"

Step four: who will ask the questions?
You?
If your organization is small, then it may be easiest for you, as the leader, to do the study yourself and keep it small. Try to set aside a part of each day to interview people. Give yourself a deadline to have the project finished.

Volunteers? Board members?
If these allies of your organization can do some of the survey themselves, it is likely to increase their involvement in and commitment to the organization. Increased interest can pay off in the long run.

For anyone who carries out interviews, it is important to be sure that what they personally want your organization to become does not get in the way of their asking objective questions. They need to understand the importance of asking all of the questions, using the same wording each time within a particular group.

Local students?
Think about using students or staff at a local university or college. They might take on the survey as part of their class work in business, marketing, sociology, psychology, or other subjects where they need to learn how to conduct surveys. Teachers or professors can tell you how many of your clients and supporters will need to be interviewed for an accurate sample of each category. Or you can learn about surveying and sampling techniques from books about marketing and statistics.

Sometimes, a business or a college or university will lend a person to help with or to conduct a short-term research project. The adviser can help refine your ideas and set up the project, perhaps for you and your staff to conduct. The adviser can also be asked to help in training others to carry out interviews.

A consultant?
You might want to ask someone entirely outside the organization to conduct the research. You may be able to find a competent person or agency familiar with such research projects. If you can afford the fee or can arrange for funding for the project, the result may carry greater weight because it is objective. That can be helpful within your organization. Staff and board members are likely to take the need for change more seriously because it comes from an "outside expert" who charged good money to provide good information. Added weight is also useful with donors. It is even better if the person doing the survey has a good reputation in the community.

It pays to shop around when looking for a consultant. Talk to your friends in other agencies about what you should be looking for and how much you would have to pay for the study you want done. Ask a foundation that supports you to suggest someone. If you are looking at several possible consultants, ask each one for a copy of a similar report he or she has produced for other agencies. (Make sure that the consultant has the agency's permission to release the reports.) Are you impressed? Do you feel comfortable with the approach to the research? Consultants too need to be good listeners, who understand your mission and the group of people who use your services. And would the consultant produce the results in a style and format that would suit your agency? In talking with a consultant, keep the kind of results you need firmly in mind. Would the consul-

Would you be willing to pay a fee for our services?

Questions for former staff
From your new perspective, how could we improve the organization?
How has your opinion of the organization changed since you left us?
Why did you leave?

Questions for volunteers
Why did you volunteer for this organization?
What could we do to make your time here more satisfying?
What improvements in our program can you suggest?
What other work could we do if we had more volunteers?
How could we use volunteers more effectively?

Other agencies in the same field
Do you see the work of our two agencies as complementary or are we competing with each other?
In what ways might we work more closely together?
What could be the benefits of cooperation?

Other agencies in the community
How is our work complementary?
In what ways might we work more closely together?
What ways would you suggest?
What might be the benefits of cooperation?

Media
What is your perception of our organization?
What do you hear other people saying about us?
Do we give you useful material about our work? Have you used any of it? If not, why not?

How could we work with you more effectively?

Individual donors
Would you tell me why you support our organization?
What would you like to see our organization do in the future?
Would you support such a program?
Would you help us find other donors?
How can we expand the support we get from people like you?

Local business donors
Would you tell me why you support our organization?
What would you like to see our organization doing in the future?
Would you support such a program?
Would you help us find other donors?
Have businesses such as yours formed partnerships with voluntary organizations?
How successful have the partnerships appeared to be?
What types of programs are businesses supporting?
How can we expand the support we get from people like you?

Potential donors (individuals or businesses)
Have you heard of our organization before? Where did you hear of it?
What is your perception of the service our organization provides in the community?
How do you think we could improve our service in the future?
Would you support such programs?
How might you give support?

International donors
Would you tell me why you support our organization?
What would you like to see our organization doing in the future?

tant's proposal produce such information?

A caution: in negotiating a first contract, consultants often see the prospect of more work with your organization and therefore may tell you only what you obviously want to hear. They may not want to risk offending you by telling you the truth. Check carefully on the reputation of possible consultants. If they are busy people with lots of clients, they will be less likely to be too dependent on assignments from your organization. (See Book 3, Chapter 21.)

Two quick, easy ways to get answers
Focus groups
You should talk to a few representatives of at least some of the groups listed above, plus any you have added. If the task looks too daunting, think of using "focus groups." This is a simple, quick technique that might give you objective opinions about your organization from at least a few of the groups whose opinions you need. It simply means bringing groups of ten or twelve people together to discuss their views of your organization. Don't try to learn too much. Three or four objectives are sufficient. Your objectives will dictate who is invited. The people can all be from one group, such as clients or individual donors, or representatives of several groups at once. Be sure that no one group could feel intimidated by any other. Focus groups are not usually suitable for surveying representatives of government, business people, or major donors. In those cases, personal interviews in their offices are usually best.

Invite people well ahead to meet in the evening in a quiet place where they will feel relaxed and comfortable. Don't use your office if there is another good location. Tell them when you invite them that the meeting will last two hours. Tell them also that you want to talk about the future of your organization, but don't give them much additional information. You don't want to treat them as special. That could distort your results. You may want to offer a token payment to ensure that they will come. Curiosity may not be enough motivation. However, it is wise to invite a few more than the ten or twelve people needed to form a good group. Inevitably, there will be cancellations.

If you can, arrange for an outside person, someone you trust, to lead but not dominate the discussion. It would be best if you do not attend: your presence might make it hard for people to be truthful. You would also likely find it hard to keep quiet. If you cannot bring in an outsider, then do it yourself. Ensure ahead of time that the session is recorded in written notes, videotape, or an audio recording.

When people come, the leader should:
- give everyone a few minutes to get acquainted
- explain the purpose of the evening
- ask well-prepared questions – six or seven at most
- step in and ask a new question if the discussion seems to be going nowhere
- remember that the group is meeting to give opinions, not to discuss issues at length
- ensure that everyone has a chance to talk

During the evening, give everyone a soft drink and something small to eat. If you promised a payment, give it before they leave and only to people who stayed the whole evening.

I was recently part of a focus group of eleven people who answered a set of questions. We talked for two hours. On the basis of what we eleven people said, our local automobile association planned to add many new services. The association has over a million members and yet the association considered eleven people to be an adequate sample. Nevertheless, I thought there should have been several more group meetings. It is too easy for one or two strong people to sway nine or ten others. So plan to do at least two sessions, more if necessary.

Be sure that the information actually gets used. Describe in a report the responses to the questions. Draw conclusions that point the way to the next steps. Share the results with participants in the focus groups and with members of the organization.

Research by dreaming
There is another easy way to begin to set your course. This method is most useful with staff and/or board – separately. It avoids the trap of looking at the past and projecting the past into the future. The group can be asked to close their eyes and forget about money and other restrictions. Ask them to ignore the past and think only of the future. Ask everyone to pretend that it is the same day two years from now. Then invite them to talk about their dreams. Ask them to describe what they have accomplished in the two years since today that makes them feel especially proud. The extension officer might say, "As a result of my farm visits and the courses I put

Would you support such a program?
Can we expand your support?
What types of projects will your agency support in the next two years?
How have you changed your mechanisms for giving aid grants?
Do you know of other donors who are interested in our field of work and might support us?
How can we work more effectively with other organizations?

Governments, national and local
How is our organization seen by your department?
Our main goals are ....; how does that match what you see as important?
What types of projects will you support in the next two years?
What changes in your programs will affect our organization?
How can we work together more effectively?

Neighbours
How can we be better neighbours?
What services could we be providing here that we don't provide now?

The board of directors
The board should consider conducting its own review without management present. Here are some questions members might ask each other:
Do we have the information we need to make responsible decisions?
Are we satisfied with our current services?
What services should we provide in the future?
What were the original goals? Have the organization's goals changed since then? In what way?
How can the commitment of the founding or previous leaders be used to advantage?

Has the original leadership passed to a new generation of leaders?
What are the beliefs of the new leaders? Does the new style suggest a refocusing of the goals of the organization? Has that happened?
Have we considered and approved the changes in management, goals, and programs? If not, how can we do this now? How can we do it regularly?
Is everyone on the board happy about the changes?
Do we have the staff to attain our program goals? What needs to be done?
Does the board have appropriate relationships with the staff?
Is the board as active as it needs to be? What other sorts of people could we enlist as board members?
Are we committed to raising money for the organization, to finding and approaching donors and to giving ourselves?
If not, what will it take to elicit that commitment?
Are we committed to investing in other income generating programs?
If not, what do we need to do?

on, 3,000 farm families are growing crops where nothing has grown for years." The director might say, "I have tripled the amount of money from local donors so we have been able to buy scooters for all the field workers so they can visit more farmers each day." The person who does the bookkeeping might say, "I have set up an excellent new accounting system that shows the cost of each of our programs." Each person will likely have a good number of dreams.

Each person talks about his or her dreams. No one is allowed to interrupt. Then everyone describes the obstacles that had to be overcome to achieve those dreams. The extension worker might say, "My biggest problem was getting information about the courses to all the farmers I serve because the leaflets were always delivered late." The director might say, "There was so much competition for money that I had to work harder than before to be sure my grant proposals were really persuasive." The bookkeeper might say, "At first, my problem was to get the field workers to tell me how much money they were spending on their visits to farmers. I started giving them weekly reminders."

As the discussion progresses, answers will emerge to many of the questions you want answered. You will also begin to form your long-term plan. Finally, after a lot of give and take and discussion about what is realistic, the dreams turn into a list of goals for the organization for the next two years. This simple technique is fun to try, will produce new ideas, will bring out the secret dreams that may never have been expressed, and get people thinking about removing obstacles to realizing their dreams. The whole exercise can be done in a day or two and can be adjusted to fit any organization.

Interviews, focus groups, and "dreaming" can all be used as parts of one study, or you can just use one or two techniques.

Wrapping up the research
While your findings are fresh in your mind, compile the results. Add your own opinions about what you have learned. What information was suspect? What was useful? What do we need to learn more about? Where should we put our emphasis in our planning? What are the priorities? You will then be able to get ready to make the plan. This topic is addressed in Chapters 11 and 12.

7 The board of directors

The board of directors is the organization's window on the world. It is also the world's window on the organization: the board stands for the organization. If the board is good at its job, the organization will be good at its job.

The role of the board

At the most basic and practical level, the board ensures that the organization survives, that its money is managed responsibly, and that funds are used effectively and for the purpose for which they were given. Being a board member is not a hobby. It is a job requiring a solid commitment of many hours each year. A board that is passive, that simply approves what the staff is doing and asks no questions, is not doing its job. Board members are accountable for the responsible operation of the organization. They should be seen by everyone to be doing that.

But a board of directors should do much more. A board should have a vision and should ensure that there is a strategy to realize that vision. While the board may be guided by the leader (likely called the executive director or manager), the board should have its own ideas and not follow the vision of the leader without question. Together management and board should be thinking about where they want the organization to be in five years, perhaps more. The vision should be reflected in the long-range plan but should go beyond the two or three years that it covers. If the board has committees, the one devoted to policy and planning should be just as important as the one concerned with finances.

Because the board is the policy-maker, it must grow as the organization grows. When an organization is small or young, the board members or group of volunteer advisers are likely to be recruited among volunteers, friends, family, or colleagues of the executive director and staff of the organization. The leader usually recruits them. Such a board gives moral support or technical advice, and approves the policies of the leader. Board members may also be very involved in the day-to-day activities of the organization, spending hours in the office helping with projects and lifting some of the work-

---

The importance of a good board for the success of an organization cannot be overemphasized. It is the board's responsibility to determine the organization's mission and purpose; select the chief executive and support his/her performance; ensure effective organizational planning; ensure adequate resources and manage them effectively, determine, monitor and strengthen the organization's programs and services; enhance the organization's public standing; ensure legal and ethical integrity; maintain accountability; recruit new board members and assess board performance. Therefore an organization is only as good as its board. How an organization performs is not only the responsibility of the staff but is the result of partnership between board and staff .... It is essential that board members take their duties seriously, give their time and effort selflessly, and have a sense of ownership.

PUSHPA SUNDAR, INDIAN CENTRE FOR PHILANTHROPY, *Sampradan*, No. 4, 1998

load from the shoulders of the staff, or they may be staff members themselves. Board members may be reluctant to challenge the friend, family member, or employer who, in effect, put them in office.

As the organization grows a little older or larger, the board members themselves may draw in their own friends and colleagues. Eventually they will propose appointments with or without the director's initiative. Only a few boards will consider inviting people in the community that they do not already know. The board may still be active in managing the organization but it may not yet have begun to govern.

When boards first begin to really govern, they may be committed to a vision of the organization, but they may not be up to the job of implementing it. They may have depended for too long on a visionary leader to do the thinking for them. They may have just followed along. Some continue in that pattern. They know the organization as it is – or as they still picture it. Like most people, they are reluctant to change. They get stuck in routine ways of dealing with issues, and avoid difficult situations that make them uncomfortable. If they cannot move at the pace the organization is moving, they will be left behind. Other boards break away from the pattern and seek new approaches and new ideas.

> *Board members who do nothing but have their names listed in the brochure are not only detrimental to the efficiency of the organization, but they can be dangerous as well. If a board member is unaware of what is going on in the organization or is unable to explain the organization's goals and objectives clearly, outsiders will begin to think that the organization must be somehow suspect.*
>
> JANE NABUNNYA MALUMBA, DENIVA NEWS, UGANDA, APRIL–JUNE 1998

The mature professional organization that eventually develops will have a professional board with people who have special, relevant skills and/or good community contacts. That is the kind of board needed for fundraising, and the kind we are talking about.

Governing means backing away from the details of management and focusing on policy – where the organization should go and how it will get there. Some boards never reach this stage. Until very recently, board members of one Canadian NGO served on the committees that hired every staff member, no matter how junior. That organization is large and has been prominent in Canada for a quarter of a century. The interest of board members should not be discouraged, but board members concerned with this level of detail cannot also consider broader issues.

Board members are not substitutes for staff members. They should not be expected to do the work the staff should do. Nor are they substitutes for a group of volunteers. Volunteers who work separately from the board, and directly with staff members if there are any, may be able to give specific kinds of help more easily than board members. In any case, board members may come to feel that too many demands are being made on their time already.

Broadening membership

As an organization matures, the board (or, often, a new executive director) recognizes that governance and credibility could be improved by enlisting new board members from outside the usual circle of friends and colleagues. People start to consider what would be an ideal board. They ask whether there is sufficient diversity on the board. They think about the groups in their society that should be represented. They recognize that new members will bring different points of view to the board's deliberations. They will also improve communications in two directions, carrying the organization's message to their communities, and reporting their community's concerns to the board. I have yet to see any board of directors that did not benefit from having board members from other sectors. Yet few development networks or individual agencies seem to welcome new voices with different ideas.

The Surplus People Project in South Africa has worked to obtain restitution for more than three million displaced people. It has a board of three non-staff and four staff members, which met annually. Such a board cannot possibly be effective in bringing the organization into the community and into fundraising.

In broadening its membership to make it more effective and credible, a board (guided often by the executive director) may decide it needs people like the following.

Seven people started our organization as a team. We can ask the board a question, and I can put the answer I expect in an envelope before a meeting. After the meeting I can open the envelope. The board members will have said what I knew they would say.

KATALIN CZIPPAN, GÖNCÖL FOUNDATION, HUNGARY

Current donors and supporters
Select people who are helping the organization already, but who differ from current board members. We all tend instead to invite people we know who are not yet active, planning to turn them into donors and workers. It is much better to look for people who have already given some sort of service or, if you have already started fundraising, have made a donation. They are already committed. I made this mistake several times. I rarely took a close enough look at generous donors as potential board members. What a resource I was ignoring!

Representatives of the people the organization is serving
Some foreign donors measure the commitment of an organization to its beneficiaries by counting how many of them are on the board of directors. There are usually very few. Is the traditional failure to include these people left over from a paternalistic, perhaps colonial, attitude that only people with money and position have the ability and the right to decide what is best for people less fortunate than they are? If so, that policy is misguided.

The people who benefit from the organization bring an important perspective to the board. They speak from personal experience about what is needed in their communities and can help to establish priorities among those needs. They also know at first hand what the organization has done for them; often they can talk about it in a very moving way. They can be very effective in building credibility, especially with people outside the organization.

It may be impractical, however, to elect representatives of the beneficiaries to the board. Board meetings may be conducted in a language the beneficiaries do not understand or in a location they cannot easily reach. In that case, the board and staff should arrange to consult regularly with the people the organization serves, so their views can influence the actions of the organization.

Business people
We have already recognized the mutual discomfort, if not outright suspicion, that may exist when development people and business people meet. Development organizations too rarely have business people on their boards, another indication of the gap between the two groups. Yet if credibility is to be gained, bridges must be built. This can be done by choosing new board members from the business community carefully. Proceed gradually, but start now. My research tells me organizations that have business people as board members are more advanced in their development than most other voluntary organizations.

You do not need to seek presidents of corporations. Many of the questions your board needs to consider relate to details of financial management and budgeting. For this, you may try to recruit accountants, small business owners, or middle-management bank employees – men and women who understand bookkeeping, how to interpret balance sheets and operating statements, and how to present accounts in a clear and convincing form. These people will be especially useful if you are thinking of starting a small business (Book 3, Chapter 12). Other questions will relate to personnel policies and the appointment of the executive director. Here again, business people with the right experience (perhaps in human resource development) can bring a useful perspective. I have found such people invaluable in managing and selecting a new director, for instance. They seem to approach the job more objectively than is possible for people within the development community.

As an organization begins fundraising programs, it will want to recruit more business representatives. It is never too soon to take the first small steps in this direction. The right business people can open doors for you. They can also carry your message to communities you are probably not reaching now and, if you educate them, carry it in the positive way you would like.

> *Some people have volunteer boards and some have local business people, an engineer for example. These are soft appointments because there is no conflict. I cannot imagine having business people on our board for ages. We could put business people on an advisory board or on a project basis where they could not influence the mission of the organization.*
>
> KATALIN CZIPPAN, GÖNCÖL FOUNDATION, HUNGARY

> *We have no business people on our board. I know them all. These people are borrowing state money to increase their income. They are big bank defaulters. Many are black marketeers, many are corrupt.*
>
> MAHMOOD HASAN, GONOSHAHAJJO SANGSTHA, BANGLADESH

Younger people
Most of the boards I have worked with had few, if any, young members. Yet it is likely that most of the people the agencies served were young. Most board members had been around a long time; they sought new members only among their own acquaintances. The members felt comfortable: they rarely challenged each other or the executive director. Because they knew their organizations well, these boards did give stable, consistent direction. But sometimes they were too comfortable, and always they were growing collectively older.

Identifying good young board members can be difficult. Integrating them into an older board may be even harder. Yet many boards which have added young men and women have found it worthwhile. One board I have served chose its youngest member as its new chairman. He provided sound leadership that was much needed and appreciated.

More women

Women are generally underrepresented on boards. They are a minority on the board even of some women's organizations and of some organizations that serve mainly women.

In some countries, a major role for women on boards may be still be in the future. You should examine social practices in your own country. In almost every country, women can take a more active role than they have been offered. By not including more women on its board, your organization may be missing an opportunity to broaden its representation and credibility. Many women hold professional positions and have experience that could be useful. Another advantage in my experience of volunteer boards is that women members come to meetings far better prepared than most men do.

Don't forget to include women if you are appointing some of the people who benefit from your services to your board.

Government representatives

This is a broad category. It can include civil servants and politicians at every level. As with corporate employees, approaches may be met with suspicion, especially if the organization has opposed government policy. Where government people are permitted to join boards, they can be valuable assets. They know government policy. They can also open doors. They may lend credibility. On the other hand, they may link the organization too closely to the government in power, and arouse suspicion among beneficiaries and donors. Obviously, it is unwise to be too closely associated with one political party, however powerful, especially if you are working in a fully democratic society. That party could be out of office any time. A decision on recruiting board members of this type must therefore be taken very carefully.

Staff representatives

Except for the executive director, who may be a non-voting member, I don't think staff should serve on a board of directors. That may be because I always feel concerned to protect the authority of the executive director. Other staff members are employed to implement policy, not to make it. Making policy is the role of the board. I believe board members in small organizations can

> *We want one-to-one linkages. We want a small group of advisers whose names will carry weight. We now have twelve board members. There are prominent people on the board but they are very busy.*
>
> *When we started, the board members all came from NGOs. Then members of the business sector were included. There were no big problems because these people had a background of volunteerism and the right feeling towards people because of their experience in Rotary and Lions, for example.*
>
> *We tried to get young people but they did not come to meetings. This was a failure on our part. Boards take their own colleagues so the members are all old.*
>
> *Eighty per cent of the groups we work with are women's groups but the committees of each organization were all men. They made all the decisions. The board of our organization has five women and seven men. The chairman is a woman. The five women are more active than the men. This gradually made the men on the committees realize they should include women.*
>
> PATMA RATNAYAKE, SOUTH ASIA PARTNERSHIP, SRI LANKA

work directly with staff members, however, even including them in board meetings about special issues when necessary. This means board members must always keep in mind that their responsibility is to the executive director, not to other staff. Some experts advise that staff members need only pay attention to decisions made by the whole board, not to statements made by individual board members. This is a way to protect staff members from interfering board members.

Keeping staff members informed about board activities is essential. The executive director should report quickly on what happens at board meetings or, at very least, circulate minutes of meetings.

We need to enlarge our board but it is difficult to find and to catch the people we want. We want to be careful about what companies are chosen. I wanted to invite a lady from Beres, a natural medicine firm, which is safe. She is vice-director. After two years we still can't get to her. We had sent her a letter asking to meet with her and explain our organization. The reply was a letter from the company's foundation saying "We cannot give you money," though we had not asked for money. She had sent our letter to the company's foundation.

Finally, I remembered I had an ex-boyfriend at the company. She is his boss. So my friend is going to speak to her.

Our director has made personal contacts and sent letters to people that she met at business sessions. Our experience is that you have to make 20 contacts to get one to help with fundraising, to be on the board, or to help with promotion.
Eventually a person might give corporate funding.

RENATA KISS, ENVIRONMENTAL PARTNERSHIP PROGRAM, HUNGARY

Others
Two categories of potential members are usually ruled out. Representatives of foreign donors have been found to exert too much influence on board deliberations. The organization is usually too accountable already to donors, and not enough to the local community and beneficiaries. The second category is people from other voluntary organizations unless, of course, the organization is itself an umbrella agency. An executive director in India cautioned against appointing colleagues from other voluntary organizations because they bring their own agendas. They may have ideas about how the board should allocate money, wanting to use it in ways that have been found best for their own organization – but that may not be best for yours. They may want to use your organization's money to benefit their friends or their own organization or to support people who think the same way they do. When it comes to fundraising, it is almost certain that their first concern will be their own organization, not yours.

Reasons people serve on boards

The motivation of board members is important, and can take many forms. In Canada, a small group raised the money to renovate a historic theatre that had been neglected for many years. The project took four years, but eventually the renovation was nearly finished. Many of the original board members were tired after working so hard for so long.

The Capitol Theatre is in Port Hope, a town with only 12,000 people, which meant it would not be easy to raise the extra money needed to complete the renovations. A revitalized board of directors was essential to ensuring that the theatre was finished and also that it stayed solvent. To attract new board members, the chairman held a weekend meeting to talk about the future of the theatre and its board. Some people who came were friends. Others were new to the community. He asked everyone several questions. Their answers illustrate the many motivations people may have for agreeing to serve on a board of directors, and the importance of channelling their interest in a constructive way. You may wish to hold similar meetings when expanding your own board.

Why are you on the board of the Capitol Theatre or why are you considering joining the board?
Have time and interest.
Want to try and make the Capitol the best it can be.
Love theatre and film.
Love the theatre. It is important to the community.
To help with fundraising.
Not sure any more, but someone has to.
Want to see excellent programming to meet the interests of a broad spectrum of the community.
To promote the theatre and the benefit of having it in this community.
Initially to see it restored, now to help support its success.
I believe in the theatre and its role in Port Hope.
Love town, love building.
To contribute my experience.

What do you hope to achieve for yourself by being on the board?
Meet more people in the community.
To feel I'm contributing to the success of the town.
To be involved with the community.
To be involved with the artistic people in town.
The satisfaction of achieving success.
Continue family tradition.
To give.
Satisfaction of seeing a job well done and being on a productive team.
A different way to stretch myself.
Curious to learn about the operation of a theatre.
Enjoy the camaraderie.
Connection to leaders in the community.
To be involved in an enterprise with which I have no previous experience.

What do you hope to achieve for the theatre by being on the board?
To help make it a success.
To help make it viable.
To complete the restoration.
To help establish it as a place of excellence.
To see the theatre restored and expanded.
To help with the workload.
To help with volunteer activities and special events.
To see the establishment of an active and dynamic working board.
To see the theatre as self sustaining and with an addition.
To increase awareness in the community.

To make an artistic and financial success.
To produce first-rate shows for all.

What do you/would you enjoy most about being on this board?
The social time after meetings.
Working with fellow committee members.
To hear from the patrons who have enjoyed themselves.
Sharing a common goal with a vibrant, intellectual, social group.
Being part of what has been accomplished.
Working with intelligent, engaging people.
Being involved in a job well done.
Attending meetings.
Contact with serious people with common vision.
Making the theatre "work."
Accomplishment.

As is evident from the replies, the satisfaction of being a board member is not always obvious, and may be very different from the reasons first given for joining.

"Committee work? Fundraising? Public accountability? You didn't tell me it was gonna be *that* kind of board!"

Recruiting members

Adding members is not a simple task. It may be difficult to identify prospective board members from new sectors of the community, especially if the present board has few acquaintances among them. Once prospective members are identified they must be persuaded to join – and the best are usually already overworked. Then it takes a while to educate them, explain the organization's programs and how they operate, and – even more fundamentally – how people in non-profit organizations think and can be motivated. Until they have that familiarity, they will not be fully effective.

These boards are very different from advisory boards, which have no legal status. When potential members are asked to consider serving on the board, they should be invited, always by the chairman, to visit the office, tour projects, meet board members, and receive an orientation package (or have an orientation session) about the organization. The legal responsibilities and liabilities of board members should be spelled out carefully. Potential directors should also know all about the actions the organization has taken to protect them from liability before they agree to serve. In many countries articles of incorporation can protect the board of directors from legal responsibility for the debts of the organization, should it have difficulties. Insurance is also often available to cover this possibility.

Most important, the orientation should describe the role of the board and what is expected of each member. Are board members to be fundraisers? That is a key question to answer clearly from the very beginning. If new board members understand exactly what is expected of them, later misunderstandings and disappointments are less likely. An active, enthusiastic board with diverse membership is one of the best demonstrations of an organization's continuing credibility.

Getting everyone headed in the same direction

Integrating representative members into an existing board is challenging and risky. It requires a good deal of patience, time, imagination, and energy. New and old members need to know and trust one another and work together effectively: this requires a special effort. Many different interests and perspectives may mean that consensus is difficult. John Carver, an American expert on board leadership, said, "An effective board has a profound sense of group responsibility. It is simply not enough for board members to be responsible as individuals, they must somehow form into a responsible group" *(Board Member,* Sept./Oct. 1996). Each person on a board must come to value the expertise of the other members. That can happen only if members speak up when their knowledge is relevant, so they gradually educate each other. This process will not happen automatically. The chairman of the board and the executive director, or another staff member, will have to encourage it. Many executive directors do so by arranging retreats, during which all board members spend a day or two together in a place where they will not be disturbed. There they can get to know one another better and review, without interruption, the organization's work and planning for the future. Occasional social gatherings, sometimes with staff members, are also a good way of bringing people together.

Further considerations

Several other practices will add to the board's effectiveness and credibility. All of these should made clear to any candidate for board membership.

1 Regular board meetings, with a majority of members present. Frequent meetings, preferably at least quarterly, are best. The board needs to be seen to work as a team and to know what is going on in the organization.

2 A membership of at least five voting members, representing a variety of interests. Larger membership – 10 to 15 – is better because it increases community representation. Boards of more than 15 members become difficult to manage, and individual members start thinking that with so many members they can miss meetings or do less without harming the organization.

3 By-laws about conflict of interest involving either board or staff. If a member of the board could benefit from any decision or action of the organization, that member should withdraw from all related discussions. For instance, if a relative is being considered for the executive director's job or someone on the board could benefit from purchases the organization may make, the board member should say so and withdraw. The same ethics apply to staff members.

On our board of directors we have a priest, the chief of the district hospital, a municipal planning and development officer, a rural planning person, and the municipal treasurer. There is not much change in membership. We did consider gender. The municipal treasurer is a woman. She is very influential on the board. Members consider their board service to be part of their jobs. All board members must be residents of the island. They are very influential in defining and guarding the direction of the organization.

Every year we have a joint staff/board review. We are together for three days of strategizing. We write a plan for the year. We even review administrative policies. The board meets every quarter. I hope that the board members all read the proposals. They watch that we don't get spread too thin.

HUR CAMPORENDONDO,
LAWIG FOUNDATION

4 Regular elections and specific terms of office – two to three years, with one additional term a possibility. Such a policy encourages the introduction of new ideas and discourages inflexibility.

5 A by-law that automatically disqualifies any director who does not attend meetings regularly without offering an acceptable reason. The by-law must state clearly how many meetings in a year a member may miss before being disqualified.

6 A by-law that specifies what constitutes a quorum. Where I live, 40 per cent of the board members must be present before a meeting is legally recognized.

7 No payment of board members beyond repayment of any actual expenses incurred by members to attend board meetings, or other expenses incurred at the specific request of the organization. Board members should receive no other remuneration for their services.

8 Clear written descriptions of the role of the board and its committees. In the context of this series, it is especially important to establish this understanding in relation to fundraising.

9 Open elections for board members, board officers, and committee members. Practice democracy from the bottom up.

10 A written record of all significant decisions in concise clear minutes. Minutes are an organization's historical record. Unpopular decisions can be recorded as group decisions; individual people need not be singled out. Oral reports after meetings tend to give only the opinions and the decisions of the most authoritative leader and not the true opinions of the members.

Responsibility for fundraising

When people are asked to serve on your board, they probably understand that the financial health of the organization will be one of their major responsibilities. That means they will be expected to review the budget to make sure the organization lives within its means. It may also mean helping to develop grant applications and calling on potential foreign donors or government officials. In the minds of board members, that financial responsibility rarely translates into actually asking for or arranging for financial support from individuals, companies, or associations in their own country and community. One reason is that prospective board members are rarely told that they will be expected to raise money themselves. This is true everywhere in the world, even where local fundraising has been going on for years.

In Book 1 our focus is on credibility as a foundation for fundraising, not fundraising directly. But the composition of a board and the attitude of its members are critical to the success of any fundraising program. It takes years to get everything right, so even if there is not yet an active fundraising program your growing need for local funding should influence your choice of new members to add to the board, as well as to the volunteer structure of the organization. For fundraising, you should be looking for people who may be different from your traditional board members, people who know potential donors in your area and will feel comfortable approaching them. At the same time, new board members should not be chosen simply because you think they might be good fundraisers. Some, including those who are on the board to represent the community, may surprise you. While some board members are naturally good at fundraising or have been successful with other organizations, most have to be taught how to do it well.

Until now, this has not mattered much in developing countries. As overseas funding decreases, however, board members will confront a new set of challenges. One of the first will be getting rid of fear of fundraising. That is not to say all members of the board will become fundraisers, though that would be ideal. Or that the board has to do all the fundraising itself. If the board is giving good leadership in other areas, don't risk alienating good board members by making demands on them that they are unwilling to meet. Think about how to build on this strength in other ways, perhaps by setting up a separate group for fundraising. Ways to do this are discussed in Book 2.

8 The value of volunteers

> *Volunteer work has always been the base of our work. Volunteers just arrive because of 30 years of work, and because of all the exposure we get through our different projects. This did not start because someone had a lot of money, but because people wanted to donate their time and work to something they believed in. The organization was born from the commitment of volunteers – manual, intellectual, and spiritual volunteers. Today there are 30 organizations in what could almost be described as a membership. They offer moral cohesion. They form the planning board in which they participate in deciding the political orientation of the organization. One hundred and fifty other members contribute material goods, knowledge, and time.*
>
> LUIS LOPEZLLERA, PROMOCION DEL DESARROLLO POPULAR, A.C., MEXICO

The late Mother Teresa began her Missionaries of Charity in India. Over the years, her movement spread around the world. In all aspects of her work she relied on volunteers. Through volunteers, money came to support her missions.

A popular musician named Bob Geldof founded Band Aid, a voluntary group that donated money to hundreds of relief and development causes in the late 1980s and early 1990s. In his book *Is that it?* he describes meeting Mother Teresa in an airport in Ethiopia. She said to him: "Remember this. I can do something you can't do and you can do something I can't do. But we both have to do it."

This often quoted statement sums up the relationship between paid workers and volunteers. It is a collaboration. "We both have to do it." Proud volunteers say "We're doing it," not "They're doing it." In non-profit organizations, volunteers and board members can be objective advisers, helpful observers, the bearers of fresh ideas, the memory of the organization, goodwill ambassadors, the friends of useful people, extra pairs of hands in the office or at events, successful fundraisers, generous donors. That is one reason such organizations are often called voluntary organizations, even when much of their work is done by paid staff. This capacity to make use of volunteer talent is a great strength and one that the for-profit world does not have to nearly the same extent.

Volunteerism has been with us always. As Sharon Capeling-Alakija of the United Nations Volunteers says, "There has never been a well dug in Africa, a new roof put on a village school in Asia, or a community health centre built in Central America without the labour, talents, skills, materials, and dedication of volunteers." She also points out that language matters. Voluntary organizations have listed these services as "in-kind support" and failed to "acknowledge or honour this important form of local initiative and participation."

Oden Grajew, president of Fundacao Abrinq Pelos Direitos Da Crianca (the Friend of Children Foundation) in Brazil, believes in volunteers. He is a volunteer himself. Eight hundred dentists volunteer their services to his organization. Each dentist agrees to care for a child free. Getting the children to their appointments is a huge problem, but it does get done. In India in one morning in December 1997, 10 million volunteers and 2 million health workers administered polio vaccine to 127 million children.

The very special strength of volunteers will be tested in the next few years as not-for-profit agencies seek more funds locally and the for-profit sector makes more use of volunteers – as interns in businesses and nursing assistants in private hospitals, to give just two examples. A good deal of volunteer work nowadays is not motivated purely by a desire to serve. Often the volunteers get specific benefits in return for giving their time. This may be time off from work, credit for a college or university course, or an opening to a career.

All over the world, organizations rely successfully on volunteers to help increase their income. However, most non-profit organizations could make greater – and better – use of volunteers for fundraising than they do. In 1998, Lions Club International studied volunteering in seven countries – Brazil, China, France, Germany, India, Japan, and the United States. More than four out of every five adults thought people should volunteer to help people less fortunate than themselves. Nearly one-half of respondents in five of the seven countries said that they would be more inclined to volunteer *if someone asked for their help*.

Nowadays, both men and women are volunteering as part of their jobs – this is usually called community service – and are giving time in the evening and on weekends to organizations that have enough imagination and flexibility to use them well. In some countries, students are also being encouraged to give time to community service.

The pros and cons of volunteers

Some organizations find volunteers a mixed blessing. They think volunteers are excellent when they are on the job, but that too often they lack real commitment. They feel volunteers are likely to disappear when another obligation or pleasure interferes. They find them unreliable.

Other organizations believe volunteers mean only trouble and don't want anything to do with them. They think volunteers are not worth the time it takes to train them. They believe only socially prominent causes attract volunteers, that volunteers want to be seen publicly to be doing good works but don't really want to get involved. In some countries, the traditional volunteer is seen as a rich, unemployed, upper class woman – an out-of-date image, indeed.

In fact, the patterns of volunteering are much the same everywhere in

---

There are potential volunteers everywhere but we need a strategy to involve them in voluntary work ....

It is particularly important in operating a volunteer program to retain a broad view of potential volunteer involvement. We should, however, not assume that the only people who are likely to volunteer for the program are the same types of people who previously volunteered for it. If you limit your focus in this way, you are likely to create a self-fulfilling prophecy.

The experience we have of programs, and this has been tested by our association in Mauritius, is that practically everyone can be persuaded to volunteer for a program if the right techniques are utilized. By retaining the broad view you will gently expand your potential targets in volunteer recruitment.

MAHENDRANATH BUSGOPAUL, HALLEY MOVEMENT, REPUBLIC OF MAURITIUS

the world, though the indications may seem contradictory. People complain, but still many of them give freely of their time to causes they believe in.

The Fiji Council of Social Services found that:

People in their twenties and thirties prefer to keep to themselves and do not care to volunteer. Eighty per cent of the people in their forties and fifties had provided some form of voluntary service or were active volunteers. However, there were signs of frustration, lethargy, and burnout .... Many complained about the lack of enthusiasm of younger people or the high costs of maintaining their interests. Almost fifty per cent of the group have already reduced their hours of involvement to half of what they used to give in time and money ten years ago because of time, money and lack of incentives. Ninety per cent of people over 60 years old said that providing free assistance to others was part of their life and they were not even aware of being a volunteer.

Executive directors of NGOs in India and Indonesia also complained that their organizations are not offering any volunteer opportunities to young people. The staff may simply be reluctant to take on the challenge.

Committed volunteers, like good staff members, are hard to find. Once found, they are often hard to enlist. The best volunteers are the ones who may take a lot of convincing. They will tell you that they are far too busy with their jobs, families, or other volunteer commitments. Such people hesitate before saying "yes." That is good. You are looking for commitment, and they are obviously taking your expectations seriously.

Volunteers need to feel useful, and to know exactly how the work they do will help the organization. Like potential board members, they also want reassurance that they will not be wasting their time by being involved in a sloppily run organization. They want to talk with pride about the organization and the contribution they are making. You, too, want them to show their pride – it is a contribution to your credibility.

The search for and selection of volunteers should be taken just as seriously as the search for and selection of staff or board members. All cost the organization money in management and training; neither group should be treated casually. Just as you hire only as many staff as you can afford to pay, you should recruit only as many volunteers as you need for the work to be done and have time to manage.

Why people volunteer

People will offer to work for your organization because they want to feel useful. They want to feel part of something large and significant beyond their own daily lives. They want to share a larger vision with others, a vision that together they can make real. They also may want to:
- feel good about themselves
- influence the direction the organization is going
- help people in need
- meet the request of a friend
- support an issue or cause that is important to them
- have a change from everyday work
- fill free time

- learn new skills
- meet new people or more people
- get a paying job

Most of these reasons for volunteering are what you might expect. Often, you won't know what exactly motivates your various volunteers. They may not know themselves. The last motivation in the list, getting a paying job, may be surprising. But whenever jobs are hard to find, volunteering can open doors to employment. In several offices I know, almost every volunteer wanted a paying job. And almost every volunteer found one. It may have taken six months to a year but, in the end, good voluntary performance and the skills learned by volunteering paid off.

It took me a long time to recognize how important a volunteer opportunity can be. Here is one example. A middle-level manager who had been released by a large public utility volunteered to fix the computer system in our office. I fell over myself being grateful. It was only when he called to ask if he could use me as a reference in a job application that I realized it was not a one-way street. I had been doing him a favour by encouraging his volunteer involvement. When he got the job, he came around at noon the first day he was working to tell us about it, and to say thank you.

Finding volunteers

Within any voluntary organization, the job of finding suitable volunteers can appear discouraging. Yet outside the organization there may be many people who want to help their community by volunteering but don't know how to go about finding the right agency. The challenge to the organization is to find these people. There are many ways to go about it:

- Ask the people you serve to be volunteers themselves and to suggest others who could volunteer.
- Ask your board and other current volunteers to find suitable people.
- Ask staff members to suggest names, including their relatives and friends.
- Ask any person who is already supporting you financially to volunteer or to suggest volunteers.
- Ask organizations (service clubs, trade associations, businesses) that are supporting you financially to suggest volunteers.
- Ask people who request information about your program if they are interested in volunteering.
- Advertise in newspapers if that is possible and affordable.
- Ask local schools and colleges to suggest "interns," young people who will work, usually for little or no money, for several months. Interns want to do useful work for a short time or gain experience that will help them in their academic pursuits or careers.

In India, volunteerism doesn't work. It is better to have paid employees. Volunteers are seen as high society ladies who want to talk in their social circles about their volunteer work. They may come only once a year. Then, women will only work from ten o'clock until two. It is too hot in the afternoon. There are volunteers who won't fill a glass or stick on a label. They just want to support charity balls.

In May, people leave the city for villages and crops and then students have holidays. Most unemployed people are illiterate and nowadays you need to be able to use a computer. In India no one is lonely so there is no need to volunteer to be with people.

Ms Malvika, South Asian Fund Raising Group, India

• Include a request for volunteers in all your printed material.
• Put a "Volunteers Needed" sign in the window of your office, in local shops, and, if it is permitted, on poles in the street.
• Post notices in post offices, markets, supermarkets, shops, recreation places, and community centres that will permit you to do so.
• Speak to groups and post notices in churches and schools.
• Post notices in factories, especially where people work at night and may have a bit of time during the day.
• Contact organizations where retired people are likely to gather and ask that a sign be posted and an announcement be made about the opportunity to work with you.
• Look for volunteers in the field in which your organization specializes or in which you mostly need help. People tend to volunteer for tasks related to their paid work. Health workers may volunteer for organizations providing health services, for example. Managers volunteer more than other people and will mostly do managerial or committee work.
• Ask businesses to encourage their staff members to do volunteer work by giving staff time off during working hours to help you. The practice of lending staff to non-profit organizations as a community service is widespread. Businesses see a benefit both to employees and to the charities they serve. Ask especially for volunteers who have the skills you need – for example, in computer training or financial planning.
• Ask local radio and television stations to put a notice on the air about your need for volunteers.
• Join service clubs. Go to the meetings. Talk to people.
• If you have e-mail, use it to reach local organizations to ask for volunteers.
• Sponsor and help out at community events organized by other groups. Favours follow favours.
• Set up a recruiting table with a sign and several volunteers to give information at a local market or major shopping area.
• Contact a volunteer bureau if there is one in your city. Volunteer bureaus act as clearinghouses for volunteers. Organizations apply to the bureau for volunteers. People interested in volunteering also fill out applications. The bureau matches the two needs. It may also advertise opportunities for volunteer work.

"Surely someone will volunteer to take the minutes."

CARTOON: CAROLE CABLE

Enlisting volunteers

Before you start meeting potential volunteers, be sure you can summarize easily what your organization does, how it meets the community's needs, and what it hopes to achieve in the future. Volunteers will be attracted if they can see right away that their contribution of time and skills will make a difference to the community you serve.

Present your invitation as an opportunity to do important work, to give an important service. Don't just invite a person to join a committee. Such an invitation sounds flat and bureaucratic. The only people that will be attracted are those who enjoy being on a committee because it makes them feel important, people who might prefer to talk rather than act. Others are likely to see committee work as mundane, routine, and bureaucratic.

When asking potential volunteers for help, make clear what you expect them to do and how much time you want them to commit. No matter what their role, volunteers have a right to know what is expected of them before they agree to help. It's essential to hold personal interviews with all potential volunteers. Many organizations go so far as to have written contracts with their volunteers. By signing, the volunteers promise to spend a certain amount of time for a certain length of time, say two hours a week for three months. This degree of formality may not suit your organization or all volunteers, but it is worth considering. Even if there is no written agreement, you should have had a chance in the interview to assess the character of the potential volunteer and to discuss the expectations on both sides.

Be positive in enlisting volunteers. It is essential that volunteers know and share your vision of the future of the organization and its programs. More specifically, it is important to get them excited about the fundraising program. Introduce volunteers to the people who benefit from your service. Give them a tour of your office and any sites where you have projects. Emphasize how their work will benefit the people who need help. Don't downplay the work you want volunteers to do. Show them they can do the job.

Don't beg. Don't twist arms – that is, put so much pressure that people feel they have to volunteer. People may agree to help you out of guilt or pressure but, very likely, they will not then stay the course.

Don't oversell your organization's program. Be honest about what it delivers. My experience is that volunteers are good detectors of the fake. If, for example, an organization says its purpose is to provide service in a particular field, but it is clear that the staff do not have the required knowledge, volunteers will detect that and will eventually leave. Disillusioned volunteers are not good ambassadors for any organization.

Right from the start – and especially during the interview – be prepared to reject unsuitable volunteers. No organization can afford fundraising volunteers who cannot or will not perform the job that is needed. That is a good reason for keeping assignments short, especially with new volunteers. You do not want to be saddled with volunteers who fail to meet expectations. But be careful. Reject or release volunteers gracefully, with gratitude. Preserve their dignity. Never embarrass them. Aside from wanting those people to think and speak well of you later, you want the volunteers who continue to work for you to know that you treat everyone decently and politely.

The work of unpaid volunteers accounts for about half the cash value of the output of [the 70,000] charitable organizations [in Canada]. The rate of volunteering by individuals other than those motivated by religion is 38 per cent [of the population], compared to 34 per cent in the United States.

RICHARD GWYN, TORONTO STAR, 1997

In Slovakia 37 per cent of organizations work with 6 to 20 volunteers, 19 per cent with 51 or more volunteers and 16 per cent with 21 to 50 volunteers.

SLOVAK ACADEMIC INFORMATION AGENCY, 1997

Be sure to keep a written file of volunteers so you will always know how to reach them and know their qualifications and interests. Keep an up-to-date list of current and past volunteers and people who have asked about being volunteers. Keep in mind that anyone who has shown interest in your organization is a potential donor.

Questions to ask potential volunteers

In your interviews with potential volunteers, you may want to ask some of the following questions. Others will occur to you.

- Why are you interested in helping us?
- What do you know of the work of our organization?
- How can you help us to achieve our dreams?
- What kind of work would you enjoy doing?
- How much time can you devote to helping us? How often? For how long?
- Have you had fundraising experience?
- What skills, hobbies, or special experience do you have that could benefit our work?
- Do you have any limitations (for instance, living far away, or a physical disability) we should take into account?

Children and young people between 15–20 years showed little enthusiasm about volunteering, as they were more pressured to obtain high marks in their studies. Seventy per cent were of the view that some kind of volunteer activity will help in moderating the pressures of school life and should form part of the studies. They were not happy with being compelled to "volunteer" in school fundraising as they were not given any chance of making decisions about their participation.

FIJI COUNCIL OF SOCIAL SERVICES VOLUNTARY ACTION NEWSLETTER, 1997

Questions volunteers should expect you to answer

Interviews are most successful when the potential volunteers have thought in advance about the experience, skills, and contacts they have to offer, how much time they can give, and what working arrangements they would prefer. But often they have not done this. If they are not certain about the extent to which they are willing to be involved, it is prudent to give them time to go away and think over what you propose. Be prepared to answer any of the following questions and others that suit your own situation.

- I want to do something worthwhile and interesting. What do you suggest?
- What goals do you have for your organization?
- Do I have a choice of volunteer jobs?
- What will you expect me to do?
- Will you give me the training I need?
- How much time do you expect me to give? How often? For one event? Or for several weeks or months?
- If we work well together, is there a possibility I might get a job here or with another organization you know? (If a job is unlikely, say so. You may offer to speak to other people about the volunteer if, after a while, things are going well. Very often, volunteering leads to a job.)
- Will you pay my expenses?

There is only one fixed rule in answering the last question. Always offer to reimburse volunteers for their out-of-pocket expenses. Some may have lots of money, yet expect their out-of-pocket costs to be covered. Others may have very little yet expect nothing. Whatever arrangement you make with volunteers, it should be private. And it should be made before the volunteer begins helping, so there are no misunderstandings later. I offered my favourite volunteer money for bus fare. "No, thank you," he said, "That is my contribution."

Occasionally you will have volunteers who are so special that you want to reward them in a special way. There is no rigid rule that volunteers should not be paid. An honorarium or some other kind of payment is often appropriate, provided it appears fair to staff and other volunteers.

Deciding what volunteers will do

All staff members in the organization should come to see the benefits of having volunteers and be prepared to adjust their working days to accommodate their new associates. They will have to be patient in explaining what needs to be done. They should be friendly, encouraging, and complimentary.

The environment in which volunteers perform is critical. The organization's openness to new ideas will get volunteers interested. Letting them take responsibility for trying out those ideas will keep them involved. However informal the arrangements may be, volunteer work should be carefully planned. The task and schedule must be tailored to the attitudes, skills, and schedules of the volunteer. If some disappear during school holidays or want to work only in the mornings or are available only in the evenings, you will have to arrange your programs to fit – provided, of course, that you think those particular volunteers are worth the investment.

Planning how to use volunteers well is the key not just to the happiness of the volunteers but also to the happiness of the staff members who work with them. The only way to ensure happiness is to write down simply and clearly:
- the goals of the volunteer program
- exactly, and in detail, each job you want volunteers to do
- the skills required
- how many hours of help you need from a volunteer and when you need it
- how volunteers will be trained
- who will keep an eye on what the volunteers are doing
- how the contribution of volunteers will be recognized
- how the volunteer program will be evaluated

Then follow the plan. Nothing creates unhappiness more quickly or more permanently than expectations and promises that are not met.

Orientation and training

The advice given to this point may seem obvious and, undoubtedly, if followed, will take time and effort. Is it worth it? Consider the hypothetical case history for "HomeLink" that follows. It combines a number of actual events.

HomeLink is an NGO that provides low-cost housing materials. It recently began a small local fundraising campaign. Two people who lived near the office knew about the campaign and volunteered to help. One was a student who would not be going back to university for four months. The other was a recently retired bookkeeper. The executive director met them on a Wednesday and suggested they come once a week. He said, "Why don't you come next Monday or Tuesday?" They both said, "Yes, that is good." "That is settled," the director said to himself, and put the volunteers out of his mind.

On Monday morning it rained heavily. The director found the two volunteers on the staircase waiting for someone to let them in. The director apologized, saying how glad he was that they had come, and ushered them in. He excused himself for a minute, went into his office, and shut the door.

The volunteers stood near the door while staff members arrived and got settled at their desks. After a few minutes, they put their umbrellas on the floor and found two chairs by the door to sit in. They felt uncomfortable because the staff members were looking at them with some curiosity, clearly wondering why they were there. Several said, "Good morning."

After a few minutes, the director came out of his office, apologizing for the delay. He said, "Now, we must organize some work for you to do. I wasn't expecting you both to come on the same day. But we certainly want to keep you busy. Do either of you know how to use a computer? No? Oh well, it doesn't matter. I'll think of something else. Ah, yes, we need to send out some receipts for donations. Perhaps you could do that. We just use a typewriter for receipts, or you can do them by hand. Now, where are the records?"

A staff member was asked to find the donation records, a task that took her fifteen minutes. It took even longer to find the receipt forms and to clear papers from a table so that both volunteers had a place to work. The director started to explain how to write the receipts. Then everyone stopped work for tea or coffee. Another search finally produced cups for the volunteers to use.

After the break, the volunteers wrote several sample receipts. One typed and the other wrote by hand. It turned out that the typewriter ribbon was worn out, and the only person who knew how to change it was away sick. Fifteen minutes passed putting in the new ribbon.

Because they had to check names and numbers carefully, it took each volunteer several attempts before each had written one correct receipt. By then, it was time for lunch. The volunteers asked where they should eat and where the washroom was. The director looked embarrassed. "I am sorry, I should have told you that before," he said.

They came back in an hour to find that the director had gone to a meeting and would be away for the afternoon. They produced a few more receipts and, in midafternoon, one said he had to leave because he had another appointment. The second volunteer left soon after. Both volunteers asked if there was a leaflet about the organization that they could read to learn more about its work. Several pamphlets were found in a drawer. The staff members suggested that the volunteers phone the director the next day to arrange when they should come the next week.

This story is not exaggerated by much. I would suggest that the chances of those two volunteers ever showing up again is not high.

Managing volunteers well depends on planning, not instinct. Like board members, volunteers should receive a small orientation package about the organization before they start work. Note the word "small": don't overload volunteers. If you give them too much information, it will never be read. Use your judgement about what is appropriate for each volunteer. The package could include several of the following:
- the history, programs, and clientele of the organization
- the latest annual report
- a current brochure describing the work of the organization (if there is no printed information, a talk with people who know the organization may take its place)
- any major policy documents, such as a three-year plan
- a list of current members of the board and staff with addresses and positions
- volunteer procedures

Fitting volunteers into the organization

Orientation involves more than explaining the vision of the organization and its programs, introducing the staff, and explaining how volunteers can help. Think of volunteers as though they are paid staff members, even if you don't in fact have any paid staff. Staff members work best when their jobs have been defined clearly, with a list of responsibilities and another list of the conditions of employment. The conditions for volunteers will not be as rigid as for staff members – you can't expect volunteers to work a full day every day of the working week, for example, and you will have to be flexible if volunteers are occasionally late or absent – but they should be set out. Make sure volunteers understand them – and recognize that by agreeing to volunteer they are committing themselves to carry out the agreement.

Orientation also means dealing with the mundane. Explain where to hang coats and store packages, the location of the washrooms, where to get food and drinks, how the cost of lunch and transportation is reimbursed. Unless volunteers join at quite different times, try to give the orientation to a group of people rather than to individuals. That is a good way to build solidarity and enthusiasm.

Volunteers will also require training in the work you are asking them to do, whatever it is. Allow time for that training. Don't expect that volunteers will be able to perform even the most routine task without a careful explanation of how it should be done in your organization. Assign a staff member or another volunteer who is patient and can communicate clearly to do the training. For clerical and similar work, assign the same person, or someone else, to check what the volunteer does in the beginning. If the work is consistently satisfactory, the monitoring can be reduced to the level that is normal in the office.

13 golden rules for keeping volunteers happy

1 Recognize that volunteers do not come free of cost. They cost time, especially at the beginning. As soon as they leave the office or a meeting,

you have to plan what they will do the next time. When they are in the office, you need to check that they are doing the right thing and doing it correctly – and happily. Volunteers are not robots on an assembly line. No two volunteers are the same, just as their reasons for being there and the amount of time they can give are not the same. Each person requires special handling. All volunteers want efficient, firm support and direction. That may come from a staff member or it could come from an experienced volunteer.

2 Volunteers need structure. As a senior volunteer with the Moral Society in Singapore said, "Volunteers must be guided and supervised. My rich sister-in-law does not know where to start." Make sure volunteers understand not just the "what" and the "who" of the organization but also the "why." People need to know more than what they are expected to do; they also need to know why they have been asked to do it a particular way. If they understand the purpose of the work they will perform it more effectively and efficiently. They may even be able to suggest better ways to do it, or new approaches to the same goal. They need to know what not to do as well. The results will be worth the investment of time.

3 Give one person the responsibility for managing the volunteers. An experienced volunteer may be great for the job, if you are lucky enough to have such a person.

"Charitable giving isn't the ultimate test of one's humility, but it gives us some numbers to play with."

4 Because volunteers come and go, you need to have some simple systems for keeping track of what they are doing. Volunteers should leave some knowledge behind when they go away. Be sure that someone writes down what each volunteer has learned, what each is doing and the procedure being used so that a second person can pick up where the first one left off. This is essential for organizations that have little or no staff and depend heavily on volunteers. Without detailed records, information and experience and history can disappear in a matter of days.

5 Hold regular meetings. Meetings have been called the glue that keeps an organization together. Meetings provide opportunities to stimulate, recognize, inform, and inspire people, to set deadlines, and to instil a shared sense of responsibility. In North America, it has been shown that the most effective volunteers are those who attend meetings regularly. Is that because meetings make volunteers more effective – perhaps because they understand more or simply because they feel more at home – or that poor volunteers avoid meetings? It is hard to know.

6 Keep meetings short. Few active volunteers want to spend time unnecessarily or in endless discussions. If key volunteers consistently miss meetings, find out why. They may find the meetings a waste of time. Consider setting a limit on the length of meetings. Then enforce the deadline, making sure decisions are reached within the time allowed.

7 Just because people are not being paid does not mean you can treat them casually. If anything, you want to treat them more carefully than peo-

ple who are paid for their services. Volunteers who come into the office to do a job should find everything ready for them to start working. Meetings should start and end on time, and have an agenda of important matters. People chairing meetings should always know what results they want so they don't let discussions drift pointlessly.

8 Keep volunteers up-to-date about what is happening. Often, volunteers will be given plenty of information about an organization when they begin helping. After that, they may be left to do their work, such as managing records or calling on donors. Since they are with you only occasionally, it is easy to forget to tell them what has been happening. Even in the course of several weeks, changes occur. People come and go. New grants may be received. New programs start.

You may feel you have told volunteers about developments because you told someone else. Volunteers get annoyed and hurt when they keep hearing, "Oh, I am sorry, I thought you knew ...." or "You mean, you didn't know that ...." Keep them up-to-date informally, regularly and frequently, or you can invite volunteers to meet regularly with staff members to talk about what is new. Another simple solution is to put up a bulletin board. Pin up interesting letters, announcements etc. Hang up a blackboard on which you can write three or four words about each of the week's happenings.

I had two recent experiences with volunteers. In one case, a volunteer for an organization called to check my address and my connection with the organization. When I said I was its president, she took my explanation well though she clearly felt foolish. But she should not have been embarrassed. Obviously, she had been given a job to do, but not enough information from which to work. In the second case, I went to a fundraising benefit for PEN International, an organization protesting persecution of writers. I asked how to join PEN and was told that all the information was in the newsletter I picked up as we talked. Only when I got home did I find there was no information at all about joining. Another case of the gap that can occur between organization and volunteer.

9 Set short-term goals. Plan volunteer activities that will last no longer than a few months. Volunteers don't want to think that a job they are doing will go on forever. If a project could last a long time, break it into small pieces so volunteers can feel rewarded with achievements frequently. Talk about what needs doing in each of the next three weeks rather than an entire project that may last six months.

10 Ensure that volunteers do not have to work for a long time in exactly the same area in which they earn their living. A person who does clerical work all day should not be asked to type all evening.

11 Be on the alert for problem volunteers – people who criticize everything, who would rather talk than work, or who make promises they do not keep. This last group may begin by saying:

No problem. Of course I can deliver these leaflets.
A month later when you ask how they are doing, they say:
Just fine. I've already delivered half of them. I'll do the rest tomorrow.
Three days later, what do you hear?

I am awfully sorry. I have been really busy and I just couldn't find the time to get out.

It may not be necessary to get rid of such people. You just need to be aware of their weaknesses and work around them. Limit the number of tickets given to the optimist. Take the critic aside before a meeting and deal with the issues he or she is likely to raise at the meeting; many may be worth listening to. Try to control talkers by giving them specific assignments on which they will report. Be firm at meetings about giving everyone an equal chance to state their opinions. Recognize that if volunteers give you excuses about why they could not do something, they are usually telling you they would prefer to be doing some other job.

12 If you know a volunteer is going to confront you about something, be sure to have someone else with you during the discussion. That way, you have a witness and can avoid the kind of later conversation that starts, without supporting evidence, "He said ...." A second person is also likely to keep the discussion on a calmer level.

13 Set group, not individual, goals. At first, it may seem a good idea to challenge people by giving them each a target, but it can destroy the team you have been building. Everyone may start thinking only of his or her own goal and not of working together towards a common goal – helping the organization. You don't want winners and losers. Everyone should feel appreciated for contributing to a team.

Recognize. Reward. Thank.
Feeling useful, working for a cause that is bigger than yourself, is rewarding in itself. Here are several suggestions about ways to ensure that volunteers feel appreciated.

- Take a personal interest in each volunteer. Every time one comes around, arrange to have a short conversation, even if it is only about the weather.
- Don't treat all volunteers the same. If poor volunteers receive the same recognition as excellent ones, it will be resented.
- Never take volunteers for granted. All volunteers, like all staff members, enjoy recognition. However, what thrills one volunteer may mean nothing to another. Try to tailor the reward to the preferences of the individual.
- Act quickly. Recognition of the best volunteers – or all volunteers – immediately after they achieved the desired result means more than recognition a year later.
- Give awards – certificates or small gifts – at appropriate times, such as the anniversary of a volunteer's service.
- Arrange for successful volunteers to be recognized by a well-known person, either at an event or by letter.
- Recognize volunteers in your annual report, in your newsletter, and any time you are talking to media people.
- Send volunteers thank-you notes regularly.
- Whenever volunteers come up with a good idea let them do what they

propose if it fits with your goals and is feasible. If you consistently ignore their suggestions, they may become discouraged, stop making suggestions, and eventually leave. On the other hand, if you follow one volunteer's suggestions, others will be encouraged to make some of their own. Make sure the person who suggested the idea gets appropriate recognition as well as those involved in carrying it out.

The signs of a successful volunteer program
Even though you chat with volunteers regularly, you may not be sure if they are finding their experience with your organization as satisfying as you would like. Every few months, speak to volunteers individually about their impression of your organization, whether they are happy working with it, and how their time with you could be improved. You will have been successful if they say:
I understand the vision of the organization. I know what it is trying to do.
I know what the goal is.
I am part of the planning.
I know what is expected of me.
I thought I could do it. And I did do it.
I like the people. I am making friends.
I learned something new.
I am having fun.
I know I help make the organization better.

9 Building credibility by finding allies

My friends don't believe in the power of the citizen. Every month 300 major environmental groups are invited to get together. Sixty come. We want to start action groups. People don't yet realize they have power in their hands.

RENATA KISS, ENVIRONMENTAL PARTNERSHIP FOR CENTRAL EUROPE, HUNGARY

One voice alone may go unheard. Even a hundred voices may be heard only softly. But a thousand voices, speaking as one, will sound loudly enough to command attention.

Building credibility on your own takes time and effort. You may not have that much time. You may not have the necessary resources at the moment. Working with others gives you strength and helps build your credibility. You might join a coalition or network of voluntary agencies through which you gain credibility by association. You may also decide to ally yourself with a large intermediary group that can help you get the resources you need. You may want to link up with and make good use of one or more other voluntary organizations that are already established and have a good reputation (See Chapter 10).

Development coalitions bring together thousands of voices. They go by many different names. Depending on their function, they are called networks, consortia, caucuses, movements, intermediaries, or umbrella groups. Other names may be used where you live. Each has a special mandate. Each focuses on that mandate, without being distracted by the local problems its member organizations must deal with. The magazine *Grassroots Development* describes intermediary organizations as the muscle tissue and nervous system of a strong civil society mobilized to solve intractable social problems.

Most coalitions of community-based organizations and NGOs have at least one severe limitation. They lack a broad community constituency. They may be known to governments, granting agencies, their beneficiaries, and other voluntary organizations but they may be invisible to average, middle-class people in their own countries. Yet this is the sector of society to which network members will increasingly have to look for support. Many networks could strengthen themselves by extending their membership. That does not mean trying to enlist organizations known to be antagonistic to the network's causes. It does mean attracting those that generally support the causes the network's members have in common. That can bring a fresh point of view, open doors, and increase the network's visibility.

Making new friends

Organizations, like people, are known by the company they keep. There may be valuable groups you have ignored in the past because their members came from different sectors of your society than yours. But since local credibility is now essential, making new friends is also essential. Many voluntary organizations have shied away, for example, from connections with the academic community and with research centres, just as they have steered clear of business and other sectors of society that intimidate them or do not agree with them on how their community should develop. This is a major weakness. There is no doubt that some academics and researchers have not gone out of their way to befriend grassroots organizations. They are often accused of doing their research in a vacuum, of being too far removed from the pressing concerns of their society. If you want to build your own credibility, you may have to take the first steps to join networks you had not considered before or to set up new exchanges that will benefit both groups. If you work in rural development or sustainable agriculture, do you tap the expertise of the agricultural scientists and economists in your area? If you are working in microcredit, do you benefit from the business management and financial knowledge of people in the area?

What is your relationship with local religious groups? They are another type of network. Sometimes, development and religious groups are on the same side in controversies over the path of civil society. Catholic priests who support "liberation theology" have been active in the civil rights movements of Latin America, for example. Other times, they are in conflict. Some development organizations have been accused of trying to destroy their country because they did not appear to support its religious leadership.

Working together in strong, supportive coalitions

There are several ways in which voluntary organizations can improve their credibility and their power. One is by joining a broad coalition of like-minded organizations that will share knowledge and speak with one voice. The other is to shelter under the umbrella of a larger organization that is able to raise money effectively for the benefit of its associated groups or members. These two kinds of joint action are discussed in this chapter; Chapter 10 discusses relationships between organizations that are more one-on-one, including alliances, mergers, etc.

Unlike umbrella groups, coalitions generally do not get involved in funding their member's programs. Instead, their mandate may be to:

• influence national development in accordance with their members' goals. These coalitions or networks may do this by lobbying their government. They may organize events such as rallies and news conferences to attract media attention. They may run educational programs and publish newsletters and brochures. They may seek representation on policy-making bodies.

The Caucus of Development NGO *Networks (*CODE-NGO*) is an umbrella organization of thirteen major development* NGOs *in the Philippines. Together, these networks – nine national and four regional – represent about 3,000 organizations ....* CODE-NGO *aims to establish non-governmental organizations as major partners in national development. Its mission is to expand the reach* *and increase the effectiveness of* NGO *development work in the country.* (CODE-NGO *publication*)

• negotiate with governments appropriate relationships with non-profit organizations. Many governments believe they are responsible for creating a sense of community in their country and for its development. They may not see NGOs or community groups as necessary or desirable in these matters. Only a concerted community effort is likely to effect any change in such an attitude.

One of the functions of the NGO-*Coordinating Committee on Rural Development is to promote understanding and cooperation between* NGOs *and government bodies working in rural development.* (NGO-Coordinating Committee, Thailand)

• develop a consensus on specific development issues. Coalitions with this goal fight for changes in the policy or activities of government or corporations. They use advocacy and protest. They may take legal action, stage rallies, seek media attention, issue publications. The issue may be environmental – for example, the protests against large tree plantations that have occurred in countries as far apart as Thailand and Brazil. Or it may be economic, a fight for the rights of small landowners or peasant farmers. There are many such issues, and for most there are networks.

The Coconut Industry Reform Movement, Inc. is a movement of three national peasant organizations and nine non-government organizations. For decades now, the coconut industry has been in crisis borne out of past policies that established control of the industry by a favoured elite, centuries-old inequity and land ownership distribution, and protectionist policies of western countries. All these have left the vast majority of the 18-20 million coconut farmers and farm workers in poverty. Hence it is crucial for us to unite to more effectively confront the challenges we face and take advantage of the space for participation in policy formulation in present democratic institutions. (Coconut Industry Reform Movement, the Philippines)

• arrange training for member organizations in all the key areas of management and fundraising. The potential for training was recognized by DENIVA, the NGO coordinating body in Uganda, after a study of its members. The study recommended that DENIVA should continue to help to build the capacity of its development-oriented member organizations. It went on to say that:

Areas for strengthening include:
  • *organizational capacities like: strategic thinking, planning and design of monitoring and impact assessment systems, report writing, fundraising, networking and*
  • *capacities directly related to project or programmes to alleviate poverty like training, management of savings and credit schemes, and management of information and documentation centres.*

The areas for capacity building in training include: carrying out training needs assessment, designing of curricula, manuals and training materials, facilitation techniques and carrying out impact assessments of the training undertaken and networking with other training institutions.

The areas for micro-finance training should include: policy development, training of clients in micro-enterprise development, developing accounting systems, designing of loan tracking systems and carrying out feasibility studies and impact assessments and collaboration and information exchange with like-minded organizations.

Areas of capacity building for research should cover the whole range of information collection, analysis, presentation, and dissemination.

The main areas under communication which require strengthening are in particular documentation, publishing and management of information and documentation centres.

• act as an information resource and exchange. The DENIVA report recommends that member organizations:
- *exchange their newsletters and other publications*
- *exchange staff*
- *visit each other for learning purposes*
- *invite each other to training sessions for communities*
- *discuss pertinent issues through the DENIVA newsletter and radio programs. Areas of sharing could include successful income generating projects, local resource mobilization strategies, management of savings and credit schemes, marketing of the organization, appropriate technologies, NGO values and good practises, and good NGO/government relationships.*
- *invite government and donors to visit member organizations to show their achievements and discuss areas of concern*

It recommends further that:

The DENIVA Resource Centre should act as the focal point for information generation and dissemination:
- *maintain a database on member organizations and donor information*
- *send relevant information to members on request*
- *develop information packages on NGO management; organizational self-assessment; management of savings and credit schemes; strategies for poverty elimination; fundraising*
- *maintain a homepage on the Internet*

Such centres are opening around the world. The Mexican Center for Philanthropy has several hundred members. It advises on organizational development, legal and accounting matters, the design of social projects, impact studies, fundraising, etc.

• act as a resource about national and local development policy. Once again, the DENIVA study provides an example:

DENIVA should encourage general debate on the role of NGOs in Uganda and their underlying values through public fora, the media and its own publications.

• develop self-regulation for credibility. Some networks have tackled the issue of credibility head on. They are training their members in financial management, accountability, and presentation of information.

CODE-NGO [in the Philippines] hopes to contribute to improving the standards of development work and to promote the transparency and accountability of development NGOs in the country. (From a CODE-NGO publication)

Accreditation is becoming popular. For example, the Ford Foundation in 1999 gave a large grant to the Philippine Council for NGO Certification to establish a self-accreditation council.

• strengthen international linkages. Small organizations cannot afford international linkages unless they receive special, usually foreign, funding. The Coconut Industry Reform Movement in the Philippines received a grant enabling the chairman and a farmer to spend 40 days in Germany lobbying for reform in the coconut industry of their country. They gave press conferences in 17 cities, resulting in a deluge of letters to the president and supreme court of the Philippines.

Choosing the right networks

Making the right connections can enhance your reputation and give you other benefits. But joining a network can bring risks as well as benefits. In Thailand, for example, protests against large tree plantations alienated people in government. As a result, development organizations, even in other areas, met resistance from government officials.

Community-based organizations must weigh carefully the benefits of membership in a particular network. Some may decide that the price of membership – reduced government interest, or even government hostility – may be too high. Others may see long-run success as worth the price.

Which networks should you join? Consider your goals carefully to see how well they fit with those of the networks around you. For every network you consider joining, ask yourself:

• Does the network operate in our organization's principal areas of concern?

• Is the network effective and well regarded by the people who know its work?

• Is the network well led? Does it have good management and a good board of directors?

• Does its membership consist only of like-minded, similar organizations? Is that a defect? Should it also represent other interests?

Kumi Naidoo, then head of the South African National NGO Coalition and now head of the international coalition called Civicus, has defined a good coalition. When answering the questions above, see how closely the coalitions you work with now, or might work with in the future, meet the standards Kumi Naidoo set. A good coalition, he said:

• respects the autonomy of members
• involves members in all activities
• ensures that the coalition can deliver measurable value. Members must know what is really in it for them other than just a warm, fuzzy feeling.

• understands the importance of a good communications strategy between and with members, donors and other social forces, including the public. (Coalitions tend to ignore the public.)

• takes risks. Balances the need for inclusiveness against being bland.

• is brave, willing to be outrageous where appropriate. Takes on things that seem impossible.

• challenges parochialism. (People can be good at meetings but can just settle back into their organizations afterwards.)

• is open, honest. Confronts diversity and deals with it. (Coalitions are often scared of diversity.)

• ensures that the coalition is greater than the sum of the parts. (People can do amazing things in their own organizations. But put these same people around a table and nothing may emerge.)

• has no permanent friends, no permanent enemies

Working with intermediary groups

Small, community-based organizations recognize that it is almost impossible for them to get funding from overseas donors and from major local donors. They do not have the resources to go hunting for donors. Even a long trip to the capital city may be beyond their means or their imagination. They may not even have built credibility with possible local supporters.

While they may have enough money as long as their needs are small, they may run into difficulties as soon as they plan a major project. A small organization in India wanted to build a school. The only industry in the town with the cash to contribute generously was a glassmaker that used child labour. The organization opposed child labour. That left only a few local sources of money such as the Rotary or Lions clubs. Money might have come from the government if there had been some way to reach the right person. The organization needed an intermediary with sources of funds beyond the community itself.

That is the role of two kinds of organization. One is the intermediary group – an organization with the contacts and expertise to secure funding, which is then distributed to the community organizations that are its members. Intermediary organizations are designed to meet the current needs of organizations that apply to them for funds. The other type of organization is discussed in Book 3, Chapter 23. It is a community foundation, or civil society resource organization, which may have significant overseas funding but is created to secure more funding for community needs from local individuals, corporations, foundations, and investment income.

Intermediary organizations are usually defined as locally owned and controlled, private, independent, and either national or local in scope. Though the term usually refers to organizations that allocate money, the intermediary may also provide its members with other resources, such as information about possible donors or training.

Intermediary organizations have been formed to build bridges between small organizations and donors, large or small, and between small communities and the outside world. Donors need intermediaries too. Judy Belk of Levi Strauss & Co. believes donors should give money directly only if they have the necessary knowledge to make gifts that will be effective. "If they don't then, as the market gets larger, they must experiment with models such

Education. Food. Shelter. Health. CRY *[Child Relief and You] tries to restore these basic rights to deprived children in rural, tribal and urban India.*

CRY does this by routing your contribution of time, skills and money to voluntary agencies working to give underprivileged children a better future.

CRY INDIA

as using intermediaries." Eugene Saldanha, of Charities Aid Foundation, South Africa, adds, "As long as there are aid agencies, there is a need for intermediaries."

> Local organizations in the countryside with only volunteers or a tiny staff and office cannot possibly write proposals. Intermediaries know everyone: they know the trends. They cannot transfer this knowledge to the small, local organizations.
>
> You have to have an image. It took us three years to realize that we needed to look like a business. Local, grassroots groups will never look like a business. That is why intermediaries are needed. (Renata Kiss, Environmental Partnership for Central Europe, Hungary)

Some of these intermediary organizations have been set up by individual people who saw a need and moved to meet it. Others have been started by a group of NGOs, a group of community-based organizations, or even by governments. Their primary purpose is to find funds to support small agencies. Intermediary groups offer a level of credibility unknown to small organizations because they are often headed by people who are:

- part of or have access to the elite of the country
- well known to foreign donors
- experienced financial managers
- living or working in cities where most donors can be found
- familiar with the languages spoken by donors, both international and local
- familiar with the vocabulary of philanthropy and of development

The arrangement sounds ideal, but, as in most things in life, where there is a benefit there is also a cost. The trade-off is that intermediary organizations can be somewhat flexible with the money they obtain. Often, it is felt, what they do with it harms the little organizations they were created to help. The "New Dawn" Association for Community Health and Development has been one such critic. It has said that:

> There is increasingly bitter criticism of the role of NGOs [that is, in this case, intermediary organizations]. There is a saying that "grassroots organizations supply the corpses while the NGOs get the money," and its expresses the contradictions existing between them. We need to undergo a thorough process of self-criticism. On occasion the NGOs have acted like ostriches, sticking their heads in fundraising and carrying out projects without looking beyond.

When an intermediary group solicits and receives a grant for a smaller organization it supports, it is entitled to keep 10 to 15 per cent of the money to cover its own administrative costs – such as office expenses, staff salaries, travel costs, and monitoring of the funded projects. That is not unreasonable, but some intermediaries were set up only to obtain this money and not really to help others. In some countries, people feel foreign donor agencies give money to intermediary groups they suspect are fraudulent simply because they have to spend their allotted funding each year.

Most intermediaries were not set up to make money for themselves, but even the 10 to 15 per cent kept by legitimate intermediaries may be resented. A small community-based organization may depend on one large intermediary for all its funding. It regularly receives more money than it could possibly raise on its own. But dependence is annoying, and many small groups understandably chafe under what they see as restrictions imposed by the intermediary. Many community groups feel that, in any dispute, overseas donors will always believe the intermediary rather than the people's organization.

There is increasing debate about the merits of the intermediary system, as seen in the quotation at right and the following example, both from the Philippines.

BavilcoI
The Bagobo Village Community Multi-purpose Cooperative Incorporated (BavilcoI) is a small village organization based near Davao City in the Philippines. It was begun by two women who thought too many children were dying of measles. They arranged an immunization program. The group has gone on to meet other health concerns and to install new wells, introduce composting, ensure that each household in the village has a pit latrine, and encourage all the children to go to school.

For two early projects, deworming and providing vitamin A for the children, they received materials from USAID. They did not receive money because, the women say, USAID feared that any cash would go to groups it considered to be communist. usaid also supplied health trainers and the materials for latrines and composting. All this aid was channelled through a large intermediary organization with more than four hundred beneficiaries in the Davao area. Eventually, BavilcoI felt confident enough to borrow money to lend to people to start small businesses – chocolate making, blacksmithing, baking. This money was repaid.

Then the women borrowed money from the intermediary to buy a piece of land to develop for income. All was well for a while, but the BavilcoI volunteers came to feel the intermediary was charging them a rate of interest on their loan that was too high for them to meet when other lenders were charging less. But they had huge difficulty in finding any group or business that would lend them money at a lower rate of interest. Having depended solely on one organization for funding, they had made no other connections. They were further disappointed when there was a change in leadership at the intermediary and a subsequent change in its interests. They felt trapped. Nevertheless, they did succeed in repaying the full loan ahead of time and in arranging less expensive financing. But they had no idea where else to look for funds in the future.

Gradually, these women went from being plain housekeepers to being community leaders. Their children are all in school. They have overcome

Community-based groups are unlettered and isolated. They can hold benefits and bingos where the profit is low. The groups are happy about having any money and they do have fun. But this is primitive fundraising. These groups know nothing about international money. Urban NGOs *have the connections. They can get international money, which trickles down to the community organizations. There is a suspicion that the money does not all trickle down. The poor unlettered group is being used by the umbrella group, which keeps a big share. It is better if each organization raises its own funds without passing through the big umbrella groups which may have 200 beneficiaries. Power corrupts.*

PROFESSOR ESPERANZA SIMON, ASSOCIATION OF RURAL WOMEN OF TARLAC AND PAMPANGA, THE PHILIPPINES

the initial anger of their husbands, who thought the whole enterprise a waste of time. And they say that they are not ashamed any more to deal with strangers, even if they cannot speak English. One of the two leaders runs a catering service. The other owns a small shop and makes hollow bricks for house building. Several years ago, they said, neither of them would ever have thought of having such ambitions.

BavilcoI could have gone on for years doing what Professor Simon called "primitive" fundraising – bake sales, bingo evenings, and so on. The group might have been happy with some money and would have also had some fun. But, because of the exceptional drive of the women who started the organization, BavilcoI was able to get money for its programs through the intermediary that, at the time, it could not likely have found anywhere else. Many people feel grants – from both foreign and local sources – should go directly to small community organizations, or to consortia of community organizations, and not through intermediary groups. Many experts see intermediary groups as temporary solutions to the credibility problems of small agencies that want to stand on their own feet. These agencies want to be capable of approaching donors directly. They think intermediary organizations will disappear as soon as community groups develop better financial management and systems of accountability, and achieve some success at local urban fundraising and finding government funding.

Community groups need to feel they will not be dependent on the intermediary agency forever. Tensions can be relieved by careful negotiations over the terms of funding from the intermediary group and by full disclosure of the intermediary group's finances. Intermediary groups can also show that they want community groups to succeed by offering them training in building credibility and conducting fundraising programs. The smaller organizations, in turn, have to recognize that, if intermediaries are to continue raising money, they do have a right to a part of every grant they obtain. Smaller organizations will also have to learn how to deal with the resentment that comes naturally with dependence on someone else. Both sides will have to show flexibility.

How long this system will endure depends very much on the attitudes of major donors, who do not want to have to deal with tens of thousands of small grant applications. Major donors have their own administrative costs, and every application for a grant – big or small – costs time and money to consider. If an application is successful, it takes more time to negotiate and manage the grant. It is cheaper for a large donor to deal with one application for a large grant than to handle dozens of small ones. For this reason major donors prefer to receive applications from intermediaries like LAWIG and the BavilcoI funder, which bring together the needs of many small organizations. It is much more efficient. I have often heard stories of organizations being refused funding because the amount of money they needed was too small for a funding agency to be able to administer economically. Nevertheless, "At the end of the day," says Mohini Mobayi of Concern India Foundation, "people want all the money to go to the beneficiary."

10 Building strategic alliances

Cooperation among voluntary organizations can take many forms. This chapter will explore the kinds of alliance that are possible, the advantages and disadvantages, and the questions that must be considered before entering into a new arrangement that has long-term benefits, especially for fundraising.

In reviewing other voluntary organizations, you may have identified some that you would be happy to work with in the future. They share your interests and philosophy. Perhaps you are in regular contact with some of them already. Before starting fundraising, it is time to consider whether you could benefit by a strategic alliance with one or more of them. You may have realized already that you will have a difficult time competing on your own for local funds with large, established groups who are mounting increasingly professional fundraising programs. The big international agencies such as UNICEF, CARE, World Vision, and Oxfam will be the dominant players in fundraising for some time to come.

This issue should be addressed before the first stages of fundraising begin. New alliances could require you to change your identity, your management, even your name. It is best to get all that done before you begin building a fundraising team, including new board members and other volunteers who may not know your organization well. You will have to acquaint them with its vision, its achievements, its potential for greater service, and what it needs to achieve that potential. If, part way through that process, you decide to make new alliances or to change your identity, you will confuse your new supporters and may weaken your organization's credibility.

Greater freedom for NGOs carries with it the obligation to become more accountable to stakeholders and more transparent to the public. Increased coordination among NGOs themselves is needed to overcome problems such as concentration in certain areas and unhealthy competition.

DR. QAZI FARIQUE AHMED, ASSOCIATION OF DEVELOPMENT AGENCIES, BANGLADESH, VOLUNTARY ACTION PULSE, NOVEMBER 1998

The reasons for considering alliances

Every day new organizations form. Every day new and old organizations compete for survival. Increasing competition for decreasing money means many organizations will disappear. There won't be enough money to support all of them. An organization is more likely to survive if its leaders learn to think in new ways and prove themselves able to manage change. If they succeed, the organization will become stronger. A stronger organization can provide better service to its clients. A stronger organization is also more credible as a fundraiser.

The chief reasons for building alliances should be to increase your organization's ability in the following areas.

• *Attract attention because of the scale of its programs.* Not long ago, I went with a Zimbabwean colleague to call on possible donors for a project in southern Africa. We had a hard time getting their attention. The project did not cost enough money to interest them.

• *Improve fundraising management and programs by drawing on the strengths of the people in more than one organization.* One partner may have more experienced managers, for example; the other may have better trained technicians. Or one may already be raising funds locally but is having problems because its program has a narrow, technical focus; the other has a program with broader public appeal but has not yet started local fundraising and expects to benefit from the experience of its new partner.

• *Build credibility and a stronger public image.* Donors can be confused when they get requests from many organizations that are competing for money. They tend to withdraw support if they see organizations are competing to provide the same services to the same people. Organizations improve their chances for support when they show that they recognize the importance of working closely together.

• *Promote your services more effectively.* With more people and a stronger financial base, you will be able to invest more in public relations and in building your fundraising capacity.

• *Enhance your image with present and future donors.* Donors will see that your organization thinks its mission is more important than its individuality, and that its managers are open to change.

• *Gain the attention of the general public by speaking with a stronger, more unified voice, thereby increasing fundraising potential*

A further reason for combining resources is to save money, especially in administration. Saving money is as effective as fundraising; it too results in more money for the program. Savings may come in two ways. In programs, it may be possible to integrate some activities and eliminate duplication. More important, you may also save overhead expenses – the routine costs of operating an organization such as rent, bookkeeping, travel, board meetings, insurance, and publications. By sharing costs, your two organizations should be able to provide the same services as they do now for less money, or provide more services with the same amount of money.

A big caution: The savings will not appear all at once. Short-term savings are unlikely because it will cost some money to set up the new arrangement. You may need new letterhead, extra meetings, or legal help, for example. It is also possible that little will be saved in the long term. Taking advantage of new opportunities for service may require all available re-

---

Organizations cannot often get it together to even know what organizations in the next town are doing. So donors are put off investing in the sector. The major problem is at the local level. The competitive spirit turns into a life and death struggle for resources that can lead to community division and even violence.

Alliances are needed for survival. They are not a luxury. Organizations have common interests. Alliances can be loose or close. Amalgamation is not necessarily best. An informal connection with a limited focus is often best.

BARRY SMITH, INTERFUND INTERNATIONAL FUNDRAISING CONSORTIUM, SOUTH AFRICA

sources. Saving money alone is rarely a sufficient reason for a new alliance. The other reasons are more important.

It is never easy to give up one's identity. But if the future looks difficult, ask yourself:

Does it really matter if my organization survives on its own and in its present form?
Is it more important that the service we provide be maintained and improved?
Are we satisfied just to survive and keep control of our destiny?
Are we willing to give up some independence to be part of a new organization that is stronger and more effective than we are on our own?

If the answer to the first and third questions is "No" and to the other questions "Yes", you are ready to start building alliances.

Initial alliances

Most voluntary agencies have taken the first step in building alliances. They have already made contact with organizations similar to themselves. After discussion agencies that have similar missions may agree to restrict their work to designated areas – that is, they agree on who does what where. Two health agencies may agree that each will work in a different town. Or one health agency may decide to specialize in prenatal care, while another handles childhood nutrition.

Dividing responsibilities in this way can ensure that an organization stays tightly focused on its mission. However, it can also restrict an excellent organization which, left to itself, might want to expand its services. Alternatives are to exchange information with others, join to press for political change, run joint training programs for professional development, or cooperate in other programs. Recognize the value of putting your toes in the water by testing a relationship with a few small projects. When everyone feels comfortable, then is the time to go swimming together.

Further types of alliance

More formal cooperation also may take many forms. Four of these are especially important.

Pooled facilities and/or administrative services

Two or more organizations agree to form a single administrative unit that will manage many of the activities they must conduct – payroll operations, communications, bookkeeping, and similar functions. This can result in big savings. It will not alter the public image of the organizations: to people outside, they still appear distinct.

Administration does not stir the heart: the program and its services, and the benefits to the community, are what attract support. Cost efficiency through sharing will, on the other hand, increase credibility and encourage donors. Several organizations may join together to apply for grants and raise funds because their services are complementary or because they have designed a joint program. Their cooperation is likely to strengthen their case for financial support. The organizations decide how the money they raise will be divided and retain control of their own programs. Churches, universities, and other voluntary organizations are all potential partners.

Affiliation
Two or more organizations form an official, formal connection for their common benefit. Each organization preserves its identity and status. However, the connection may be recognized on the stationery of one or both organizations, in their publications and in conversation. People may be appointed from one board to another. In affiliations, there may be little integration of programs or none at all.

A link of this kind can give credibility to a new or relatively unknown organization. It can open doors for small organizations that they could not open on their own. Affiliations are less frightening and easier to negotiate than the closer types of alliances below, but the benefits can be significant.

Merger
Several more or less equal organizations join to create an entirely new organization. They have decided, individually and collectively, that as one larger body they can raise money and provide services beyond what each of them can do on its own.

Mergers are not without cost. If the new organization has a new name, it must invest time and money in establishing its identity and re-establishing its credibility. Unless the terms of the merger are fair, a smaller organization may feel it has been taken over, perhaps losing more control than it wanted. To a small organization, a merger can feel the same as an acquisition.

Acquisition
One organization takes over another smaller, perhaps weaker, organization. This should not be a hostile acquisition, as when one business corporation takes over another against its will. The smaller organization should be willing to be acquired, to ensure its financial stability and expand the scope of its work and its contacts. It must recognize that its services mean more than the risk of losing its identity.

Don't wait for a miracle

Like many organizations, yours may be breaking even financially, but only by cutting expenses and programs. If so, this is a good time to start looking around for partners.

Many organizations wait too long to say, "It cannot be business as usual any more. We had better find a bigger organization to help us." They may know in their hearts that they are on shaky ground. Yet they hope every day that a grant application will be approved, a big donation will appear, or the government will give them money. Eventually, everyone in the organization recognizes that no saviour is in sight, that no miracle will happen. Only at this point are most organizations willing to consider seriously a whole new way of doing business. By then, however, it may already be too late: they are operating from weakness rather than from strength. The prospect of change, always threatening to many people, will then appear even more threatening. Staff morale will drop, and vulnerability will reduce the number of options available. Potential partners may make demands that could have been refused a year earlier.

It is never too early to start planning alliances. The time to think about a new structure is when your organization and your commitment to your vision are strong. The decision should be made as part of a well-thought-out plan for future growth. Realignment will then be seen as a sign of strength, of the leaders' ability to understand the climate in which they will have to operate in future, and to adjust accordingly. Change at the right time can be invigorating, giving new energy to an already lively organization.

It can be useful to tell your current donors you are considering an alliance with another agency. Most believe cooperation is a good thing and will cheer you on. They may also be willing to give some financial support for your efforts. Investigating a merger or an affiliation can cost money. The biggest investment is in time but it may be necessary to get some extra help or travel to another centre to meet with a potential partner. Several foundations I talked to thought the voluntary organizations they supported should be pushing them for funding to investigate possible new arrangements.

In the early 1990s, a staff member at the Canadian International Development Agency suggested that I, as executive director of a development agency with a staff of ten (and a deficit), should consider merging with a larger, more secure organization. I thought it was a good idea – some time in the future. I wanted first to build our program further and pay off the deficit through fundraising. I hoped a major change in status would be unnecessary. The economy was strong at the time.

I finally decided to take up the suggestion some years later after reading the financial projections our treasurer prepared. While we were not in a desperate position, his calculations showed we would just barely survive if we kept on the way we were going. We simply could not bring in enough money, at a low enough cost, to maintain the program at its current level – which both our staff and board already considered inadequate. By then, the organization had dropped to seven staff members and was heavily dependent on several excellent, committed volunteers. In the years when we thought we would be able to effect a miracle, the Canadian economy had turned downwards and government funding of all agencies had been cut.

When we started looking for a partner, no organization felt as confident about merging as it might have felt some years earlier, when we were all much more secure financially. I spent the next three years and a good deal of money pursuing mergers. We got close to a deal with three different agencies but never found the proper match. The opportunity was lost, per-

"When charities measure their success only in terms of 'lives changed,' it's a sign that they didn't meet their fundraising goals."

haps permanently. And the organization's work is restricted, perhaps permanently.

Would a change of direction be good for us?
In approaching an alliance of any sort, your organization needs a clear sense of its purpose. Are your goals more likely to be realized in a new arrangement? Ask yourself the following questions. Your answers will tell you what to do.

The financial future
What do our financial projections tell us? What can we learn from a realistic estimate of our costs and revenue over the next five years, under existing arrangements? Are we large enough and strong enough financially to continue as we are? Are we large enough and strong enough financially to expand our program during the next five years?
Are our major donors pushing us to change the way we look for funds? Have they indicated that they will be reducing their grants in the future?
Even if we think we can succeed in the short term, how will we survive in the long term, given the increasing competition for funds from larger, richer, better-known organizations?
Can we survive alone in the long term, given the increasing competition from agencies close to us that are doing similar work? What are the reasons for thinking we can, or can't?
What are we doing to ensure that we do not lose our position?

Cooperation in income-generating activities
What possibilities are there for cooperating with other agencies in developing and promoting programs that will generate income?
What would be the benefits?
What would be the disadvantages?
If we decided to go ahead, how long might it take to set up the program? How long might each step take?

Division of territories
Does it make sense to divide our area of work geographically with other agencies to avoid inappropriate competition? What agencies might we be able to work with in this way? How would we best arrange a division for the common benefit?
What would be the benefits of such an arrangement?
What could be the disadvantages?
If we decide to go ahead, how long might it take to set up the program? How long might each step take?

Joint fundraising
What would be the advantages/disadvantages of joining with one or more agencies for fundraising?

If we decided to join with one or more agencies to increase our income, what obstacles would we have to overcome?
How would we see such a program operating?
If we decide to go ahead, how long might it take to set up the program? How long might each step take?
If we succeed, would we conduct joint programs? How would these be managed?

Umbrella/intermediary groups
Is there an umbrella/intermediary organization through which we might be able to receive funds? What is it? What do we know about it? How would we apply for funding from it?
What obstacles would we have to overcome to receive funds in this way?
How much might we benefit financially?
What would be the disadvantages?
(For further discussion of umbrella and intermediary groups see Chapter 9.)

Pooled facilities and administrative services
What facilities/services would we be prepared to share?
What organizations might we share them with?
What arrangement do we think would work best?
What would be the plan and schedule for making this arrangement?

Affiliation/association
Could we strengthen our organization by making an unofficial, informal connection with an agency that has a vision similar to ours?
Could the right affiliate introduce us to useful people?
What valuable connections might be lost?
What would be the advantages and disadvantages?
What steps do we need to take now to form an affiliation?
What would be the schedule for making this arrangement?

Merger/acquisition
Are we prepared to put the value of our program ahead of the identity of our organization?
Are there organizations with which we feel comfortable that might also want to consolidate or expand their programs by joining with us?
What strengths would we bring?
What would be the advantages?
What would be the disadvantages?
How might our staff and board view a new arrangement?
How would our donors/supporters feel?
How could we calm the likely fears? What would we need to do to ensure strong support for the idea?
How would the staff and board of the other organization view it?
How would we want such an arrangement to work?
What would be the advantages?

What would be the disadvantages?
What would be the schedule for making this arrangement?

Conclusion
Are there any other arrangements we could make with other organizations that would strengthen our program in the long term?
What steps should we take next?

What to look for in a partner

Any potential partner should meet certain basic criteria.

1 *A similar or compatible mission.* People often think the mission of each partner must be precisely the same. In fact, most organizations that have considered merging have found that the new arrangement was worth pursuing as long as the missions were just compatible – that is, not identical but well suited to each other. I found there were fewer discussions about mission than any other aspect of merging, perhaps because many mission statements are so broad that they can accommodate a wide variety of approaches and programs.

2 *Compatible programs and services.* The most appropriate partners are not your direct competitors. With them, it may be difficult to overcome long-standing suspicions and rivalries. Think instead about joining with organizations whose work is similar to yours but not exactly the same or in exactly the same place.

3 *Financial stability.* You don't want to be responsible in any way for rescuing an organization that is in bad financial circumstances. Its failure could drag you down as well.

4 *Stable and diversified sources of revenue.* You don't want to get too close to an organization whose existence is precarious because it is unduly dependent on only one or two donors. Investigate the likely future status of any potential partner as well as its present situation. It may have five or six donors now, but three grants are coming to an end in a year and no new donors are in sight. Just because you want to work with another organization, don't ignore signs of trouble ahead.

5 *A good reputation in the community.* You cannot afford to damage your own organization's credibility with your supporters and community by association with another organization that has a questionable reputation, no matter how rich, powerful or well connected it may appear to be.

If an organization meets these criteria, further investigation is worthwhile. Other, less fundamental, issues will emerge gradually. Some of these can make or break an arrangement, as discussed in the following sections.

It may not be love at first sight

Even with favourable economic conditions, it takes time to find the right partner. It takes even longer to negotiate any arrangement. The steps described here apply mostly to acquisitions and mergers, though many are useful in planning any kind of cooperation.

1 *Agreeing on a timetable.* Do the boards and staff members of each or-

ganization share a sense of urgency about getting together, or does one organization want to move more cautiously than the other? Agreement on the speed of exploration and negotiation is essential. When organizations operate on different schedules, misunderstandings and friction can result.

Tackle the big issues early. Decide which of the issues that follow are most important for your organization. How willing are they to compromise about leadership? name? fundraising? If you cannot resolve several major issues quickly, then it is unlikely a new arrangement is possible. Learning that will save you a lot of time.

At some point you may feel you have run into a stone wall in the discussions, with neither side willing to change its position. That may be a signal to break off and seek another partner. But first you might consider asking someone outside both organizations to take a look at the outstanding issues and to mediate the discussions with a view to establishing trust.

2 Telling the staff. The negotiators for both organizations should agree on a date when the idea of a new arrangement will be discussed with the staff members of both organizations. There is no wrong or right time to tell the staff, but it is hard to keep secrets in any organization, especially a small one. I favour telling the truth from the start. Leaders can go only where others will follow. People are more likely to follow happily if they have been consulted about the direction they are being asked to go. Even in societies in which the management style is top-down, the natural fears of the staff about any change should be addressed.

Begin the process by setting some target dates for the steps to be followed: making a preliminary plan for the new arrangement, discussing it with everyone affected, finalizing the plan, and putting it into effect. This will be a balancing act. If you move too slowly, worries can build as people find more and more problems to debate. If you move too fast, people will feel that you are not consulting with them enough and are taking too many chances. A year may be needed just to complete the first stages, and longer if the organizations are large and complex. Even after full agreement is reached on terms, putting the new arrangement into effect will be a continuing process of learning and change.

3 Drafting the joint mission statement. Significant obstacles may arise in combining missions even when the missions of the individual organizations are complementary. My experience suggests it is not difficult to join together the missions of similar organizations. The job still needs doing, however. Working on a mission statement together is a good way to expose and resolve any differences in approach. The job is easy because only broadly expressed ideas are involved, not personalities or power.

4 Building trust. It is difficult enough to build trust with people you don't know at all or know a little but already like. It is even more difficult to build trust with groups you have disagreed with in the past. But circumstances may dictate that such an attempt be made. Without trust, there can be no workable partnership, no matter what structure is chosen, be it cooperating on programs or effecting a full-scale merger.

Governance, overall management, program management, financial management and responsibility, staffing, salary levels and personnel policies, office arrangement, the use of volunteers – all must be negotiated and may change, perhaps dramatically. Amidst all these other adjustments, the fundraising programs may also change. Who will do the fundraising in the future? What will each organization have to pay? Who will allocate revenue? Will each organization be treated fairly?

One major obstacle to building trust is a fear that the change in structure will prove harmful. In the exploration my own organization carried out, both sides feared loss of control. Would we merge completely? Would one organization become a department of the other? Would there be two boards or one? If there were one board, how would the interests of each organization be protected? The answer, of course, was that existing arrangements could not be fully preserved. Each organization would have to give up some autonomy. We spent hours tinkering with the mechanisms. Staff members were fearful that their own interests had not and would not be recognized – so fearful that they failed to see the potential of an alliance. I realized later that none of us had ever expressed our fears openly so they could be dealt with specifically and some reassurance offered.

Provided they consult fully with everyone affected, only a few board and staff members on each side need be involved in the detailed negotiations for any new arrangement. If the project is small, negotiations are more likely to go smoothly. In bigger projects with more people involved and more complex programs to coordinate, confidence is more difficult to build. In such cases, it is a good idea to bring everyone involved together frequently, especially at the beginning of the process, and to encourage them to get to know one another. A few meals together can do wonders for breaking down mistrust.

5 *Budgeting for cooperation.* Trust will build more easily if all the papers are on the table, that is, if everyone can see in detail the financial position of each organization involved. The sources of revenue that will be combined are critical. You will want to be sure there are enough sources that the new organization will remain solvent, even if several grants run out or are cancelled. Equally, you will want to know what obligations you might be undertaking. You need to know, for example, what bills are outstanding against the other organization and what future financial commitments, such as leases, it has made. Perhaps someone on your board will know how to make this kind of analysis and how to make the necessary inquiries from persons other than the potential partner (a process called "due diligence"). Otherwise ask your bank manager, accountant, or a lawyer for help.

Building a budget should be a part of the negotiations for the new arrangement. With all the facts about each organization's financial position available, that will be much easier.

6 *Who will be in charge?* Negotiations for a merger or affiliation are normally conducted by the senior staff person in each agency. A board member may be involved but may not have the time to take part in detailed discussions. Naturally, neither executive director is likely to feel comfortable discussing who will end up running the organization. This decision prop-

erly belongs with the two boards, but they may not become involved soon enough. In that case, negotiations may stall while the chief executives circle around like competing males in a mating ritual.

As the director of a small agency, I could never imagine myself reporting to the executive director of the bigger agency with whom we were in negotiation. But I never came right out and said that. Nor did the board of either organization ever discuss it, either separately or, as they should have done, together. They should have made a clear decision early on, because one person must be in charge to move the process along. Instead, we all danced around the issue for two years without reaching agreement.

7 *Choosing the board.* Each partner in a merger will want to be represented on the new, combined board. Agreement on how that board will be composed may prove difficult to achieve, however, if either side fears loss of control. One way to resolve the issue is to agree that the original organizations will be formally represented for only the first few years. After that, the only criterion for membership in the board will be suitability; efforts will be made to get the best people in the community, without concern for their connection with either of the old bodies. If agreement cannot be reached on the composition of the governing body, the whole idea of partnership should be reconsidered and, perhaps, rejected.

In my own negotiations, the question of leadership would have been easier to settle if the boards had agreed on how they would fit together. Having done that, two boards can begin making joint decisions. They never reached that stage.

8 *Choosing a name for the new organization.* Choosing a name for the new partnership is a good way to focus on the mission and the image that each organization has of itself and of its possible partner. A new name can unify the groups. It can also cause problems. Will it still be possible to recognize the old organization in the new name? If your favourite detergent changes the look of its package completely, it will be a while before you recognize it in the shop. So, too, your beneficiaries and your funders will need time to adjust to a new name. If your detergent box shows much the same label but announces that the contents are new and improved, you will have less trouble identifying it. Perhaps you can find a name that makes the change apparent but does not eliminate the identity of either organization. Be careful, however. It's easy to come up with a name so unwieldy that it is laughed at.

Keeping the same look of the detergent box suggests the product inside is the same thing you have been buying for years. I believe that some change in name or logo or both is, on balance, a good idea.

9 *Recognizing that oil and water won't mix.* The most significant questions, and some of the most difficult to determine, concern the "culture" of the other organization. How does an organization you have seen only from the outside really work on the inside? Do you like the people? Do you share the same political views? Do you think the same things are funny? It may sound trivial, but it is essential to get along easily with the people you may be working with daily for years to come.

I negotiated with one executive director for months and months. The situation seemed promising. I kept asking for assurances that the staff members of his organization were happy about the merger, because I seldom saw any of them. They never came to our meetings. Many travelled frequently. Eventually, when I insisted on a meeting with the staff, I found that they had not been told in any detail, let alone consulted, about any of the possible new arrangements for partnership. Naturally, they felt resentful and threatened. That was understandable. However, I could tell that their resistance was unlikely to be overcome, given the top-down style of management in that organization. Among themselves, the staff members were united: they were just not united with the director. They feared their programs, even their salaries, might be cut to cover any costs of making the new arrangement and expanding areas of service. That made our organization uncomfortable. We did not want to be part of an organization where the director appeared to set one course and the staff another. Besides, we and the people in the other organization did not think the same things were funny.

How could I have found out about these bumps in the road before I started to walk along it? I could have talked to former staff members and volunteers of the other organization to find out how things worked inside. I might have received an unfairly negative picture, but it would at least have made me aware of what to look for. Can you think of other steps I might have taken?

What happens next?
Let's assume every problem has been solved and everyone agrees to proceed – that none of the hurdles has proved too great to overcome. All the necessary new arrangements have been discussed at one time or another during the process. Moreover, everything that has been decided is recorded in a written agreement, so there can be no misunderstandings later on. This is most important. Depending on the new arrangement, you may want a lawyer to help with the agreement, or you may be able to write it yourselves. It should include, among other matters: financial considerations (a list of outstanding debts, committed revenues, and capital assets; a five-year financial projection; a plan to raise funds locally and through grants; agreement on division of revenue): personnel policies (salaries, benefits, reporting arrangements), and governance (board membership and policies).

Be positive. Celebrate the new arrangement. Launch the venture with publicity, a party for everyone involved, a plant or a flower for every staff member and volunteer.

Don't allow either organization to disappear completely. Keep some of the customs, rituals, and distinctive ways of each.

Once the integration is under way, allow time for everything and everyone to settle down. Some people may not have a job under the new arrangement; there may be resentment among the remaining staff members. Some jobs may change. Some small programs may be ended or absorbed in a new, bigger program. There will be plenty of bumps on the adjustment road, too. Staff morale may sink for a while after the excitement of change wears off. Frank, open discussion all the way along will smooth the transition. Active interest from the new board will help.

Evaluating the process
After a year or so, look back at what you wanted to achieve when you went in a new direction and think about the results.
Have you improved management and programs? Have you saved money as well? Are you serving more people?
Have you increased credibility and built a stronger public image? Has media coverage increased? Do more people know about your work? Have you gained prestige in the community?
Are you promoting your services more effectively? Are your services more in demand? Are people coming to your organization to suggest projects you might undertake? Are other organizations asking you to give them training or other professional help? Have you enhanced your image with present and future donors? Have you attracted more donations and other kinds of financial support?

The answers will identify the areas where more work needs to be done. If you find it hard to be objective, think of asking someone from outside to take a look.

11 Writing a long-range plan

The study you completed (Chapters 4–6) is the foundation on which you will build a plan for the future. You have gathered a great deal of information. Now you need to organize it into a long-range plan for the agency as a whole and, later, for each project, new or old. A few members of the board and the senior staff should help put it together for the consideration of the whole board. Once the board approves it, you will want to show parts of the plan to possible donors. That is an extra reason for writing it as well as possible. The plan should cover all activities including administration, financial planning, and fundraising.

While you are planning and writing, keep in the back of your mind the possible strengths and weaknesses described in Chapters 4 and 5. Build on the strengths and plan to overcome the weaknesses.

Your plan should be as short as you can make it. Think of a document of not more than ten to twenty pages, plus a budget. You may also need a few appendices. For example, you may want a separate appendix for each project included in the total plan.

You may find it is more difficult than you expect to write a short document. A famous author once wrote to a friend, "I am sorry this letter is so long. I didn't have time to write a short one." A brief, easy-to-read document requires more work than one that is long and rambling. It takes concentration to make every word matter, but it is worth the effort.

A plan that is brief and well organized earns the respect of the reader. It is convincing because it demonstrates an organization's abilities in management and communication. On the other hand, a document that has too many words, or that is vague and poorly organized, has the opposite effect. Readers will grow impatient; they will have a poor impression of you and your organization; they may stop reading before they reach the end.

The plan should be reviewed every year to take account of changed circumstances.

What to include
Your long-range plan should:
- describe why your organization exists
- tell what the organization has accomplished
- describe who you will serve
- describe the services you will provide, how, when, and to how many people

- show the benefits to the people you will serve
- show how you will measure the results
- show how and to whom you will communicate the results
- define the resources – staff, equipment, money, time – you will need to provide the services, showing what resources you have already and what will have to be added
- describe administrative improvements needed to carry out the projects
- provide an overall budget
- outline the fundraising plan

You will see from the list that the general plan will include only an outline of what you intend to do to raise money. You will have to write a second, separate plan, in greater detail, about fundraising. This planning exercise will be especially important if your organization is new to fundraising. The fundraising plan should be considered separately by the board. It is so important that it deserves special attention.

Once the general plan is complete, you will have all the information you need to put together proposals for potential donors. You may use the whole document or excerpts. You may change the emphasis or revise the document in other ways to fit a specific proposal. In some cases, you will want to give the whole plan to a possible supporter. Book 3 talks about how to make the best use of your plan in your fundraising programs.

Once the general plan is complete, you will have all the information you need to put together proposals for potential donors.

Getting started

The examples in the next chapter do not include as much detail as you will need in your real plan. They simply give an idea of how you might use each of the headings in the list above. Use these headings to write about the plan for the agency as a whole. Use the same headings, or as many of them as you need, to describe each individual project. For projects, however, you may prefer to describe the objectives rather than write a mission statement.

For the overall plan, you can begin with your mission statement and work your way through the list of topics. Or you can begin work with separate projects and complete the other sections later. That is often the better way, especially if your organization has a number of projects that must be combined in the overall plan. It is usually easier to start off by writing about a single project than about the whole organization. But if you do choose this course, keep the goals of your agency in your mind all the time. If you are writing about existing projects, you need to show how they support your goals. If you are asking for funding for new projects, in general you should not stray from your stated goals. Each project should follow logically from your mission statement.

If a project you want to take on does not fit logically into the mission statement, you should have a very good reason for including it. It may be tempting to include a project that falls outside the organization's mission and expertise because:

- it seems likely to be funded and the money is needed
- it could bring good publicity
- it looks interesting or exciting

An experiment now and then is a good idea. But keep the risk small.

How long is long range?

When they talk about long-range planning, people usually mean somewhere between two and five years. Planning experts often say that, in our uncertain world, it makes no sense to plan for more than three years. They say this is as far ahead as anyone is able to predict anything. Other experts say it is impossible to plan even that many years ahead.

Many donors give grants for only two or three years. They want the receiving organization to guarantee that the project or perhaps the whole organization will become self-sustaining in that time. If you are in that situation and if you can indeed satisfy that requirement, then your plan may be limited to two or three years.

In many cases, however, you know it may be four or five years before you can hope to have even a small measure of financial independence. In that case, you may want to extend the plan. Naturally there are a huge number of unknowns when you think about your programs far into the future. The more years ahead you plan in a budget, the more likely it is that you will be wrong. Costs may go up more than you have allowed for, or expected revenues may drop, or new needs may arise. But you can only do your best. At least there is a chance you will be able to persuade a reluctant donor to support a project and fund it for a longer time than normal if you show where you are headed.

A plan is only a statement of what you intend to do. It is not a prison. It is a framework to be reviewed and adjusted annually to take account of changed circumstances. That does not mean it should be taken lightly. It should be taken seriously, especially by the board. Eventually a responsible board of directors will judge the management by how well the plan has succeeded. So will grantors, who may agree to pay a grant in three or four instalments and refuse to pay an instalment until an agreed stage in the project has been achieved. They may even cancel the grant if the project is far behind schedule.

Preparation and planning = power

This section on preparation and planning is intended specifically for the chief executive officer or the plan leader.

You may be asking yourself whether this whole planning process is worthwhile. It is, because it can give you some control over the destiny of the organization. As a leader, you should always know what you want to accomplish. Before you discuss the need for a plan with anyone, you should have a clear idea of what it will eventually contain. Think about meetings where no one seems quite sure what to do. You look around. What do you see? Blank faces. Then a well-prepared person presents a clear case for a certain course of action. That person usually carries the day. The same thing happens with long-range plans. If you are well prepared, if you know what you want to achieve, you will have a measure of control. People want direction. If you don't give it, someone else will. That person may lead the organization where you do not want it to go.

Write down what you want to see happen. Present it persuasively. Use the information you have collected from staff, board, people the organization serves, and others. If the plan seems reasonable, it is very likely to be accepted. To be persuasive, you should:
- express a clear vision of the future of the organization
- sound enthusiastic about the future
- explain carefully what you want to do and why you want to do it
- show how the plan builds on the strengths of the organization
- keep the document short

Why your organization exists: the mission statement

A clear mission statement, or a statement of goals, is helpful to just about any organization, even a small group of volunteers. It explains why the organization exists. This one clear message describes your work in simple terms; it should be effective for a long time and should be used everywhere. Don't change it easily. Think of advertising slogans. They take years to get established.

Perhaps you already have such a statement. If you do, it may be time to examine it again. It can be out of date simply because it does not reflect your current priorities. Your research may have uncovered new needs. Old goals may no longer seem as important. They may even have been achieved and new goals must be set.

For example, you may have been putting increasing effort into meeting the special needs of women. But that concern may not be reflected in your mission statement. I worked for years in an agency that consistently tried to meet the needs of rural women. Most of the staff were women. Yet we had never included helping rural women in our mandate. We thought it was obvious that we cared. The stated mandate was changed only after a major donor insisted on it.

Writing a mission statement can be as important as having one. There is an expression in English: "It is the journey, not the destination, that matters." In this case, both matter. Writing a mission statement makes people, especially leaders, think about the purpose of the organization. Often it draws out contradictions and confusion in the way people think about the organization. It may even unveil basic disagreements about the purpose of the organization that no one understood or wanted to recognize. Working together to reach agreement on a short statement can pull everyone together and head the team in the same direction. It can act like a magnet, attracting people to the cause and holding their interest. After the agreement, the planning becomes much easier.

A lot of people worry about defining missions, goals, and objectives for their organization. They think it sounds hard. They don't know what the three words mean. They may have heard that this exercise can cause a lot of arguments. One reason it does cause arguments is that almost no one can figure out the differences among the three terms. As a result, meetings are spent arguing over which is which instead of making a plan.

At this point, you may want to look back to the section at the end of Chapter 6 on planning by dreaming. It shows you how to avoid these traps. In case you do need to define mission, goal, and objectives, here are some guidelines:

- *Missions or goals* are what we want to do in a general way. They are difficult, sometimes impossible, to measure. Here are examples of mission statements from two organizations in Anambra State in Nigeria:

> *The Urueze Women Improvement Welfare Group believes in womanhood and has the goal of the total empowerment of women especially in the socio-economic sphere. One of the dreams of the Group is to build women who are poor today into entrepreneurs of tomorrow.*
>
> *The Crown Women Co-operative Organization creates, develops, demonstrates and disseminates, worldwide, innovative programs to eliminate chronic hunger by providing resources and information that empower the poorest families and communities to help themselves.*

- *Objectives* are what we are actually going to do. They have a timetable; they can be measured; they are affordable; someone can be given the responsibility for reaching them. Reaching objectives or failing to reach them is how we can tell if we are succeeding in our plan. Here is the main objective that supports the Urueze Women Improvement Welfare Group mission statement:

> *The success of the process is that the business members think for themselves, strengthen basic business skills, and establish an enterprise using their own creativity, knowledge and technical skill. It is expected that people who hitherto suffered due to lack of skills to compete in the informal section could now earn a living ....*

Modern managers are not too concerned about the distinctions between missions, goals, and objectives. In many cases, including the ones above, mission statements are so vague that they are meaningless, whereas statements of objectives can have real force because they are more specific. My experience is that people in an organization will often write a vague, pretentious mission statement. Then they follow it with a more specific statement that has real meat in it. I often think it would be best to drop the first statement and depend on the second, which communicates the mission far more effectively.

Here is the second-level statement from the Crown Women Co-operative Organization. Though longer than necessary, it is much more specific – and more helpful and interesting.

> *Our work ... supports self-help groups of poor people, particularly women. We help these groups provide their members with cash, credit, and non-formal education. The credit enables participants to increase their income-earning and savings opportunities so they can buy or grow more and better food. The education enhances their money management and offers knowledge and motivation to improve their health, nutrition, and family planning practices. Par-*

ticipants learn to identify and solve their problems. By increasing income, knowledge, and solidarity, participants are empowered to change their lives. An empowered person is a "learning ready" person, open to new ideas that can lead to a better life ....

What you need for both your own organization and for fundraising is one powerful statement of what you want to do – whatever it is called.

The next chapters are about long-range planning for a mythical voluntary organization called WaterLink.

Putting words on paper

The mission statement should:
- be short, three sentences at most
- state the vision of the organization

  or
- summarize what the organization stands for
- reflect its unique quality
- show how your organization differs from others
- reflect what the organization is doing now, not just some goal you may never be able to reach
- be simple, so that it can be kept in mind every day by everyone involved with the organization
- *not* read like an advertising slogan
- inspire supporters

The mission statement is dealt with in this chapter because it is the basis for everything else that is written. Other parts of the plan are discussed in the next chapter. But first, here is some advice that can help make everything you write more effective and more convincing.

WaterLink's mission statement

WaterLink aims to ensure that village people have one of the bases of all life – safe, convenient, dependable water – and, as a result, will lead healthier, more productive lives.

Use the right words

You want people to be interested in your plan, and to read it. To achieve both goals you need some writing skills. You do not have to be an expert communicator, but you should follow some useful rules that are not difficult to learn. They will make a great difference in the way your plan – and everything else you write – is received.

Remember, you want people to read all of your plan. They won't get to the end if your writing is difficult to understand. They won't be interested if you bore them.

Here are ten basic rules to make all your writing more effective. Similar rules and additional examples are given in Book 2, Chapter 12.

  1 *Think of the reader*. Picture a typical reader of your plan. Perhaps it is one of your board members – not the one who is most interested and knows what you are going to say already – but, let us say, a businesswoman who is new to the organization. It is always easier to write with only one person in mind. It is much more difficult to write for a group of people with different personalities and different lives.

  2 *Avoid jargon*. The kind of language that has grown up in government and is popular in development is often called "jargon." It tries to make its

writer sound important. Long words are used to sound impressive even though simpler ones have the same meaning. Several words are used when one would do the job. Shorter sentences and simpler words are easier to read. Here is a real example from a development plan:

It must be emphasized that nothing in this plan is self-fulfilling and the plan is only as good as its implementation. Formulation of the plan is one thing and operationalization is another thing.

What does that mean? Would you understand it more easily if the author had used simple language? Those two difficult sentences only mean:

It is not enough to make this plan. It must be carried out.

You may need to add some long words to sound impressive when you write a grant application for a donor agency that likes that sort of presentation. Many big agencies seem to be impressed with big words. But don't clutter your own plan with jargon. It will simply confuse you. It may even prevent you from seeing problems or omissions. Remember that, once you start local fundraising, you have a variety of new audiences. Your board members, especially those from outside the development community, will not be comfortable with page after page of development jargon, nor will most of the donors you want to attract.

3 *Avoid initials.* Use the full names of organizations and the full technical terms – at least the first few times until the reader becomes familiar with them. After all, how many people are likely to know IPM means integrated pest management? Or that CSO means civil society organization?

People may not ask for an explanation because they don't want to appear ignorant. But if they don't ask, they may not be able to understand what you have written and won't be able to discuss your plan usefully. If they do ask, they may feel silly. In either case, they will certainly resent being put in such a position.

When you do use initials, make sure you explain what they mean. One good rule is to use the full name the first time. This can be followed by the initials in brackets, but only if the organization will be mentioned again later. Otherwise, don't clutter the document with initials.

Official Development Assistance (ODA)
United Nations Development Programme (UNDP)

In long plans, it is sometimes useful to include a list of initials that you have used and what they mean. Put it near the front of the document so people will be sure to see it.

4 *Keep sentences short.* Use a sentence to tell one idea. If you have two ideas, use two sentences. If there is too much in a sentence, it is hard to understand. A good rule is to write so that your average English sentence is only about 20 words long.

5 *Look for short, simple words.* They are easier to understand and take less time to read than long words. And they don't complicate the message. Remember that you may be writing in a language that is your second language, for readers who must use their second language to read what you have written.

6 *Remove unnecessary words.* More words than necessary slow down the

reader and confuse the message. An effective written document is as streamlined as a jet plane.

7 *Add details to make sure the reader understands.* When you write, you want the reader to understand exactly what you are trying to say.

Be sure to define any technical term that may be unfamiliar to your reader. For example, you may have to explain that Integrated Pest Management is a system that helps farmers recognize and manage pests in ways that are safe, healthy, and economical.

Use words that present a clear picture of what is in your mind. If I write, "We want to provide water to the villagers" you know my intention. But you will have a much better understanding if I write, "We want to provide clean, safe water to the villagers so they will be healthier. There will be enough water for them to grow more vegetables."

8 *Be positive and straightforward.* You are trying to convince people that your plan is a good idea. Don't make claims you can't prove. But don't sound uncertain when you are sure something is true.

Don't say: "At the time of writing, evidence suggests that dirty water is one of the main causes of sickness in the villages." Instead, write: "It is clear that dirty water is one of the main causes of sickness in the villages." Or, better still, just state the fact you know is true: "Dirty water is one of the main causes of sickness in the villages."

9 *Try to make your writing sound as close as possible to the way you talk.* Spoken language is simple and straightforward. When I am having trouble writing something simply, I ask myself: "How would I say this to a friend?" That usually solves the problem.

Try reading what you have written out loud. If you run out of breath before the end of a sentence, that sentence is probably too long. If you have difficulty saying the words, they are probably too complicated. If the sentence doesn't sound right, it is probably hard to read.

10 *Assume readers and listeners don't know what you are talking about.* Keep asking yourself: "Will the reader understand this? Does the reader have the necessary knowledge? Have I written enough explanation?" Readers who don't understand quickly stop reading.

If possible, put your plan aside for a few days after writing it. Then read it again. You may find points that are not as clear as they seemed earlier – even to you. Ask two or three people who know nothing about your organization if they can understand what you have written. If they can, then your board members and anyone else who reads your plan should be able to understand it.

Make your document attractive

Readers get a first impression of your organization and your ability to plan the minute they pick up one of your documents. If the document is ugly or messy, they will think poorly of your organization and of you. If it looks cluttered or confusing, they will think your plan is poorly organized and not well thought out. These first impressions may be very wrong, but it will take extra work to overcome them.

It is not difficult to prepare documents that look attractive and efficient. Here are ten more rules to follow that will make your writing more effective through its appearance.

1 *Make sure the letters are big enough for people to read easily.* Use 12 point type if possible, as shown in the example.

2 *Use the style of type you see in this publication.* It is called serif type. The serifs are the little lines at the top and bottom of the letters. They make words and paragraphs easier to read.

3 *Choose a serif type that is easy to read.* Modern computers offer a big choice of letter forms. Not all are easy to read, but you can always rely on Times, or Times Roman, or Times New Roman.

This is "Times New Roman" in 12 point type.

Sans serif type like this, with no serifs, is more difficult for most people to read.

Serifs

No (sans) serifs

Serif styles:
This is regular (Roman)
This is bold
This is Italic

Sans serif styles:
This is regular (Roman)
This is bold
This is Italic (oblique)

HEADINGS AND SENTENCES ALL IN CAPITALS ARE HARD TO READ.

4 *Use only one typeface and only one size of type, unless you have professional help.* With computers, it is easy to use many different kinds of type in one document. But if you use too many, you just confuse the reader. Keep the document simple.

5 *Avoid italic type (slanted like this).* It is difficult to read in large amounts. Use it only for headings, for examples, or for occasional emphasis.

6 *Don't put too many words on a page.* Leave generous space on all sides.

7 *Make sure lines are neither too short, nor too long.* Ideally a line should not contain more than sixty-five characters (including punctuation and spaces), or less than 25 characters.

8 *Avoid long paragraphs.* They look hard to read and scare off readers. Break the text into short paragraphs, just as you try to keep sentences short.

9 *Use headings to show the reader where you are going.* A good set of headings is like a road map. Make them stand out by underlining or using **boldface** (the extra-black letters used for headings in this book).

10 *Don't write headings or sentences all in capitals to give emphasis.* Headings and sentences written in small letters (lower case) are easier to read. If you want to give emphasis, use **boldface** or *italic* type.

12 Writing a plan: an example

This chapter lays out a simple long-range plan for an imaginary organization called WaterLink. Each section contains suggestions for ways you may write about your own organization. The plan is shorter and has less detail than you may need.

In writing any document, the intended audience must be kept in mind every minute. A long-range plan is no exception. In the past WaterLink used such a document for internal use and to show granting agencies. But now that it is seeking local public support, WaterLink writes the three-year plan from a different viewpoint. The new audiences will be much broader and more diverse, and the plan must be written to interest and convince them. The language must be clear and simple, the benefits easy to appreciate.

While WaterLink is imaginary, much of the information in this chapter is from proposals and criteria drawn up by Watercan, a Canadian voluntary organization, and its southern partners including Canadian Physicians for Aid and Relief, Uganda.

If you think this plan reads somewhat like a proposal for major funding, you are right. WaterLink will use this plan as the basis of all grant proposals or requests for donations in the next few years. They will use a paragraph here, a section there, and for some major donors, almost the whole document. Here is a table of contents for the WaterLink plan:

Why WaterLink exists: the mission statement
What the organization has accomplished
The people WaterLink serves
The three-year program: the opportunity
The resources required for the program
Special concerns that will be addressed
   Protecting the environment
   Involving both women and men
   Bringing children into the picture
   Sustaining the programs
   Influencing national water policies
The three-year program: objectives and activities
Improving techniques
Challenges/solutions
The benefits to the people: measuring the results
Communicating the results
Improving the administration

Building on strengths
Overcoming weaknesses
Taking up opportunities
Threats to success
The three-year plan: the budget

Why WaterLink exists: the mission statement

Make this statement as strong – and as simple – as possible. You will want to use it over and over, with staff, volunteers, donors, and every other person whose good opinion you want.

WaterLink aims to ensure that village people have one of the bases of all life – safe, convenient, dependable water and, as a result, will lead healthier, more productive lives.

What the organization has accomplished

Many documents about organizations give the organization's entire history right at the beginning. This is a mistake. People want specific evidence that your programs are useful and that you are worth supporting. But they do not want to read details about what the organization has been doing ever since its founding. Avoid beginning with sentences such as: "WaterLink was established in 1975 ...." People will be bored immediately. Your organization's history is important but it is background information. It should be put towards the end of your plan, not at the beginning. You could consider making it an appendix.

Some examples of what you have achieved should appear early in the plan, however. They establish your credibility and show what your organization can do in the future – whenever possible, what you can do better than other organizations. If you can, include four or five points here about your successes. Keep them brief. Even though you know the first audience for your plan is internal – staff, board, volunteers – you should always keep in mind that they need good examples when they talk with other people about your work. Think also of possible external readers such as donors, potential donors, and government officials. You want to remind people who know your work that you have the experience and the knowledge to succeed in what you want to do. You will talk about your strengths in any grant proposal and in every piece of promotional or fundraising literature that you produce about your organization. To people who are unfamiliar with your work, proof of your success is essential if you want to gain their interest and support. Make it part of your overall plan – for reference and to remind yourself, if necessary.

"Waterlink's record of success" provides an example:

WaterLink is the most respected agency in water management and sanitation in the country. In just one district, WaterLink has constructed 82 shallow wells, 54 rainwater collection and storage tanks, and 15 protected springs since 1992. Working with other groups including international funders, WaterLink has helped build 6,347 pit latrines in the same district.

WaterLink has also provided sanitation and health education to families and primary school children, and technical assistance to both the community and the district water staff. As a result, the incidence of diarrhoea declined 25 per cent between 1993 and 1996. People also suffered fewer skin diseases, fevers, and less weight loss.

All projects have been undertaken at the request of community leaders. Projects were agreed upon only after thorough study of the daily practices and real needs of community members, especially women. WaterLink projects have won significant local recognition for the high level of community participation. Local people received significant training. They formed community councils to work with local water and health authorities to plan all projects. As a result, the communities themselves controlled these assets and contributed to their operation and their maintenance. Gradually, the communities have taken financial responsibility for the management of their water supply.

WaterLink has always provided training in constructing and maintaining the equipment. All the installations function properly because WaterLink and the people responsible for maintenance inspect and repair the wells frequently. The services are reliable, affordable, and sustainable.

Objective evaluations of these projects have shown that each was well managed and achieved the hoped-for results.

The people WaterLink serves

Everything you write in your long-term plan should centre on the people you will serve and how your agency's projects will improve their lives. Be very clear exactly who it is you wish to serve. It is tempting to try to do too much, to try to meet too many needs. But it is essential, from the mission statement at the beginning to the smallest administrative change at the end of the plan, to keep the organization and the plan tightly focused. Keep your mission and the people you want to help constantly in mind.

Colonial attitudes often dictated how development happened. People were rarely asked what they needed or wanted. They were just told what they were going to get, often by people who did not know the problems well enough to design the right solutions. In some cases, decisions were made by people who never visited the sites of projects. Fortunately, that way of working is disappearing. Nowadays, it is essential in planning to include and to talk to the people who will be affected by your work and plan how they will participate in it.

Be as precise as possible. Show that you know the people who want your help and that you are really responding to their needs, not making only a gesture. Stephen Huddle, a Canadian professor, remarked that, "The NGO often sets the playing field before the village has an opportunity to define its needs, priorities, desires, etc. I reviewed a plan for 60 wells. The plan had token community participation in identifying sites, committee oversight of operation and maintenance, and training for maintenance. What the plan did not address was that women were already making the economic choice to use undeveloped water sources (holes in low-lying areas) rather than walk to the existing wells. The choice of technology was made by the NGO before the villagers were approached. If the full set of options were given to the village, what choice would they make? Given access to the full range of options with the costs and benefits shown, it is likely that the villagers would have chosen a combination of strategically placed deep wells for long-term water security and a network of improved shallow wells to improve access to safe, potable water."

Saying in the plan that the technology was chosen by the community and is affordable is not enough nowadays. Real, not token involvement of the beneficiaries must be clear, especially to local donors. In the plan the community itself must be clearly seen to be deciding on the service it needs, where the service should be delivered, the order in which projects are carried out, what technologies will be used, what results matter most.

Give details about the people who need your service. They will make your plan come alive to all its various readers. Details paint a picture that is convincing. They also show that you have thought carefully about your program.

In the district north of the capital, there are only 13 sources of safe water for some 35,000 people. Seventy-five per cent of these people still walk nearly a kilometre for safe water. Less than half the population use pit latrines.

A group of community councillors asked WaterLink to help them get more water and improve sanitation. Together with WaterLink, a survey of 100 women, 100 men, and 50 school children was conducted to ensure that their real needs will be met.

Chose the right name. If you can, give each project an appealing name that says this project will help people solve a problem. A good name did not matter as much when a planning document was seen only by members of the organization and by foreign granting agencies. But, now, engaging community interest is a priority. A good name will help with public relations and fundraising. But be careful. An inappropriate name or one that sounds like an advertising slogan will not be helpful. As you read this section, think of a good name for WaterLink's project. How about "Clean water: fresh hope"?

The three-year program: the opportunity
You will have identified opportunities to improve your program from the answers given in your survey. But any changes in direction should be consistent with your mission statement.

Because of increasing demands, you may see an opportunity to expand or improve your existing services. Or you may have discovered that people in your community badly need a service no organization is providing. Any changes in services should be planned with members of the community.

As a result of surveys and consultation, you may get an entirely new perspective on the community you serve. You may become convinced that you need to look at the quality of life in the community and not just at its needs for a service that has been your traditional concern.

Program goal
At present, only one-third of the villages have adequate, convenient, safe water and adequate sanitation facilities. Within three years, WaterLink will

ensure that 75% of the villages have clean water within less than 500 metres and pit latrines and other facilities for personal hygiene. These projects will include training to ensure that the communities can manage and sustain the new installations. Training programs will also include education in good personal hygiene, especially for primary school children.

The resources required for the program

In approving your plan, your board members and donors will want to know that you can do what you say you can do. You need to reassure them that you have considered exactly what you will need to meet the commitments you want to make. But also your plans may require working more closely with other agencies. For both your board and these agencies, you will need to show that you have:
- enthusiastic participation of the people who want the service
- enough well trained, experienced staff
- access to necessary technology
- enough time to devote to managing the project
- necessary arrangements with affiliated organizations to do the whole job
- the right equipment on the sites and in the office
- administrative, accounting, and clerical support

WaterLink and its affiliated organizations have demonstrated that they have the expertise and experience to conduct this project successfully. The people in the villages will contribute their labour to the program and will manage the projects on a continuing basis. WaterLink will provide the technical skills needed to construct the water points and the sanitation facilities.

We will form an alliance with BestHealth, a newly-formed local organization, that will advise on planning the hygiene programs and supply a trainer, training materials, and classroom space for the annual training sessions in the community and in the schools. BestHealth will also monitor the results of these programs regularly in the third year of the program.

Special concerns that will be addressed

The plan will establish objectives for your organization for the next three years. In doing so you will need to think carefully about the circumstances in which your organization works. It is time for a fresh look. You will need to consider broad social concerns. Your research will have told you what special issues you need to address in your planning. There may be new government priorities, for instance. You may have other concerns as well. Even if your organization does not address these directly, they are issues that should inform all your program planning. WaterLink decided that providing clean water is not enough. In this section six concerns are talked about: protecting the environment, establishing good hygiene and sanitation practices, involving both women and men, bringing children into the picture, sustaining the program after three years, and influencing national water policies.

Nowadays, developing sources of safe drinking water alone is not seen as a pana-

cea for reducing water-borne diseases. Other factors, including sanitation and hygiene practices and cultural factors, affect the quality of water used in a household. Developing safe water should therefore be part of an integrated program of safe, convenient drinking water, environmental sanitation, hygiene education, and developing local competence.

Protecting the environment
Every development plan should include an examination of its effect on both the physical and the social environment. At the very least, they should not damage the environment. At best, any damage should be repaired.

Objective 1: to develop and protect 67 safe springs, shallow wells, and rainwater tanks in the target district

The wells are too shallow to tap the aquifer and will not therefore endanger the long-term water supply. To prevent erosion, runoff from water points, especially shallow wells and springs, will be contained and used to grow vegetables and trees.

Objective 2: to promote good hygiene and sanitation practices, increasing pit latrine use from 27% to 55% at the end of three years

These projects are similar to programs WaterLink has conducted for ten years without causing environmental damage.

Involving both women and men
Development priorities have included the special needs of women for some time. But the unequal burden that women carry – poor health, inadequate education, lack of opportunity, long hours of work – compared to men still needs to be addressed. Are women involved both in the planning of the programs and in conducting them? How are they affected by the projects? Are there constraints in involving women? How can they be overcome?

Objective 3: to increase the ability of both women and men to share in planning, managing, repairing, and sustaining water points

Bringing children into the picture
Improving the welfare of children is an important goal of development programs worldwide.

Objective 4: to promote cleanliness and good hygiene among children in the 20 primary schools

Education programs for children in schools will foster good sanitation and hand and body washing. Children will then be able to pass this information on to their families and to other children. WaterLink will also promote proper storage of food and water and safe disposal of waste.

Sustaining the programs
You will need to consider how the local community will maintain the programs once your organization is no longer involved. What skills will the people need to sustain the new service? How can enthusiasm be maintained? How will the community build the necessary support? What training will people need to do that?

The community will also need to think about the ways its members can contribute to the projects – by donating their labour to operate, maintain, administer, and police the services, by paying small fees, by spending time attending training programs, by conducting public education programs after their training and so on.

An organization will also need to look for other supporters to sustain the programs. What assistance, if any, can be expected from government? Does the government have enough resources to take over the program? Can you be sure the government will become involved in an effective way? Could the government train community members to sustain the programs? What support can be attracted from the private sector? Could the private sector take over some of the programs?

Objective 5: to equip the local communities to sustain water points and other programs after the WaterLink projects are completed

We will work with local committees to develop skills in management, maintenance, administration, and financial operations.

Influencing national water policies

You may have decided that managing specific projects is not enough; you may want to persuade the government to give higher priority to finding long-term solutions to the problems of the people you exist to serve. That could mean working more closely with government and other agencies, and with the business community.

Objective 6: to ensure that within two years government officials approve in principle a sustainable national water policy

The three-year program: objectives and activities

In your plan be specific about what you are going to do and when you are going to do it. If there is uncertainty about timing, say so. Discussing these questions in your plan shows, once again, that you have thought through a project carefully.

Objective 1: to develop and protect 67 safe springs, shallow wells, and rainwater tanks in the target district

Activities

First steps:
- *conduct water source survey*
- *mobilize community leaders and other villagers to support improving their water supply*

Second steps:
- *purchase drilling rig*
- *purchase hardware and spare parts*

Third steps:
- *construct 22 shallow wells*
- *protect 30 springs*
- *construct 15 rainwater tanks*
- *increase average yield per water point by 15% by rehabilitating existing wells*

Fourth steps:
- conduct market study on viability of selling spare parts on the open market

Objective 2: to promote good hygiene and sanitation practices, increasing pit latrine use from 27% to 55% at the end of three years
  Activities
  First steps:
  - promote with local leaders the need for good sanitation and hygiene practices in each of their communities
  - mobilize community members to construct the latrines
  - construct 3,000 pit latrines for distribution to families, schools, etc.
  - produce 1,000 sanitary platforms to fit over waste pits

  Second steps:
  - train 25 women and 25 men to conduct home hygiene improvement programs, including the use of drying racks and rubbish pits
  - train 20 health promoters (45% women) and provide each promoter with a bicycle and information materials
  - conduct hygiene and sanitation training for 40% of community members
  - conduct home environmental competitions

Objective 3: to increase the ability of both women and men to share in planning, managing, repairing, and sustaining water points
  Activities
  First steps:
  - conduct two gender analysis workshops
  - send five WaterLink members to workshops on gender and community development
  - train 20 local councillors in the resources needed for rural water development and primary health care
  - train 40 religious leaders to promote good sanitation and hygiene practices in their communities

Objective 4: to promote cleanliness and good hygiene among children in the 20 primary schools
  Activities
  - conduct workshops for science teachers and head teachers to promote sanitation and hygiene in the schools
  - train 600 children in good hygiene, who will then educate their families and other children
  - schedule regular dramas and songs to reinforce the messages
  - set up 100 demonstration hand-washing facilities
  - construct 40 demonstration vip latrines

Objective 5: to equip the local communities to sustain water points and other programs after the WaterLink projects are completed
  Activities
  First steps:
  - each village will set up a community council with 10 members to work with WaterLink, the private sector, and local water authorities

on all aspects of the project

Second steps:
- *the council will take over the management of the training programs*
- *train 67 water source caretakers to carry out daily operations and maintenance*
- *select and train 11 pump mechanics and equip them with repair tool kits*
- *train two government health assistants to test water quality accurately at the 67 points*

Third steps:
- *the council will take over the on-going maintenance program*
- *the council will assume responsibility for financing the water management program, setting up a fee schedule, establishing a collection system, a retail spare parts outlet, etc.*

Objective 6: to ensure that within two years government officials approve in principle a sustainable national water policy

  Activities
- *develop with other agencies an advocacy program called "Water for All"*
- *prepare annual papers on water policy for local and national politicians and civil servants*
- *meet monthly with local representatives in national assembly to discuss advancing a national water policy*
- *promote media coverage of advocacy activities when appropriate*

Improving techniques

Don't be afraid to admit a past mistake and describe how it will be corrected in future projects. Development is a process of experimentation. If everything we tried worked perfectly, more people would be healthy, well educated, and prosperous.

The head of an agency in Harare that works primarily on water projects was asked recently by the director of an international funding agency how the agency's work was progressing. His reply was anything but honest. He said: "Everything is going very well. Our projects are all successful." The director lost interest immediately, I thought. She knew the projects of such an agency could not all be equally successful and that she was not hearing an honest answer. Sensible people know that mistakes are made. Since they may know all about your mistakes already, it is better to be direct about them rather than pretend they never happened.

  In the past we used pumps that were recommended by numerous international experts. The pumps did not live up to their reputation. They required expensive maintenance. We will test several new types of pumps for six months in one village. Very soon, we will be able to ensure that any pumps installed by villagers in our projects will be inexpensive and easy to maintain.

It is also essential that board members and other volunteers know about past problems and problems that could arise. When they are making a case for public support, there should be no surprises.

Challenges/solutions
Don't forget to deal with threats to the success of each project – the risks you may have to take. It is good to show that you have anticipated what can go wrong. That is much better than having board members or donors raise objections to a project because they can see threats you appear not to have recognized. Explain whatever threats there are to reaching each of the objectives, and how you plan to overcome them in a positive way.

Challenge: The government may take control of the projects. If this happens, the government officers may not consult with or involve the villagers in the projects. In that event, the villagers may not receive the proper training and therefore will not maintain the wells in the long term.

Solution: The community councils have agreed that, together with WaterLink, they will negotiate with the government before the projects start to ensure that local officials will understand and cooperate.

The benefits to the people: measuring the results
People talk about results when they really mean "activities." Keep in mind that results are always external to an organization. Holding a series of training workshops is an activity. It is not a result. A result is the change in the community that will happen when the participants go home from the workshop and set to work applying what they learned.

These days the phrase "results-based management" appears in almost every development project document. In the past, development agencies might have felt proud to include in their report of a project that they had installed 100 tube wells. That is no longer enough. Board members and donors now want to know the extent to which the project has benefited the whole community. You will want them to have that evidence because it will help them feel comfortable when they are persuading potential donors to support your organization's work.

In writing your plan, you must explain what specific results you expect to achieve in a form that can eventually be tested by measurement. At the most basic level, people will want to know that what you have said you would do is actually being done at the basic, technical level. Were the water points installed? Do they work properly? Did they produce the projected amount of water? Did the children learn to wash their hands when they need to? Did fewer people get sick each year? Did the women gain the "free" time the wells were supposed to give them? Were the communities more productive? Donors want statistics that prove the people served are healthier, or better off, or better educated, or in some other ways have had their lives improved. They want details. They want to know not just that results were measured but what methods were used to take the measurements.

At the next level, they will want to know how the whole community is affected. What is the impact of your work? Impact is often difficult to measure statistically. Impact may be a change in attitude, or a new way of conducting local business or community management. You will need to look at your expectations in the widest context – the life of the whole village, if not the whole region where you will be working. How are people benefiting overall? Are the villagers affected in the positive ways the organization promised? How has the governance of the community changed?

Objective 1: to develop and protect 67 safe springs, shallow wells, and rainwater tanks in the target district

Expected results:
- *3350 households with some 27,000 people and other adults and children coming into the community will all have safe water nearby. Women and young girls will spend less time fetching water. As a result, kitchen garden productivity will increase by 10%*

Expected impact:
- *water-borne diseases will be reduced by 27%*

Objective 2: to promote good hygiene and sanitation practices, increasing pit latrine use from 27% to 55% at the end of three years

Expected results:
- *50% of households will have pit latrines and use them correctly*
- *40% of community members will know the importance of good sanitation practices*
- *30% more women will be involved in the planning and management of health and sanitation activities*

Expected impact:
- *the incidence of water-borne diseases will be reduced by 27% among 30,000 community members*

Objective 3: to increase the ability of both women and men to share in the planning, management, repairing, and sustaining water points

Expected results:
- *67 reliable, well-maintained water points*
- *200 women will be involved in the management of water and sanitation activities*
- *women will form at least half the membership on the community councils*

Expected impact:
- *an increasing sense of control of their environment among community members*

Objective 4: to promote cleanliness and good hygiene in the 20 primary schools in the district

Expected results:
- *80% of children will practice good hygiene every day*

Expected impact:
- *30% reduction in water-borne diseases among school-age children*

Objective 5: to equip the local communities to sustain water points and other programs after the WaterLink projects are completed

Expected results:
- *two-thirds of the villages will be able to plan, manage, maintain, and sustain financially their own water supply and their sanitation and hygiene programs*

Expected impact:
- *villages will be more secure economically*
- *villages will have better health and greater productivity*

Objective 6: to ensure that within two years government officials approve in principle a sustainable national water policy
Expected results:
- *the national government approves a national policy*

Expected impact:
- *too long term to measure in this plan*

In this section, it is important to say by whom and how the evaluations will be done. It is also important to be clear about what will be evaluated. You want the reader of your plan to know that you understand the implications of your work.

WaterLink staff will be responsible for supervising and monitoring the program, based on a sampling of the practices and needs of the community. Before the program begins, an outside water expert, two community leaders, and an agricultural expert who speaks the local language will conduct a survey to establish the baseline against which the progress of the program will be measured. They will design detailed monitoring forms based on the objectives for each activity. These four people will be part of the monitoring team throughout the project.

Internal evaluation will be continuous. BestHealth will monitor the results of the sanitation training programs. WaterLink staff members will produce quarterly and annual reports for the board of directors and for all donors. These reports will show whether the projects are being carried out as planned. External evaluators who have not been involved with the program will assess its results at the end of three years. The environmental consequences of the programs will also be assessed. All monitoring and evaluation activities will include both women and men.

Communicating the results

Development worldwide has been far too slow. One reason is that so many of the lessons learned by community development agencies never go beyond their organizations. Development agencies rarely include communications in their planning or in their budgets. As a result, no one else is able to apply the lessons learned because they cannot find out what the lessons were. But we owe each other the chance to share what we have learned. Think first of all about the other groups who could make good use of your experience in their own work. Think too of the people you want to think well of your work. Successes and failures can be communicated in many ways.

We will give:
- *regular progress reports to the agencies funding the projects*
- *a progress report on the projects at a meeting of local ngos next year*
- *summaries of the project plans and of the evaluations to agencies similar to ours in other parts of our country*
- *regular reports to appropriate international agencies, asking them to report the results in their publications*
- *press releases to the media describing the measures we have promoted so that other people can try the same techniques*

- *reports to donors and other supporters, in person and through our newsletter, of all activities, including advocacy activities*

Improving the administration

Once you have completed the presentation of the mission statement, the people you will serve, the list of the projects you plan to undertake, and the intended results, you may turn to the internal, administrative improvements you want to make to support your organization's services. Many of the ideas you want to try will have come to you from the answers to the questions discussed in Chapter 6.

This section, which relies on the SWOT analysis you conducted earlier about your organization, is solely for internal use, including the board of directors. It is probably not to be shown to donors.

Some of these ideas may improve your relationships with your board and other volunteers, and with other organizations. Unless these changes involve major restructuring, the board of directors may say, as mine did, "It is interesting to learn about the changes you are planning. However, we don't need to deal with that part of the plan. Those changes are up to you to make." Still, this is an important way to let them know your ideas.

Building on strengths

Think about SWOT again. When you were doing your research, what strengths did you find that you now want to build on?

An outside engineering study confirmed our belief that the equipment we installed has a lower than average need for repairs. We should analyse the reasons for this good result to ensure that future projects incorporate the benefits of this equipment. We should also share this information with other water agencies.

WaterLink has three staff members with years of high-level technical experience in water projects. We will also emphasize their skills when we describe the projects we can undertake successfully.

Overcoming weaknesses

What improvements do you need to make to eliminate the weaknesses you uncovered in your survey? Discussing weaknesses this way emphasizes your positive attitude.

These three experts need further management training if they are to contribute more to the organization by taking on additional responsibilities. Each will attend a year-long management training course one evening a week at the local business college.

We should put more emphasis on the skills of our expert staff when we describe the projects we can undertake successfully.

We need to improve relationships between management and staff members by holding more staff meetings. We should meet at least every two weeks.

You may have been going along happily doing the same thing over and over. You may realize that you have not been keeping up to date on changing development priorities.

than cutting the wages of an already underpaid staff.) By establishing targets for revenue and spending, budgets not only set financial limits but tell staff members what their managers expect of them. Once the budget is established, regular reports provide information about shortfalls in income or excesses in expenditure. They also raise signals when too little is being spent in key areas of program or staff development. They are essential instruments for managers and for the management committee of the board. Finally, financial reports of all kinds are the principal media by which major donors are likely to evaluate the credibility of a voluntary organization. They use them to decide whether the organization represents a good investment of their contributions. No one wants to give to an organization that is seen to be ill-managed financially.

Financial reports have four principal purposes. These are:
1 to show what you expect to be able to do in the near future – an annual budget and forecast of cash flow for the coming year
2 to show where you hope to go – a business plan for the next three to five years
3 to show where you are this year – account books, operating reports, responsibility reports, cash flow for current year
4 to show where you have been – balance sheet, statement of revenue and expenditures for the previous year(s) (in commerce, known as profit-and-loss)

Many of these reports require the same basic skills used in planning a household budget or keeping track of the money you have in the bank. A few are more complicated. All involve detailed record keeping on a regular basis – daily if there is a lot of activity, weekly if there is little. The methods used in preparing them must be consistent: accounting procedures should not change from year to year. They may have to meet standards established by the accounting profession or the government. They require speed and regularity in their preparation: sporadic, out-of-date financial reports aren't much help to anyone. They may have to be subjected to an annual independent audit. Computers have made the task of financial reporting much easier than in the past, but using them requires special skills. As a result, most voluntary organizations need some professional help, such as a trained bookkeeper and the advice of an accountant, in establishing and maintaining their systems of financial reporting. Outside professionals can only advise, however. The organization and its staff are responsible for the completeness and accuracy of its financial reports.

While a trained bookkeeper may prepare them, financial reports are intended for others in the organization to use. The executive director must be able to read them and understand their messages – they can warn of trouble on the horizon. In large organizations, middle managers must receive them to monitor the performance of their own departments and respond to problems. The fundraisers who approach business people must understand the financial reports well enough to be able to explain them and answer any questions.

What follows may seem overly complex. But it is, if anything, too simple in its examples. Unfortunately, there is no easy approach to financial record keeping. It requires careful, regular, attention to details – and the consequences are serious if that attention is not given. In the short term, the organization will face financial difficulties. In the longer term it may well lose financial credibility.

This chapter cannot go into all the details of bookkeeping procedures. Many books are available on the topic. If you need help, check a local library, or ask an accountant or businessperson in your community. Here, we are most concerned with the reports that will help to establish credibility with potential donors and business partners, and how they should be constructed to achieve that goal.

As an example, we will follow the statements of another hypothetical organization called BookLink. It requires an introduction.

About BookLink

BookLink is an intermediary NGO, based in a big city.[1] It exists to encourage literacy and rural development through establishing village libraries and stocking them with books, mostly in local languages. It works through local partners, typically NGOs active in other areas of rural development that will take responsibility for establishing libraries in villages in their geographic area. To facilitate inter-library circulation of books and reduce administrative costs, libraries are typically established in clusters of ten neighbouring villages. The local partner is expected to:
- identify villages that want and need libraries
- identify suitable persons to work as librarians
- procure suitable accommodation for the library, usually a room or small building, preferably in the centre of the village
- see that a Village Library Committee is constituted and a bank account opened, and provide continuing guidance to the librarian
- help generate resources (cash and in-kind) for the library and make it self-sustaining as soon as possible
  BookLink provides the initial funding for the libraries:
- furniture: racks, table, chair, name-board, clock, maps
- a collection of 350 to 400 books
- initial stationery (accession register, loan register, receipt book, membership cards, book labels, minute book, etc.)
- funds to maintain the library for its first two years

At the end of two years, the village library is expected to have built up a small operating fund from memberships, municipal grants, and donations.

---

1 BookLink's projects are modelled upon the Village Library program that was started in India in 1992 by the Machwe Foundation in collaboration with the Rajiv Gandhi Foundation. BookLink's policies are not exactly the same, however, and its financial statements are pure fiction, in no way reflecting the experience of the Indian agencies.

Thereafter it is expected to be financially self-supporting from the same sources of revenue.

Before a library is established, the local partner visits the village and discusses the idea with the community. A library is established only if it is seen to have the support of the community. A representative Village Library Committee is formed to decide policy on day-to-day operations including membership fees, hours of operation, lending periods, the need for more books, and similar policies. With the librarian, it is responsible for publicizing the library and encouraging membership. The committee raises funds locally, with the assistance of the local partner NGO.

The libraries are not intended as reading rooms. They are lending libraries. There is not enough accommodation in most villages for reading rooms. Also, there is concern that women might hesitate to use a reading room that becomes a place where men congregate.

The librarian is a local person, preferably a woman, who is on duty for a few hours every day. BookLink provides brief training in procedures before the library opens. The librarian receives a small honorarium for services.

Villagers pay a small fee to become library members. It is low enough that it will not be a bar to membership. Members receive a library card and the right to take out books. The conditions of lending vary, but normally a member may take out one book at a time and must return it within one week.

A bank account is opened in a nearby bank/post office to receive all membership fees and donations. The librarian and one other member of the Village Library Committee are signing officers; both must sign to withdraw money.

The libraries cater to the literate and the neo-literate. Most of the books are chosen by the villagers. When possible, BookLink organizes book exhibits in a village cluster; at other times, villagers must choose from catalogues. The books are varied in topic. Most of the books are fiction, but BookLink encourages villagers to choose other books on subjects of special interest to women, such as health, nutrition, general housekeeping, consumer protection, and family planning. Most libraries include a small selection of books on starting small businesses and good farming practices, and a special section for children and young adults. Efforts are made to integrate the collection with other rural development projects being carried out by the local NGO partner. The libraries are encouraged to exchange books after a certain time. This gives readers a wider choice at no extra cost.

Over the last five years BookLink has helped to establish 230 libraries. It hopes to establish 40 more in the current year and in each of the next three years, depending on its success in finding funding and local partners.

BookLink's finances, as seen in the following pages, are simpler and appear to be much more comfortable than those of many real voluntary organizations. It is worth emphasizing that BookLink's financial reports are only examples of how such reports may be prepared and presented. They are positive in their projections because BookLink is a positive-thinking organization, and positive thinking is important for success in fundraising.

Looking ahead one year: the budget

The budget is a prediction of income and expenses during the coming year. It is prepared for approval by the board, which is responsible for ensuring that its forecasts of revenue and expenditure are realistic. Once the budget has been approved, it provides a target for raising revenue and an authorization to the staff to spend money in accord with its estimates. Because it consists of easily recognizable amounts (we need to sell this many greeting cards, we should not spend more than so much on office supplies), a budget is a powerful way to motivate staff and volunteers to work towards the goals of the organization. For the same reason, it provides an easily understood basis for comparing planned performance with actual achievements. On the basis of that comparison, it should be reviewed regularly during the year to see whether its assumptions remain correct. Donors will be interested in knowing how closely the organization follows its budget plan. A realistic budget is therefore one element in financial credibility.

All senior staff members should be involved in preparing the budget, because each should be responsible for his or her part of it – whether that means achieving an agreed upon target for revenue or ensuring that expenses remain within an agreed amount. Budgets imposed from the top down do not build morale. Too often they contain flaws that could have been avoided if the advice of hands-on workers had been sought. On the other hand, budget making is not a task that can be delegated by the boss. I once heard an executive director tell his board he had not seen the budget until the meeting at which it was submitted to the board for approval. This did nothing to build the board's confidence in him or in the budget – which the board members themselves were expected to support through fundraising efforts.

The final budget should be acceptable to all those who have participated in its preparation. To reach consensus requires more than writing amounts on a spreadsheet. It may take hours of discussion, but it is usually worth it. By working together on the budget, staff members come to understand how all the efforts of a large organization with different divisions fit together. Managers of core programs will no longer see fundraisers as rivals for available funding but as allies. Fundraisers, in turn, will learn exactly how the money they secure will be used and will be reminded that the heart of the organization is its programs. (This last lesson, while obvious, sometimes is forgotten.)

Work on the budget should start as much as six months before the beginning of the next financial year. It takes time to find out what a major funder may be planning for the future, to make plans for alternative fundraising if necessary, and to establish priorities for expenditures. If there is likely to be a major change in funding, an early start is essential.

Many expenses can be estimated based on previous experience – what the same items cost last year and what they cost now. Allow adequately for inflation, and for any changes in government policy on such matters as sales taxes and minimum wages. New projects or new fundraising initiatives will require research into probable costs.

Income may prove more difficult to estimate. Government funding agencies are notoriously slow in telling voluntary organizations how much they may expect in the coming year, and often announce a cut in grants only at the eleventh hour. Local fundraising can be affected by a sudden change in the price of a staple crop, a drop in worldwide demand for an important export commodity, a rise in imported fuel costs, a new tax policy from the national government, or speculation in a foreign stock exchange. Budgeters therefore must be well aware of economic trends and forces outside their own community.

Rules for budgeting

Here are six good rules for budgeting.

1 Be sure to include every possible item of expense and income.

2 Break down major areas of expenditure. Under travel, for example, have separate lines for meals, accommodation, taxis, and/or per diem allowances. Under staff, distinguish between full-time staff and part-time staff, staff with general administrative functions and staff assigned to specific programs such as projects or fundraising. In each of these categories have a separate line for each major planned expense.

3 Explain the reasons for each budget line in words.

4 Err on the side of caution. Estimate high for expenses, low for revenue.

5 Double-check the figures.

6 Make sure everyone responsible for achieving the budget in the coming year understands what is expected and agrees to it.

Donor agencies and corporate donors distrust vague budget items such as "contingency funds," "overhead," and "miscellaneous." They think of them as blanket terms – warm and comforting to the budgeter but possibly covering a multitude of sins. Avoid such categories in budgeting. Show office expenses under specific headings such as "salaries," "benefits," "rent," "telephone," "stationery and other office supplies." Instead of showing "contingency funds," be cautious in estimating revenue and expenses (Rule 4, above).

It may be necessary to budget for a deficit at the end of one year, but such a step is undesirable. It should not be undertaken unless there is some considerable certainty that the amount will be repaid in the following year. More commonly, deficits arise at the end of a year because costs have risen, a grant is late in arriving, financial management has been loose, or some emergency has arisen. On any such occasion it may be necessary to negotiate a short-term bank loan if the organization can raise the required assurance, perhaps by arranging for one of the board members to act as co-sponsor and guarantor. But bank loans must be repaid with interest; no organization should start borrowing without strong reason to believe that it will be able to pay back the loan in a short time. Members of the board of directors should be aware that all of them may be held responsible for paying any debts, including loans, incurred by the voluntary organization.

Voluntary organizations sometimes adopt a process, which is becoming more common in commercial businesses, called "zero-based budgeting."

This method does not use the current level of expenditures as a starting point. Instead, it pretends the organization is beginning all over again. Each expense item is analysed and discussed as if it were a new idea. Only after considerable thought is a budget value placed upon it. This forces everyone to scrutinize the expense and not accept it because "that's the way we've always done it." The process takes a lot of time and is not always practical, especially as a budget deadline approaches. But it can be valuable from time to time, especially if an organization is facing a major drop in revenue.

Many organizations try to build a reserve fund to protect themselves against unexpected falls in revenue or increases in costs. They transfer any money left at the end of the year to this fund, and draw upon it only when necessary. It is unusual to secure funds from a donor specifically for a reserve fund. However, special appeals may be made to foundations or granting agencies for money to start a fundraising program, and if that program is successful it can contribute to a reserve fund.

Some organizations also try to build an endowment fund to ensure a constant source of revenue. The capital in the fund is not used for operating expenses (except as an extraordinary measure); instead it is invested. The income it earns becomes part of the annual budget. Special appeals for endowment funds may be made to all sources of funds, including granting agencies that are reducing their operating grants. Endowment funds may be particularly appealing to supporters who are considering leaving money to a voluntary organization in their will.

BookLink's budget

The executive director of BookLink started working on the budget for the current year with the secretary-bookkeeper five months before the end of the previous financial year. The board approved it a month before it came into effect. Table 1a gives a detailed list, by type, of estimated revenues and expenses in the current year. Those estimates are summarized in Table 1b, which shows the overall budget.

Up until now, BookLink has been able to rely on a major grant from a North American government agency for two-thirds of its funding. Last year the grant totalled $\Sigma 200,000$ out of a total income of just under $\Sigma 300,000$.[2] A European government agency made up most of the difference with a grant of $\Sigma 75,000$. The first agency has had its own budget reduced, however. Last year, it announced that BookLink's annual grant would be cut by $\Sigma 50,000$ a year, beginning in the current year, until it had been reduced to $\Sigma 50,000$. After that the agency could not make promises but hoped it could continue to support BookLink at the same level, one-quarter of what it had originally provided. This was a terrible blow to the board of directors. They had recognized foreign aid might not continue forever but had not foreseen anything so drastic. Fortunately, the European government agency said it

---

[2] In this chapter, currency is quoted in a universal currency called the sigma, represented by the symbol Σ. The sigma bears no relation to dollars, pounds, piastres, nairas, pesos, rupees or any other actual currency, nor do the revenues or costs shown bear any relation to actual revenues and costs in any country.

Table 1a: Projected revenue and expenses for current year

	Last year actual	This year budget
Revenue		
Foreign sources		
North American aid agency	200,000	150,000
European aid agency	75,000	75,000
Community-based campaigns		
Donation boxes	3,500	4,000
Personal appeals		10,000
Local foundations		2,000
Corporate appeals		5,000
Income-generating activities		
Advertising book		16,000
Greeting cards	9,500	11,000
Religious organizations		
Local church	8,500	8,500
Interest		2,151
Non-cash contributions		
In-kind	6,600	6,800
Volunteer time	11,429	12,000
Total revenue*	**296,500**	**283,651**
Expenses		
Program expenses		
Furniture for new libraries	79,545	70,000
Stationery for new libraries	4,091	3,600
Books for new libraries	36,364	29,600
Training librarians	13,636	12,000
Sustaining libraries for 2 years	40,909	45,000
Total program expenses	174,545	160,200
Fundraising expenses		
Community-based campaigns		
Donation boxes	700	2,000
Personal appeals		500
Corporate appeals		100
Income-generating activities		
Advertising book		6,000
Greeting cards	4,750	5,500
Total fundraising expenses	5,450	14,100
Administration		
Staff (salaries and benefits)	60,571	63,600
Rent	10,909	12,000
Printed materials	5,000	5,500
Travel	4,500	5,000
Postage and telephone	800	1,000
Electricity	648	720
Office supplies	170	200
Office repairs	50	60
Staff training	500	500
Audit & accounting	350	350
Bank loan (including interest)	1,237	0
Amortization	1,000	1,000
Total administration expenses	85,735	89,930
Non-cash contributions		
In-kind contributions	6,600	6,800
Volunteer time	11,429	12,000
Total non-cash contributions	18,029	18,800
Total expenses*	**265,730**	**264,230**

* excluding in-kind contributions and volunteer time

Table 1b: BookLink budget for current year

	Last year actual	This year budget
Revenue		
Foreign sources	275,000	225,000
Community-based campaigns	3,500	21,000
Income-generating activities	9,500	27,000
Religious organizations	8,500	8,500
Interest	0	2,151
Non-cash contributions	18,029	18,800
Total revenue*	296,500	283,651
Expenses		
Program	174,545	160,200
Fundraising	5,450	14,100
Administration	85,735	89,930
Non-cash contributions	18,029	18,800
Total expenses*	265,730	264,230
Income less expenses	30,770	19,421
Cash balance at first of year	0	30,770
Transfer to/(from) reserve		18,000
Cash balance at year end		32,191
Reserve fund at year end		18,000

* excluding in-kind contributions and volunteer time

believed in the program so much that it would do all it could to maintain its support unchanged for at least another three years.

As soon as it heard the bad news, BookLink began planning how to raise funds elsewhere. It had started raising some money locally a few years before by placing donation boxes in various shops and banks around its city, and by producing and selling greeting cards. A local church had been collecting money for BookLink from its parishioners as well. These three local sources of income amounted to Σ21,500 last year. BookLink planned to increase that amount by roughly 10 per cent in the new year by increasing the number of donation boxes and marketing its cards more aggressively. More important, it planned to begin a major campaign of appeals to individuals, corporations, and local foundations. It also planned to publish an annual book of illustrated folk tales for which it would sell advertisements. (These various fundraising techniques, and their budgeting, are described in more detail in Book 3 of this series.) In addition, it began applying to foundations in the North that had shown an interest in encouraging literacy.

This was an ambitious program of fundraising, possible only because BookLink had been building support in the community since it was founded. Too, from the beginning it had recruited a number of enthusiastic volunteers. The program is more than most voluntary organizations should, or can, undertake in a single year.

Filling in the numbers

BookLink's expenses fall mainly into two areas: program costs for establishing village libraries, and salaries and benefits for its own staff. The libraries are expected to be self-sufficient financially after the first two years. The BookLink staff is small and hard working. It consists only of an executive director, who oversees operations and works with the board, and whose attention now must be directed mainly to fundraising; a projects coordinator, who works with the local partner NGOs, trains the new village librarians, and monitors the work of the libraries; and a secretary who doubles as bookkeeper.

This year, BookLink hopes to establish 40 new libraries, in four administrative/geographic clusters. It has budgeted accordingly. Each new library, it estimates, will cost a total of Σ2,880: Σ1,750 for furniture, Σ90 for stationery, Σ740 for books, and Σ300 for training a librarian. (At an average cost of Σ2.00 per book, this works out to only 370 books per library, down from the 400 books given to each new library in the previous year. The number of new libraries has also shrunk, from 50 last year. The organization and its beneficiaries are already feeling the cut in the North American grant.)

The rate of inflation during the previous year was 10 per cent. In view of the reduced grant, the board has decided to increase salaries and benefits of its staff by only 5 per cent. This was not an easy decision, but the board recognized that it could no longer pay the staff at somewhat more than national levels (as it had in the past, thanks to the foreign grant) and that it was essential to build up a small reserve fund. If the budget is met, BookLink will be able to transfer Σ18,000 to the reserve fund at the end of the year (Table 1b).

In this budget, the executive director and the board clearly established their priorities. They want, first, to build a reserve fund against future unpleasant surprises. After that, they want to support the program of village libraries to the greatest extent possible. To achieve both these goals, they are committed to a more aggressive program of fundraising. And, finally, they are asking staff members to accept a reduced level of income because salaries and benefits will not rise as fast as the cost of living.

The other lines of the budget were relatively easy to establish. There is provision for the cost of making new donation boxes. Donation boxes require year-round servicing, so provision was also made to reimburse volunteers for incidental expenses (bus fare, snacks) incurred in visiting the boxes regularly to collect the money in them. The much shorter campaign for funds from individuals and corporations will also involve expenses of board members and other volunteers, which should be repaid, but these are relatively small. The cost of printing the advertising book is based on an estimate from a reliable printer. (When the time comes to produce the book, the organization will ask three printers to submit bids, but one realistic estimate is enough for budgeting. See Book 3, Chapter 4.) The retail price of the greeting cards is roughly twice the cost of manufacturing them. In the quantities that are being sold it is economical to print a new supply every year; the cost of cards is therefore budgeted at half the budgeted sales revenue.

The administrative costs are normal. BookLink does not own its own building but rents quarters at an especially low rate; otherwise it might consider finding more economical space. (The difference between the rent and market value is recorded under "in-kind" contributions.) The printed materials for which it has budgeted include a promotional brochure, annual report, advertising for greeting cards, and similar items.

Two years ago BookLink exceeded its budget and had to take out a small bank loan. That was repaid in full last year. This year it will earn interest on the money in its bank account.

The organization has little in the way of fixed assets – furniture, computers, other office equipment – and the allowance for amortization (that is, for reducing the value of the fixed assets in the organization's accounts) is small. BookLink uses a common style of amortization. If it decides a piece of equipment should be paid off in five years, it allows one-fifth of the purchase value each year for amortization. BookLink does not own its own vehicle but uses public transport to visit the villages it serves.

Recording non-cash contributions

To show the extent of the public support they receive, many voluntary organizations put a value on the non-cash contributions they receive in the form of volunteer time and donated goods and services (such as gifts of furniture or office equipment, the design of greeting cards, or the printing of a brochure). This record is particularly important to many foreign granting agencies. They feel that the value of an organization is demonstrated by the amount of support it receives from the community in which it operates or which it serves – the extent to which those communities are prepared to get involved and accept some responsibility for the organization's financial well-being. In fact, some granting agencies credit non-cash contributions as if they were cash in analysing the merits of a grant application.

The methods of showing non-cash contributions vary, and can be controversial. Because no cash is involved, there is no need to include volunteer time and in-kind contributions in normal budgets. But BookLink does include them; then it does not have to prepare separate budgets for some donors. It feels any donor, foreign or local, who is interested enough to study the budget will be impressed with BookLink's success in securing community support.

How then did it place values on non-cash contributions? It assigned a fair market value to in-kind donations. It estimated that the number of hours worked by volunteers totalled approximately one full year, and assigned a value equal to the cost of hiring a junior staff member for one year. It did not include either of these kinds of donations in its "total revenue" because no actual money was involved. To balance its books it showed the same amounts as expenditures, but again did not include them in "total expenses."

Looking ahead one year: projecting cash flow

A balanced budget tells you that, if all goes well, you will have enough money to meet all your expenses for the year. But bills must be paid every month, and revenue does not flow evenly. You need to know when you will have to pay out money, and when you can expect to receive it. Will there be a period when the cash runs out? Can you plan to avoid that by delaying an expenditure or by advancing plans for a fundraising campaign?

Nothing is worse than running out of money to pay salaries, rent, program costs, and routine business operations. When commercial businesses are short of funds, they often can negotiate a short-term bank loan. Few small voluntary organizations have that flexibility. Banks do not always consider them good credit risks and they have little property to put up as collateral. It is essential therefore to plot the flow of cash, month by month, to ensure against surprises. This should be a part of the budgeting process.

Cash flow projections are prepared in three parts:
1 an estimate of how much money will be received in each month from all sources
2 an estimate of how much money will have to be paid out in each month for all purposes
3 a table combining the totals of the first two estimates, showing for each month the opening balance (cash on hand), expected receipts, expected expenditures, and closing balance

They include rent, salaries, and utilities. Failing to pay them on time can seriously affect your program. On the other hand, it may be possible to negotiate delays in paying other expenses, such as a printer's bill. At the same time, some revenue can be scheduled with reasonable certainty (the month when a promised foreign grant is due to arrive, for example). Other revenue can be expected to arrive regularly throughout the year (money from donation boxes or church collections). Still other sources can be planned to occur when they are most needed to avoid a shortfall – a fundraising event, for example. The cash-flow projection is a tool to help you plot a fundraising course through these shoals.

For voluntary organizations that get most of their income from a few sources with regularly scheduled payments, it is probably best to begin by setting out how much money is expected each month. Then, if possible, major expenditures can be scheduled to follow large grants. (BookLink is an example of such an organization.)

For voluntary organizations that receive their income from a large number of sources in a relatively even flow throughout the year, it is usually best to begin with a table of expenditures. Fundraising efforts then may be scheduled to avoid running out of money in a particular month.

Once again, it is important to be conservative in estimating income and expenditures. You did this in calculating the total income and expenses in each line of the budget. In projecting cash flow, it's a good idea to plan that at least some money will be slower in coming than you might expect. For example, merchants advertising in the program of an event may not pay for their advertisements until at least a month after the program has been distributed. Or grants from foreign agencies may be delayed. Perhaps the funder will be late in sending the money or there will be a holdup within your own nation's bureaucracy. Experience may show that an instalment of a grant promised in one month should not be entered in the cash flow projection until one or two months later.

BookLink's cash-flow projection

BookLink's cash flow projection has been set out in the three parts listed above (see Tables 2a, b, c). Most of the money in this budget year will come in large scheduled instalments – two of Σ75,000 each from the North American agency, two of half that much from the European agency. Money from the donation boxes and the local church will flow in fairly regularly throughout the year. Personal and corporate donations will follow a short campaign in Month 6; the money will not come in all at once, however. Publication of the advertising book is planned for Month 3, around the time of a major religious festival. But many of its supporters will not pay until a month or two later, despite the organization's efforts to get cash in advance. Income from greeting cards will also come throughout the year but not evenly. It will peak in the month of the country's major festival and in Months 11 and 12 just before a big holiday season.

BookLink's major program costs are establishing libraries and supporting existing ones. These are scheduled in the months after it receives its largest grants. It orders the furniture, stationery, and books as soon as it has confirmation that the grant has been received. (It would place the orders sooner, but knows that grants are sometimes late.) It expects the orders to be delivered within two months of the receipt of the grants, and budgets payments accordingly. In that same month it will pay maintenance expenses to the libraries that are already established. They will just be entering their first or second year. It will train the village librarians before their libraries open.

In Month 2, it budgets to pay for additional donation boxes, in order to increase revenue from that source. It will pay the incidental expenses of canvassers in the campaign in Month 6, as soon as they are incurred: it doesn't want its volunteers to be unhappy or out of pocket. For the advertising book, it will have to pay the printer a deposit in advance in Month 2 and will pay the rest in the month following delivery. It plans to print all the greeting cards for the year at one time, when stocks are getting low. Administration expenses are budgeted more or less evenly throughout the year. In some months BookLink may actually have to pay slightly more for postage than in other months, for example, but the difference is not worth worrying about except at a peak period around the fundraising campaign and in Month 11, when there will be a special promotion of greeting cards.

The organization will begin Month 1 with a healthy balance. It will not have spent all the large grants received only three months earlier from the North American aid agency and one month earlier from the European one. Thereafter it expects to have cash on hand at the end of every month. In some months the balance will be low, however, and the organization remains afloat only because of fundraising ventures such as the advertising book in Month 3 and the personal and corporate campaign in Month 6.

Table 2a: Cash receipts for the current budget year

	Month 1	Month 2	Month 3	Month 4
Foreign sources				
Aid agencies				75,000
Community-based campaigns				
Donation boxes	300	350	350	300
Personal appeals				
Local foundations				
Corporate appeals				
Income-generating activities				
Advertising book			8,000	6,000
Greeting cards	600	600	2,000	600
Religious organizations				
Local church	500	500	1,500	500
Interest	160	132	39	67
Total revenue	**1,560**	**1,582**	**11,889**	**82,467**

Table 2b: Cash expenses for the current budget year

	Month 1	Month 2	Month 3	Month 4
Program expenditures				
Furniture for new libraries				
Stationery for new libraries				
Books for new libraries				
Training librarians				
Sustaining libraries for 2 years				
Fundraising expenditures				
Community-based campaigns				
Donation boxes	50	1,450	50	50
Personal appeals				
Corporate appeals				
Income-generating activities				
Advertising book		3,000		3,000
Greeting cards		5,500		
Administration				
Staff (salaries and benefits)	5,300	5,300	5,300	5,300
Rent	1,000	1,000	1,000	1,000
Printed materials	500	1,000		
Travel		1,000		
Postage and telephone	70	70	70	70
Electricity	60	60	60	60
Office supplies	15	15	15	15
Office repairs	5	5	5	5
Staff training		500		
Audit & accounting		350		
Bank loan (incl interest)				
Amortization	85	85	85	85
Total expenses	**7,085**	**19,335**	**6,585**	**9,585**

Table 2c: Cash flow in current budget year

	Month 1	Month 2	Month 3	Month 4
Opening balance	30,770	25,245	7,492	12,796
Cash receipts (Table 2a)	1,560	1,582	11,889	82,467
Cash expenses (Table 2b)	7,085	19,335	6,585	9,585
Closing balance	25,245	7,492	12,796	85,678

	Month 5	Month 6	Month 7	Month 8	Month 9	Month 10	Month 11	Month 12
		37,500				75,000		37,500
	350	300	300	350	350	300	350	400
		4,000	3,000	1,000	1,000	500	500	
	1,000			1,000				
				3,500	1,000	500		
	2,000							
	600	600	600	600	600	700	1,500	2,000
	500	500	500	500	500	500	500	2,000
	447	381	59	48	45	29	399	345
	4,897	43,281	4,459	6,998	3,495	77,529	3,249	42,245

	Month 5	Month 6	Month 7	Month 8	Month 9	Month 10	Month 11	Month 12
		35,000						35,000
		1,800						1,800
		14,800						14,800
	6,000						6,000	
		45,000						
	50	50	50	50	50	50	50	50
		500						
		100						
	5,300	5,300	5,300	5,300	5,300	5,300	5,300	5,300
	1,000	1,000	1,000	1,000	1,000	1,000	1,000	1,000
	4,000							
	1,000	1,000		1,000			1,000	
	70	200	70	70	70	70	100	70
	60	60	60	60	60	60	60	60
	15	30	15	15	15	15	20	15
	5	5	5	5	5	5	5	5
	85	85	85	85	85	85	85	65
	17,585	104,930	6,585	7,585	6,585	6,585	13,620	58,165

	Month 5	Month 6	Month 7	Month 8	Month 9	Month 10	Month 11	Month 12
	85,678	72,990	11,341	9,215	8,628	5,538	76,482	66,111
	4,897	43,281	4,459	6,998	3,495	77,529	3,249	42,245
	17,585	104,930	6,585	7,585	6,585	6,585	13,620	58,165
	72,990	11,341	9,215	8,628	5,538	76,482	66,111	50,191

FINANCIAL CREDIBILITY

Looking further into the future: the long-range plan

A long-range plan allows you to chart a course some years into the future. Its importance has already been explained in this book, along with the way to set about writing one. Once the goals and objectives have been established, it is time to put a price on each aspect. How much can be accomplished in each year of the plan and what will it cost in staff and staff salaries? in materials? in office quarters and supplies? in travel and equipment? in all the other elements that must be combined to reach the goal? And then where will the money come from? How much will have to be raised each year? Is it reasonable to think that much can in fact be raised? If not, what changes can be made in the program? How much can we save in each category of cost? Gradually, the current year's budget is extended and adapted.

This course will carry you into waters that grow more murky with each year of the plan. Looking into the future means making assumptions that can only be based on the past. A long-range plan has to take inflation into account – but how much will prices go up? And how much can wages and benefits be raised to keep up with inflation? Will a strong public awareness campaign lead to increased donations? What will the climate of giving be like two or three years from now: will people be more generous, or less? What will the national economy be like: buoyant or depressed? What will the world economy be like?

We can only guess the answers to these and similar questions, using all the information at our disposal. If we try hard, we may be able to guess fairly accurately one year into the future, but the chances of being wrong increase with each following year. That is why many people do not believe in making a long-range plan for more than three years ahead. That is also why it is important to review the plan regularly and adjust it to meet changing conditions.

With so much uncertainty, why bother making a long-range financial plan? There are three reasons. First, to see what problems lie ahead. Second, to have the time to make plans to deal with those problems. Third, to set targets that can be achieved gradually. A manager I knew used to tell his staff: "I hate surprises. Tell me about any problems before they become too difficult to resolve easily. Don't surprise me." A long-range plan is a recipe against unpleasant surprises.

Guidelines for planning

As always in budgeting, be conservative in making the plan and involve others in its preparation.

1 List every possible type of expense. Estimate how much you will have to spend on each during the next three years to achieve your goals and objectives. Group expenses according to classifications (for example, program, personnel, office operations, fundraising) so that you can easily recognize areas that have high priority and/or high cost. Be cautious; allow for unexpected costs.

2 Allow sufficiently for inflation. Build an annual increase in costs into your plan.

3 Do everything you can to increase staff wages and benefits in line with inflation, to maintain morale. If this proves impossible, try to find more economical ways to maintain morale with small gifts or social events, or by giving the staff extra days off.

4 List every possible source of revenue. Be realistic in estimating how much is likely to be obtained.

5 Try to build a reserve against surprises you haven't thought of and can't reasonably predict. A fundraising event may be rained out, a grant may be reduced, costs may suddenly rise because of government policies or currency devaluation.

6 Bring your senior staff – everyone responsible for any part of the budget – into the planning process. A long-range plan should not be made by the executive director or the board in isolation. It must be based on the best possible information, the broadest experience (in the field as well as in the office), the greatest possible opportunities for incorporating new ideas and approaches. Most important, it must have the commitment of all those who will have to carry it out. They must feel part of the planning process. They must recognize their own responsibility for the plan's success.

7 If the first estimate of costs is greater than the revenue that can reasonably be expected, make adjustments. Reduce costs in some areas. Or add new sources of revenue. But be careful. It is much easier to budget for revenue than it is to raise the actual cash. Too often voluntary organizations spend as if they have already raised as much as they hope to – and then fail to find the extra money. That is the route to bankruptcy. It is usually more prudent to reduce costs.

8 Explain the plan, once it has been drafted, to the entire staff. They want to know where the organization is going. They want to feel part of its progress. They may need to be convinced that an unpopular decision – such as low wage increases, or the reduction or cancellation of a program – is really unavoidable. There is nothing worse for employees' morale than feeling they are being ignored when important decisions are being made that they don't understand but that will almost certainly affect them and their jobs.

The initial long-range planning should be carried out entirely by the staff. Once the plan has taken shape one or two board members might be brought into the process – the chairman or, if there is a separate finance committee, its head. The head of a fundraising committee, if there is one, could also be included. There is no point in bringing a financial plan to the board that does not have the support of these key people. Once the plan is complete, it must be submitted to the full board for approval. There it should be explained in detail. The members of the board must also feel a sense of commitment to it and responsibility for its success. It is the board's obligation, ultimately, to ensure the organization's financial health.

BookLink's long-range plan

BookLink already was operating under a three-year financial plan, part of a long-range plan that set out goals and objectives and the resulting requirements in personnel and other resources. In fact, that was BookLink's second three-year plan. But it assumed the grant from the North American aid agency would remain constant at Σ200,000. Now that the grant was being reduced, a new plan was needed. The executive director set to work on it once her budgeting for the current year was well under way.

Revising a long-term financial plan is very much like creating one in the first place. The advantage is that you have some experience in the process. Also, the financial records of previous years give a basis for projections.

The executive director began by looking at places to reduce costs. The staff was about as small as possible, so there could be no cutting there. Some saving could be made in salaries and benefits, however, if she and the others would continue to accept increases that were less than the rate of inflation. There was only one way to save large amounts of money, though. That was by cutting the number of new libraries established each year and the number of books they received to begin with.

She discussed the situation with the chair of the board and the head of the finance committee. All three recognized they could make up for the loss in income simply by cutting the program. But if they did so, they agreed, BookLink would have little reason to exist. It would soon be spending more on its own operations (salaries and office operations) than on its village libraries.

They decided the only solution was to commit themselves much more actively to fundraising locally and internationally. They wrote to four or five foundations seeking support. The head of the regional office of a large northern foundation was interested in their program but asked what chance they had of existing without the large grant they were accustomed to. His foundation could not make up all the difference. He also asked whether BookLink had the support of its own community, and emphasized how important that was. Finally, he said he would recommend to his foundation that it match all the money BookLink could raise locally, up to a total of Σ60,000 a year. The BookLink officers went away feeling encouraged but facing a major challenge.

They decided they were already active in several areas of local fundraising – donation boxes, personal appeals, corporate appeals, the advertising book, and greeting cards. They could not easily take on more, given the small staff and the limited number of enthusiastic volunteers. However, they could hope to build up these activities, some of which were just starting. Too, they could ask the board and other senior volunteers to recruit more volunteers to help with them. The chairman said he would approach the regional and municipal governments for support. They also decided the project coordinator could spend a little less time visiting libraries, and could offer one or two training courses a year to other organizations that would pay fees to attend.

They tried, as realistically as possible, to estimate the probable income from all these sources. The result appears in Table 3a. If they can find the additional volunteers, if they keep up the energy level, if there are no unexpected economic crises, they think they can exceed the target set for local fundraising by the foundation. They decided to plan on that basis and to include Σ60,000 a year from that source in their new long-term plan.

Making the plan credible
At this point the head of the finance committee, a local businessperson, emphasized that major donors will need to be assured about the credibility of the plan and the long-term future of the organization. He suggested that BookLink:
    1 add to its new reserve fund every year, even if that means some reduction in the program
    2 explain to its volunteers, so they can explain to donors, that the organization is operating in modest quarters with the fewest possible staff members, who are accepting salary and wages increases below the level of inflation.

He said the first suggestion, if followed, will produce a reserve that will be able to support the program if funding is cut further in the future. The second will assure possible donors that any contributions will be well spent.

The executive director then prepared a budget of expenses (also Table 3a). She allowed for inflation of 10 per cent each year in the cost of program items (library furniture, books, stationery) and in rent, and 4 per cent in salaries and benefits. These are the organization's major items of expense. She estimated roughly what expenses were likely to be in other areas for the next three years. She then combined projected revenue and estimated expenses (Table 3b).

The two tables do not show her first attempt at a long-range plan. Those calculations were based on maintaining the current program. They hit a roadblock. The projected increases in revenue would simply not keep up with the increased costs of operation, given inflation. She did not think it was realistic to expect revenues to increase more than shown, and realized she would have to cut further than she had hoped into the program.

In its previous three-year plan, BookLink had planned to establish 50 new village libraries each year. In the current year, after the first drop in the North American grant, that number had been reduced to 40. If all goes well, BookLink should be able to establish 40 new libraries again in Year 1 of the new plan, but in the second and third years the executive director calculated that the number will have to drop to 30. The number of books given to each new library will also have to drop, from 370 in the current year to 350 in Year 1 and 300 in Years 2 and 3. With these cuts, it will be possible to add each year to the reserve fund, so long as the fundraising is successful.

The project coordinator then asked, "I understand why we want to build a reserve fund, but does it have to grow so quickly? Couldn't we reduce the amount for reserve and put more into program?" The executive director explained, "As you can see, in the current year the cost of establishing a new library is Σ2,880. Since the program is based on establishing libraries in clusters of 10, if we start a new cluster it will cost Σ28,800. By Year 2, the cost of each new cluster will have increased with inflation to nearly Σ35,000. That is more than all the money we are putting aside for the reserve."

Table 3a: BookLink long-range plan - revenue and expenses

	Budget this year	Long-range plan Year 1	Long-range plan Year 2	Long-range plan Year 3
Revenue				
Foreign sources				
North American aid agency	150,000	100,000	50,000	50,000
European aid agency	75,000	75,000	75,000	75,000
Foundations		60,000	60,000	60,000
National/state/municipal governments		5,000	8,000	10,000
Community-based campaigns				
Donation boxes	4,000	4,700	5,300	5,500
Personal appeals	10,000	14,000	18,000	21,000
Local foundations	2,000	4,000	5,000	6,500
Corporate appeals	5,000	9,000	13,000	15,000
Income-generating activities				
Advertising book	16,000	20,000	23,000	22,000
Greeting cards	11,000	13,500	15,000	17,000
Religious organizations				
Local church	8,500	8,700	9,000	9,000
Training programs in librarianship		5,000	8,000	12,000
Interest	2,151	3,024	9,486	13,800
Non-cash contributions				
In-kind	6,800	7,000	7,100	7,300
Volunteer time	12,000	14,000	17,000	20,000
Total revenue*	**283,651**	**321,924**	**298,786**	**316,800**
Expenses				
Program expenses				
Furniture for new libraries	70,000	77,000	63,525	69,878
Stationery for new libraries	3,600	3,960	3,267	3,594
Books for new libraries	29,600	30,800	21,780	23,958
Training librarians	12,000	13,200	10,890	11,979
Sustaining libraries for 2 years	45,000	49,500	48,400	46,585
Total program expenses	160,200	174,460	147,862	155,994
Fundraising expenses				
Community-based campaigns				
Donation boxes	2,000	2,200	800	800
Personal appeals	500	750	1,000	1,250
Corporate appeals	100	150	200	250
Income-generating activities				
Advertising book	6,000	7,500	9,000	9,900
Greeting cards	5,500	6,750	7,500	8,500
Training courses	0	1,500	2,400	3,600
Total fundraising expenses	14,100	18,850	20,900	24,300
Administration				
Staff (salaries and benefits)	63,600	66,144	68,790	71,541
Rent	12,000	13,200	14,520	15,972
Printed materials	5,500	6,500	6,500	6,500
Travel	5,000	5,500	6,000	6,000
Postage and telephone	1,000	1,050	1,092	1,136
Electricity	720	720	720	720
Office supplies	200	220	240	240
Office repairs	60	60	60	60
Staff training	500	500		
Audit & accounting	350	400	450	500
Bank loan (incl interest)				
Amortization	1,000	1,000	1,000	1,000
Total administration expenses	89,930	95,294	99,372	103,669
Non-cash contributions				
In-kind contributions	6,800	7,000	7,100	7,300
Volunteer time	12,000	14,000	17,000	20,000
Total non-cash contributions	18,800	21,000	24,100	27,300
Total expenses*	**264,230**	**288,604**	**268,134**	**283,963**

* excluding in-kind contributions and volunteer time

Table 3b: BookLink long-range plan

	Budget this year	Long-range plan Year 1	Long-range plan Year 2	Long-range plan Year 3
Revenue				
Foreign sources	225,000	235,000	185,000	185,000
National/state/municipal governments	0	5,000	8,000	10,000
Community-based campaigns	21,000	31,700	41,300	48,000
Income-generating activities	27,000	33,500	38,000	39,000
Religious organizations	8,500	8,700	9,000	9,000
Training programs in librarianship	0	5,000	8,000	12,000
Interest	2,151	3,024	9,486	13,800
Non-cash contributions	18,800	21,000	24,100	27,300
Total revenue*	283,651	321,924	298,786	316,800
Expenses				
Program	160,200	174,460	147,862	155,994
Fundraising	14,100	18,850	20,900	24,300
Administration	89,930	95,294	99,372	103,669
Non-cash contributions	18,800	21,000	24,100	27,300
Total expenses*	264,230	288,604	268,134	283,963
Income less expenses	19,421	33,320	30,652	32,837
Cash balance at first of year	30,770	32,191	31,511	31,163
Transfer to/(from) reserve	18,000	34,000	31,000	33,000
Cash balance at year end	32,191	31,511	31,163	31,000
Reserve fund at year end	18,000	52,000	83,000	116,000

* excluding in-kind contributions and volunteer time

The project coordinator then said, "But couldn't we just make each new cluster bigger, say 11 or 12 libraries?" The executive director replied: "We could, but there is a danger that the villages then will be too widely spread for an easy exchange of books, another key element in our program. Also, we can't be sure we will raise all the money we hope to, so there may be less to put in the reserve fund than we think. And our board insists that we do all we can to build that safety cushion for the future."

She also pointed out that the reserve fund would be earning income each year. She had estimated that interest earned by the reserve fund would average 14 per cent per year (4 per cent above the rate of inflation). In her calculations she had also included the interest that would be earned on cash in BookLink's current bank account. By Year 3, according to the plan, the interest from the reserve fund would be enough to buy nearly all the books needed for 15 new libraries.

By Year 3, the reserve fund should have grown to Σ116,000. The organization could thus survive, for at least a year or two, even if foreign funding were reduced again. By that time, too, the executive director hoped to have obtained support from other foreign sources.

BookLink's long-range plan is ambitious. If all goes well, BookLink's reliance on foreign funding will have dropped, in just five years, from more than 90 per cent of cash revenue in the year before the current year to less than 60 per cent in Year 3 of the plan. Local funding will have increased slightly more than six times in the same period, from Σ21,500 to just over

$132,000. In addition, community involvement will have increased in the form of non-cash support.

What donors want to know
Most donors, and major donors in particular, are concerned that the money they give is being well used. They want to feel that it is going into the programs that are the reason for the voluntary organization's existence. They want to be sure it won't be wasted in unnecessary administrative expenses or inefficient efforts to raise more money. Many experts suggest that at least 60 per cent of an organization's annual budget should go into programs. That is a target to aim for in long-range planning.

To show how administrative costs will be spent, divide them among the major categories of the budget. For example, in calculating the proportion of the budget devoted to program activities, be sure to include a reasonable proportion of staff time and office expenses. Allocate staff and office costs proportionately also to fundraising and general administration. If non-program costs are greater than 40 per cent, look for ways to reduce them.

BookLink recognizes that some donors want to know how much of the money they give is spent just to raise more money, rather than on core programs. Before BookLink began active fundraising, its expenses in this area were minimal – the cost of servicing donation boxes and producing greeting cards, and a bit of the executive director's time – but so was the return. By Year 3, the executive director calculated, she would be spending close to 70 per cent of her time on fundraising, the projects coordinator would be spending 10 per cent of his time in revenue-generating training courses, and the secretary would be spending 15 per cent of her time (with volunteer help) keeping records of fundraising. That amounted to a good-sized allotment of staff salaries – just over $28,000 – but, together with the cash expenditures under "fundraising" and a small portion of the office expenses, the costs of fundraising would amount to only about 17 per cent of all BookLink's cash revenue. Most major donors would consider that an acceptable proportion.

Donors are also concerned about the amount of revenue spent on routine operations other than program. BookLink's plan assumes that by Year 3 such routine administration will occupy 25 per cent of the executive director's time, 10 per cent of the project coordinator's time, and 65 per cent of the secretary-bookkeeper's time ($19,640 of staff salaries) plus 70 per cent of all non-staff costs listed under administration ($22,489). That amounts to about 13 per cent of total cash revenue.

Just over 10 per cent of total cash revenue is to be transferred to the reserve fund. This leaves 60 per cent of all cash revenue to be devoted to program. That is a proportion that is generally accepted as a target for allocation of resources by voluntary organizations engaged in fundraising.

A final warning about long-term plans
A plan is not reality. I have known more than one voluntary organization in North America that followed a plan based on expected revenue, even when the revenue didn't arrive. They spent their money according to the plan, but

failed in fundraising. One changed in a single year from having a small surplus to having a debt half as big as its operating budget. In another, after several applications for grants were not approved as quickly as expected, the executive director gave up his salary for several months to keep the office operating.

A three-year plan is only as good as the assumptions underlying it. It must be checked regularly. Is inflation higher than expected? Are donations dropping? If it looks as if targets are not being met, adjustments should be made as soon as possible. That may mean changing the plan to reduce costs. More positively, it can mean renewed efforts in fundraising.

BookLink knows this. It will revise the plan each time a budget is prepared for the coming year. It will examine its own performance regularly against its budget and against the assumptions of the plan. This is possible because of the detailed records it keeps of its day-to-day operations.

Looking at the present: monthly operating reports

A budget, no matter how carefully prepared, is only a plan, an estimate of what is expected. And, as a saying in English goes, there may be many a slip between the cup and the lip. Costs may be higher than expected, revenues lower than expected. Of course, the opposite may also happen. That is good news, but unfortunately it seems to happen less frequently.

It is essential therefore to keep track of expenses and revenue regularly, and to compare them to what was planned in the budget. This comparison is the most important part of the report. Simply knowing how much has been received or spent does not help in managing finances.

There are two ways to record expenses and revenue.

• The *cash method* shows how much money has actually been paid out and how much has actually come in. It reports your cash position (in effect, how much money you have in the bank) at any one time.

• The *accrual method* records expenditures and revenues *as soon as they are incurred*, regardless of when the bills will actually be paid or when the cash will actually be received. This method keeps track of income that is expected and the amount of money that will be needed to pay future bills.

Accountants prefer the second method, and it is not hard to see why. It is a more accurate picture of a firm's true financial strength or weakness. With the cash method, it is possible for an organization to present a statement at year end that shows a lot of money in the bank – but does not show that the organization owes a great deal of money or has a number of commitments. (The organization mentioned previously, whose executive director had to go several months without pay, used the cash method. The audited statements prepared at the end of its financial year showed a cash balance large enough to keep the organization in business for at least six months. What the statements did not show was that a good deal of that large balance was already committed to support projects, and would soon have to be transmitted to the recipients. Within three months, the organization was in a financial crisis. The problem would have been evident if the organization had been using accrual accounting.) Of course, the opposite can occur; the cash method may paint a much darker picture than is true. An organization may appear to have too little money in the bank to pay its debts at the end of a month – when in fact it will definitely be receiving a large amount of money in the next month and can postpone payment of some bills until that money is received.

If the accrual method is used, it is necessary to prepare a second projection of month-by-month income and expenses at the time of yearly budgeting. This one will be similar in form to the cash-flow projection. But it will not show when cash is expected to be received and spent. Instead it will show when expenses are committed (that is, when an order will be placed for materials or for services such as printing) and when revenue has been promised to be paid, *regardless of when the actual bills will be paid or when the cash will be received*. These figures will then appear as the "budgeted" amounts in the monthly operating reports. (With the cash method of accounting, the budgeted amounts will be based on the actual cash-flow projection.)

Keeping a watchful eye
Many organizations believe income and expenses should be monitored every month in a report that consists of three parts (Table 4):

1 the month just past: budgeted amounts and actual amounts
2 the year to date: budgeted amounts and actual amounts, plus the variance (that is, the difference between the budgeted and actual figures)
3 forecast to the end of the year based on evidence to date and any new information: budgeted and actual amounts and variance

The third part is in many ways the most important of the three. A shortfall in revenue or an unexpected increase in costs at the first of the year may spell problems that will escalate. On the other hand, some differences between budgeted and actual amounts in any one month can be ignored, at least for the time being. It is likely they will be balanced by other differences before the end of the year. (For example, a new supply of stationery may have to be bought three months earlier than planned, but the total bill for the year for office supplies will be about the same as budgeted.) The year-end forecast in the monthly report requires careful preparation and an understanding of annual cash flow. It cannot be done mechanically on the basis of performance in any single month.

In a monthly report of this kind, the budgeted amounts (columns 1, 3, and 6) are based on the amounts already established in the current year's budget (the month-by-month projection of income and receipts, prepared for accrual or cash reporting depending on the organization's policy). The actual amounts (columns 2 and 4) are based on separate records. These should be kept for every amount of money received and spent, listed under the appropriate categories. The best way to keep accounts up to date is to do it every day, in separate records for receipts and expenses. An organization that runs a small business, such as selling greeting cards from its office, will likely want to have a separate book for that purpose. This can be used to record receipts of small amounts of money and to issue receipts to customers; then daily totals can be entered in the main record of revenue.

Table 4: BookLink monthly operating report for Month 4

	Current month			Year to date				Year end		
	Budget	Actual		Budget	Actual	Variance		Budget	Forecast	Variance
Revenue										
Foreign sources										
Aid agencies	75,000	75,000		75,000	75,000	0		225,000	225,000	0
Foundations										
Community-based campaigns										
Donation boxes	300	297		1,300	1,273	(27)		4,000	4,000	0
Personal appeals								10,000	10,000	0
Local foundations								2,000	2,000	0
Corporate appeals								5,000	5,000	0
Income-generating activities										
Advertising book				16,000	16,500	500		16,000	16,500	500
Greeting cards	600	482		3,800	3,742	(58)		11,000	10,700	(300)
Religious organizations										
Local church	500	496		3,000	3,089	89		8,500	8,500	0
Interest	67	68		398	401	3		2,151	2,151	0
Total revenue	76,467	76,343		99,498	100,005	507		283,651	283,851	200
Expenses										
Program expenditures										
Furniture for new libraries	35,000	34,775		35,000	34,775	(225)		70,000	70,000	0
Stationery for new libraries	1,800	1,840		1,800	1,840	40		3,600	3,800	200
Books for new libraries	14,800	14,765		14,800	14,765	(35)		29,600	29,600	0
Training librarians								12,000	12,000	0
Sustaining libraries for 2 years								45,000	45,000	0
Fundraising expenditures										
Community-based campaigns										
Donation boxes	50	45		1,600	1,721	121		2,000	2,120	120
Personal appeals								500	500	0
Corporate appeals								100	100	0
Income-generating activities										
Advertising book				6,000	6,123	123		6,000	6,123	123
Greeting cards				5,500	5,622	122		5,500	5,622	122
Administration										
Staff (salaries and benefits)	5,300	5,300		21,200	21,200	0		63,600	63,600	0
Rent	1,000	1,000		4,000	4,000	0		12,000	12,000	0
Printed materials				1,500	1,623	123		5,500	6,000	500
Travel				1,000	873	(127)		5,000	5,000	0
Postage and telephone	70	68		280	274	(6)		1,000	1,000	0
Electricity	60	60		240	240	0		720	720	0
Office supplies	15	12		60	65	5		200	200	0
Office repairs	5	0		20	10	(10)		60	60	0
Staff training				500	320	(180)		500	500	0
Audit & accounting				350	345	(5)		350	350	0
Bank loan (incl interest)										
Amortization	85	85		340	340	0		1,000	1,000	0
Total expenses	58,185	57,950		94,190	94,136	(54)		264,230	265,295	1,065

The variances may be shown as amounts (the actual difference between budget and actual) or percentages (for example, if the budget allowed Σ100 to be spent and the actual cost was Σ110, the variance would appear as Σ 10 per cent). Accountants don't agree on which is better. Some think percentages make it easier to spot major variances. However, a variance of 50 per cent on a budgeted item of Σ20 is less significant to financial health than a 5 per cent variance on an item of Σ20,000. I prefer to see variances given as amounts.

Of course, knowing the amount of a variance is of little value without knowing the reason for it. Financial officers or managers should be ready to explain why a significant variance has occurred. Their reasons may be included with the operating report. Some possible explanations of variances (apart from loose management) are:

• *for a shortfall in revenue*: a temporary problem; a delay in receiving grants; donors who are not honouring pledges; outstanding invoices that are not being paid in time; an error in accounting that will be corrected next month; membership fees that are so late in being paid that it should be assumed the memberships will not be renewed

• *for greater than budgeted expenses*: a temporary or seasonal problem; an unauthorized expenditure (a problem that will not be repeated); unexpected costs that could not have been foreseen in the budget

• *for greater revenue than expected*: a temporary situation; a long-term gain that should be used to balance unforeseen expenses, invested in projects, or deposited in the reserve fund

• *for a shortfall in expenses*: postponement of some expenditures; unavailability of supplies; departure or non-hiring of staff

A relatively small organization, such as BookLink, may need to prepare only one operating report each month. Larger, more complex organizations should prepare one for their overall operation as well as sub-reports for each project and department.

The report for each project or department should be sent promptly to the person who heads it. That is the only way managers can know of any growing financial problems and act to meet them. All reports should also go to the chief executive officer. Too often they sit in the bookkeeper's office, where they are of little use to anyone. The reports should be prepared and distributed as quickly as possible after the end of the month, so that managers will have as much time as possible to respond to any problems that are revealed. Out-of-date reports are of little value.

Donor agencies and corporations know regular monthly reports are essential for efficient operations. By showing that they prepare such reports and use them effectively, voluntary organizations can prove to potential donors that they are financially responsible.

BookLink's monthly operating report
BookLink uses the accrual method of accounting. Therefore the total anticipated income from the advertising book is shown in its monthly operating report (Table 4) as revenue under "year to date" even though the last of

the money is still to come in. For the same reason, the cost of furniture, stationery, and books for 20 new libraries is shown as an expense. Even though the bills will not be paid until after the items are received, the items were ordered after the grant was received in Month 4.

The volunteers sold $\Sigma 500$ more advertising for the book than budgeted. That is shown as a plus in the variances for the year to date and in the year-end forecast. Sales of greeting cards have been down slightly in the first four months; this drop may not persist, but BookLink is cautious in its budgeting and predicts a small shortfall in total annual sales. (If the financial officer were extra cautious, she might provide for the possibility of some non-payment and estimate year-end revenue for advertising as only $\Sigma 16,000$.)

The new donation boxes have cost slightly more than budgeted. More serious is an increase in the local cost of paper. As a result, the costs of producing greeting cards, the advertising book, and promotional printed materials have all been higher than expected, and so is the cost of stationery for new libraries. The advertising book and the year's supply of greeting cards have already been delivered, so their actual cost can be predicted accurately in the year-end forecast. BookLink's bookkeeper has estimated how much the rise in paper costs will also affect future purchases of printing and stationery during the year.

BookLink has kept within budget during the first four months of the current year, mainly because costs were significantly lower than expected in two areas, staff training and travel. The apparent saving may not be good. It may mean the staff is not getting training it needs, for example, in better use of computer programs. It may mean the project coordinator is not spending enough time in the field monitoring the performance of the village libraries. The year-end forecast assumes the total budgeted amount will be spent in these areas.

At the end of Month 4, it appears that by the end of its financial year BookLink will have received $\Sigma 200$ more than expected but will have spent $\Sigma 1,065$ more than budgeted. This is a variance of less than one-third of one per cent on the total budget, which is a highly credible performance. The predicted shortfall may, however, spur the volunteers on to even more determined canvassing when the annual campaign for personal donations begins.

Looking back: the balance sheet

The balance sheet is a statement of the financial position of an organization at a given date – usually the end of its financial year. In that sense it is a static document, a snapshot at one moment that can be compared to the financial position at an earlier date, usually the end of the previous financial year. The balance sheet is not as important for day-to-day management as other financial reports already discussed, but it is useful for demonstrating the financial strength (or weakness) of an organization.

The balance sheet is the first thing business people are likely to ask to see. A fundraising consultant in South Africa was interested in increasing her personal donations. She asked ten organizations to send her their financial information, including their balance sheets. Only two sent balance sheets, so they received all her donations that year.

The form of the balance sheet may vary according to accounting practices in particular countries. All balance sheets have certain characteristics in common, however. Basically, they present the assets and liabilities of the organization, show whether or not it is solvent, and compare its position to the previous accounting period. Balance sheets may be prepared at the end of each month, but more often are prepared only annually. In the following paragraphs, it is assumed that the accounting period is a complete financial year.

Assets are usually divided between those that are *fixed* (that is, they are part of the organization's permanent assets) and those that are *current* (they may change almost daily). Fixed assets include property, vehicles, and office equipment and furniture. These assets are shown at their value after the annual allowance for amortization. (In many countries, the rate of amortization for different kinds of fixed assets is established by the government.) Fixed assets also include long-term investments and long-term loans to other organizations. Current assets include cash on hand and in the bank on the day of the balance sheet, the value of goods that are in stock then but have not yet been sold, accounts receivable (money owed by other people that will be paid within the next 12 months), and any pre-payments for goods that have not yet been supplied.

Voluntary organizations that receive grants for specific projects may show their short-term assets under two headings: restricted and unrestricted. Restricted funds are money that has been given for specific projects; it may be spent for no other purpose. Unrestricted funds, as the name suggests, may be spent for any purpose, including routine operating costs such as staff salaries and office supplies. (In negotiating grants, try to have a reasonable share of any restricted funds assigned to routine operating costs. Otherwise, the granting agency is not providing full support for the program in which it is interested.)

Liabilities are also classified as long term and short term. Long-term liabilities are money that is owed to other parties but does not have to be paid during the next 12 months. Short-term liabilities include accounts payable (money owed to others on the day of the balance sheet that must be paid within the next 12 months), any bank loans or overdrafts then owing, and any taxes that may have to be paid in the next 12 months.

BookLink's balance sheet

BookLink has adopted a simple form of balance sheet (Table 5) that is acceptable in many countries for voluntary organizations. The amounts under the various headings show that BookLink achieved the budget and cash-flow projections set out at the first of the year. (Note: in an actual balance sheet, the columns would be headed by the actual years – for example, 2002 and 2001 – and the date of the balance sheet would be the last day of the financial year just ended. The balance sheet would be supported by year-end documents listing sources of revenue and areas of expenditure.)

Table 5: BookLink's balance sheet at year-end

Balance Sheet
as at (date: end of financial year)

	(Year just ended)	(Preceding year)
Assets		
Current assets		
Accounts receivable	350	450
Inventory	1,250	1,350
Cash in bank and at hand	31,841	30,319
	33,441	32,119
Fixed assets		
Office equipment and furniture	4,500	5,500
Reserve fund	18,000	0
	22,500	5,500
Total Assets	55,941	37,619
Liabilities		
Bank loans	0	0
Accounts payable	200	400
	200	400
Surplus (loss)	55,741	37,219

At the end of BookLink's financial year, one of the businesses that bought space in the advertising book still had not paid its bill. This is shown as an account receivable. There are a number of greeting cards in stock and not yet sold; these are valued as inventory at the cost of manufacturing them. The organization has a sizeable amount of cash in the bank, from which it will have to pay its operating expenses until the next grants are received.

BookLink amortizes its office furniture and equipment at a rate of Σ1,000 per year. The value of those assets therefore declines each year by that amount, unless new equipment is bought. The reserve fund is shown as a fixed asset because it has been invested in long-term securities.

The organization has few liabilities – only a few bills for office supplies and for services that were delivered in the final month of the financial year but have not yet been paid.

The surplus has grown substantially over the past year, demonstrating BookLink's resolve to improve its financial security and reduce its dependence on foreign grants.

Suggested reading and Web sites

Check with major aid agencies, foreign foundations, embassies, high commissions, large libraries, and your funders, who may have or be able to get some of these publications, especially the reference books. Many of the Web sites (including those listed with the books) include a variety of information for fundraisers. However, World Wide Web addresses change frequently; in this case a search engine may help. Since prices also change, they are not included. Books may be ordered by mail, by e-mail from the publishers, from Web sites, from some urban bookstores, or from a Web bookstore such as http://amazon.com or http://amazon.co.uk. See also the Web sites in Book 2, Chapter 24.

Alternative financing of third world development organizations and NGOs, Vols. 1 (445 pages), and 2 (300 pages), by Fernand Vincent. 1995. Geneva, Switzerland: Development Innovations and Networks (IRED), 3 rue de Varembé, P.O. Box 116-1211, Geneva 20, Switzerland.
ISBN 2 88368 005 1
E-mail: ired@worldcom.ch

@t ease with e-mail: A handbook on using electronic mail for NGOs in developing countries. New York: The United Nations Non-Governmental Liaison Service and The Friedrich Ebert Foundation. 1998. Free from The United Nations Non-Governmental Liaison Service, Palais des Nations, CH-1211 Geneva 10, Switzerland. (Also available online; see list of Web sites below.) 130 pages. ISBN 0 9645188 5 6
Web site: http://ngls.tad.ch

Charity shops, by Hilary Bloom. London: The Charities Advisory Trust. 1995. London: Directory of Social Change, 24 Stephenson Way, London NW1 2DP, UK. 160 pages. ISBN 1 873860 77 3
E-mail: webmaster@d-s-c.demon.co.uk
Web site: http://www.d-s-c.demon.co.uk

Chronicle of Philanthropy, the newspaper of the non-profit world, published bi-weekly. 1255 23rd Street, Washington NW 20037, USA.
E-mail: subscriptions@philanthropy.com
Web site: http://www.philanthropy.com

Community participation and financial sustainability, compiled and edited by James Taylor, Dirk Marais, and Stephen Heyns. Action-learning series case studies and lessons from development practice. 1998. Published by Juta and Co. Ltd., Mercury Crescent, Hillstar Industrial Estate, Wetton, South Africa, 7780, in association with Community Development Resource Association, PO Box 221, Woodstock, South Africa 7915. 126 pages. ISBN 0 7021 4629 3
E-mail: info@cdra.org.za
Web site: http://www.cdra.org.za

Corporate responsibility: Philanthropy, self-interest and bribery, by Delwin Roy, former president of the Hitachi Foundation. 1999. Kluwer Law International, Distribution Centre, PO Box 322, 3300 AH Dordrecht, The Netherlands. ISBN 90 411 9645 5
E-mail: services@wkap.nl
Web site: http://kluwerlaw.com

Creating effective partnerships with business, a guide for charities and non-profits in Canada. 1996. Toronto: Imagine, a program of the Canadian Centre for Philanthropy, 425 University Avenue, Suite 700, Toronto M5G 1T6, Canada. 84 pages. ISBN 0 921295 37 7
E-mail: imagine@ccp.ca Web site: http://www.ccp.ca/imagine

The DIY guide to public relations for charities, voluntary organizations, and community groups, by Moi Ali. London: Directory of Social Change, 24 Stephenson Way, London, NW1 2DP, UK. 184 pages.
ISBN 1 873860 80 3
E-mail: webmaster@d-s-c.demon.co.uk
Web site: http://www.d-s-c.demon.co.uk

Face-to-face, how to get bigger donations from very generous people, by Ken Wyman. See list of Web sites below.

The five most important questions you will ever ask about your non-profit organization: Participant's workbook. The Drucker Foundation (http://www.pfdf.org) self-assessment tool for non-profit organizations. 1993. San Francisco: Jossey-Bass Publishers, 350 Sansome Street, San Francisco 94104, USA. 62 pages. ISBN 1 55542 595 X
E-mail: info@josseybass.com
Web site: http://www.josseybass.com

Fund-raising and the nonprofit board member, by Fisher Howe. A booklet in the governance series published by the National Center for Nonprofit Boards, Suite 510, 2000 L Street NW, Washington DC 20036-4907, USA. ISBN 0 925299 02 2
E-mail: info@ncnb.org
Web site: http://www.ncnb.org/main.htm

Fundraising for social change, by Kim Klein. 1996. Berkeley, California: Chardon Press, 3781 Broadway, Oakland, California 94611, USA. 350 pages. ISBN 0 9620222 3 3
E-mail: info@chardonpress.com
Web site: http://www.chardonpress.com

Fundraising ideas that work for grassroots groups, by Ken Wyman. See list of Web sites below.

The grass roots fundraising book: How to raise money in your community, by Joan Flanagan. 1992. Chicago: Contemporary Books, Inc., Two Prudential Plaza, Chicago, Illinois 60601-6790, USA. 332 pages. ISBN 0 8092 5746 7
E-mail: ntcpub@tribune.com
Web site: www.contemporarybooks.com

Guide to special event fundraising, by Ken Wyman. See list of Web sites below.

Managing your solvency, by Michael Norton. 1994. London: Directory of Social Change, 24 Stephenson Way, London, NW1 2DP, UK. 160 pages. ISBN 1 873860 25 8
E-mail: webmaster@d-s-c.demon.co.uk
Web site: http://www.d-s-c.demon.co.uk

Manual of practical management for Third World rural development associations, by Fernand Vincent. Vols. 1 (Organization, administration, communication. 240 pages. ISBN 1 85339 404 1) and 2 (Financial management. 208 pages. ISBN 1 85339 405 X). 1997. Originally published by IRED, republished by Intermediate Technology Publications Ltd, 103-105 Southampton Row, London WC1B 4HH, UK.
E-mail: itpubs@itpubs.org.uk
Web site: http://www.oneworld.org/itdg/publications

The raising of money: Thirty-five essentials every trustee should know, by James Gregory Lord. 1996. Third Sector Press, 28050 S. Woodland Rd., Cleveland OH 44124, USA. 128 pages. ISBN 0 939120 02 X
E-mail: quest@lord.org

Relationship fundraising, a donor-based approach to the business of raising money, by Ken Burnett. 1992. The White Lion Press Limited in association with the International Fundraising Group. White Lion Press, White Lion Court, 74 Rivington Street, London, EC2A 3AY UK. 330 pages. ISBN 0 9518971 0
E-mail: mikek@burnettassociates.com
Web site: http://www.burnettassociates.com

Successful fundraising: A complete handbook for volunteers and professionals, by Joan Flanagan. 1993. Contemporary Books, Inc., Two Prudential Plaza, Chicago, Illinois, USA 60601-6790. 306 pages. ISBN 0 8092 3812 8
E-mail: ntcpub@tribune.com
Web site: www.contemporarybooks.com

Towards greater financial autonomy, a manual on financing strategies and techniques for development NGOs and community organizations, by Fernand Vincent and Piers Campbell. 1989. Geneva, Development Innovations and Networks (IRED), 3 rue de Varembé, P.O. Box 116-1211, Geneva 20, Switzerland. 225 pages. ISBN 2 88368 003 5
E-mail: ired@worldcom.ch

The worldwide fundraiser's handbook, a guide to fundraising for Southern NGOs and voluntary organizations, by Michael Norton. 1996. London: Directory of Social Change in association with the International Fund Raising Group, 295 Kennington Road, London SE11 4QE, UK. 270 pages. ISBN 1 873860 75 7
E-mail: webmaster@d-s-c.demon.co.uk
Web site: http://www.d-s-c.demon.co.uk

Reference

The directory of American grantmakers that fund charitable organizations and individuals outside the USA 2000, edited by Nancy Bikson and David Wickert. Chapel & York Ltd., P.O. Box 50, Lingfield RH7 6FT, United Kingdom. ISBN 1 90329 300 6
E-mail: info@chapel-york.com
Web site: http://www.chapel-york.com

Directory of international corporate giving in America and abroad 2000. Tracks 650 companies with international connections. 75% give directly. The Taft Group, P.O. Box 9187, Farmington Hills, Michigan 48333-9187. ISBN 1 56995 336 8
E-mail: international@gale.com
Web site: http://www.taftgroup.com/taft/about.html

The directory of international funding organizations, a guide for the non-profit sector. London: Charities Aid Foundation, 1997. Order from CAF, Kings Hill, West Malling, Kent ME19 4TA, UK. ISBN 1 85934 031 8
E-mail: international@caf.charitynet.org
Web site: http://www.ngobooks.org

The European grants index. The first statistical analysis of the funding interests of foundations and corporate funders active in Europe, as well as Japan and the USA. Data said to be current, with 75 per cent of listings containing information for 1996, 1997, or 1998. European Foundation Centre: Fax: 32 2 512 3265.

E-mail: efc@efc.be
Web site: http://www.efc.be

Guide to funding for international and foreign programs, 2000.
The Foundation Center, 79 5th Avenue, New York City 10003-3076.
358 pages. ISBN 0 87954 903 3
E-mail: orders@fdncenter.org
Web site: http://www.fdncenter.org

The International Foundation Directory, 1998. Europa Publications,
P.O. Box 97974, Pittsburgh, PA 15227, US. Lists 1,500 foundations,
trusts and non-profit institutions in over 100 countries that operate
internationally. 817 pages. ISBN 1 85743 054 9
E-mail: sales@europublications.com
Web site: http://www.europapublications.com/

International fundraising for not-for profits: A country by country profile, by
Tom Harris. What a fundraiser must know when preparing for an
international fundraising campaign. 1999. John Wiley and Sons,
605 Third Avenue, New York, NY 10158-0012. 439 pages.
ISBN 0 471244 52 X
E-mail: catalogue@wiley.com
Web site: http://www.wiley.com

International grant guides. Foreign and international programs. 345 pages.
International grantmaking: A report on U.S. foundation trends, including
profiles of more than 500 leading foundations, 1997. The Foundation
Center, 79 5th Avenue, New York City 10003-3076. 170 pages.
ISBN 0 87954 760 X
E-mail: orders@fdncenter.org
Web site: http://www.fdncenter.org

The international guide to nonprofit law, by Lester Salamon. 1997. Analyses
the legal status of non-profit organizations in 22 countries. John Wiley
and Sons, 605 Third Avenue, New York 10158-0012. 400 pages.
ISBN 0 47105518 2
E-mail: catalogue@wiley.com
Web site: http://www.wiley.com

WWW.Grantmakers: directory of funders' Web Sites, 2000. Lists 1,000
organizations in North America and Europe that fund internationally.
Published by Chapel & York (see first reference listing). 109 pages.
ISBN 1 903 903293 01 4.

Useful Web sites
Most sites in this list were suggested by Ken Wyman, a Canadian fundraising consultant. Many also have e-mail discussion groups that you can join.

www.charitynet.org
Information and financial resources for a better world. The voluntary action site of CAF (Charities Aid Foundation, UK)
http://www.CAFonline.org

www.charityvillage.com
One of Canada's – maybe the world's – most notable sites. How-to articles, current information on non-profit news, books, careers, professional associations, online publications.

www.chardonpress.com
Fundraising for social change is the theme of this American site from Kim Klein, publisher of the *Grassroots Fundraising Journal*, among other good print material. Online stories, free newsletter, non-profit links, and book catalogue where you can browse selections or search by topic, author, title, or organization.

www.charitychannel.com
Many non-profit discussion forums on specific topics, and Guestshare, a space to share documents among non-profit professionals trying to solve similar problems.

www.electroniccommunity.org
Intends to become the premier Internet portal for civil society organizations involved in the development of Africa. Interactive.

www.fundersonline.org
The European Foundation Centre provides a free toolkit and templates for setting up a Web site.

www.fundraising.co.uk
This Web site has developed a strong worldwide following based on its library services and in-depth coverage of events, jobs, news, grants, funding, compilation of sites. It also has a great feature called "stay in touch" which e-mails you about site updates.

www.fundsnetservices.com
Research and locate international funding: 1,500 sources are listed.

www.idealist.org
Rich collection of non-profit resources. Offers training for non-profit and community organizations on how to use the Internet.

www.ncnb.org
The National Center for Nonprofit Boards (in the United States) has extensive resources on board development including an answering service for e-mail questions

http://ngls.tad.ch/english/pubs/at/ateng.html
@t ease with e-mail: A handbook on using electronic mail for NGOs in *developing countries* (see reading list above).
www.nonprofits.org
Huge site from the Internet Nonprofit Center with information for and about non-profit organizations.

www.nutsbolts.com
Practical "how-to" management tips. Browse some of the articles from current and back issues of their printed monthly newsletter, *Nuts & Bolts*, for the busy non-profit professional.

www.oneworld.net/production/supportcentre.html
Includes lists of organization whose lists you can join. The "support centre" offers help in setting up a Web site.

www.pactworld.org
Lists many useful resources. Look at www.pactworld.org/toolbox.html for development expert Richard Holloway's Civil Society Toolbox, including a section on financing civil society organizations.

www.pch.gc.ca/cp-pc/ComPartnE/pub_list.htm
Three excellent books to download, published on the Web by the Community Partnership Program, Canadian Heritage, Government of Canada:
Face-to-face, how to get bigger donations from very generous people, by Ken Wyman. 1993. 192 pages.
Fundraising ideas that work for grassroots groups, by Ken Wyman. 1995. 156 pages.
Guide to special event fundraising, by Ken Wyman. 1990. 170 pages.

www.philanthropy.com
Online source for Internet resources, and current and back issues of the American newspaper, *The Chronicle of Philanthropy*. Some information is available only to subscribers.

www.vita.org
Keep track of the plan by United States organization VITA, Volunteers in Technical Assistance, to bring low cost e-mail services to rural and isolated areas in developing countries.

List of Topics

This list contains page references to all three books. The Roman numeral is the volume number, I, II, and III. The Arabic number is the page number, e.g. III/224.

Advertising for donations
in the media III/70
directories III/71

Advertising books
scheduling for success III/24
contracts with advertisers III/28
editorial section III/30
volunteer activities III/31
follow-up after publication III/36

Alliances
presenting a united front I/44
making new friends I/88
supportive coalitions I/89
valuable networks I/92
intermediary groups I/93
advantages of alliances I/97
types of alliances I/99
mergers and acquisitions I/100
criteria for partnerships I/104
conditions for success I/104

Annual reports
attractive reports III/19
contents II/154
saying thank you II/155
covering fundraising news III/19

Audiovisual presentations
reinforcing words visually II/105
choosing illustrations II/110

choosing photographs II/111
taking good photographs II/113
working with photographers and artists II/114
getting started II/116
the right location II/117
who is the audience? II/118
making the presentation II/118
slide presentations II/120
audiotapes II/122
films and videotapes II/122
presentation books II/123
using images III/16
computer presentations II/122, III/21

Boards of directors
commitment I/33
failures of leadership I/48
strengthening governance I/48
role of board of directors I/63
broadening the membership I/64, II/43
reasons for service I/69
recruiting members I/70, II/46
adding business people I/66, II/44
responsibilities for fundraising I/72, II/35, 38
building a fundraising board II/39, 43, 48
alternatives to board fundraising II/52
using celebrities II/57

Business giving
building alliances with other organizations III/162
engaging a company's interest III/163
cash contributions III/164
employee contributions III/164
employees as volunteers III/167
matching grants III/167
in-kind contributions III/168
sponsorships III/170
social marketing III/173
facing the realities III/175
roadblocks by voluntary organizations III/178
looking at attitudes III/183
building corporate relationships III/184
researching the prospects III/186
being businesslike III/186
effective proposals III/188
following up III/195
corporate complaints III/199

Businesses for fundraising
kinds of fundraising businesses III/98
planning, management, governance III/100
what can go wrong III/102
separating business and services III/103
advantages of commercial activities III/104
requirements for success III/105
dealing with governments III/107
building a budget III/109
selling services III/115
making a business plan III/116

Challenges in the future
building links with the community III/248
building leadership III/249
ethical standards III/249
informing governments III/251
better networks and services III/251
better information sources III/254
expanding overseas III/255

Communicating
public image I/18
communicating regularly I/28
capturing attention II/79
importance of research II/81
choosing the message II/83
choosing target audiences II/84
selecting the media II/86
communications budget II/89
17 paths to effective communication II/91
thinking of the audience II/91
avoiding jargon II/93
keeping it simple II/94
See also annual reports, audiovisual presentations, media, newsletters, printed materials, speeches

Credibility
goals on the path I/9
becoming known I/10
reasons needed to give I/11
gaining new credibility I/15
14 assets for credibility I/17
good personal reputations I/2
in local community II/29

Direct mail
getting started III/120
will direct mail work? III/123
budgeting for direct mail III/127
permission to mail III/128
mailing to the right people III/129
sharing lists III/130
timing of mailings III/133
mailing envelopes II/133
appealing letters III/135
pitfalls in letter writing III/139
response forms III/142
reply envelopes III/143
sample letters and forms III/140, 145, 189, 190
an extra promotion III/146
thanking donors III/147
keeping good records III/149
compiling the responses III/150
testing for effectiveness III/151
planning the next mailings III/152
See also communicating, printed materials

Donation boxes
rules for success III/78

Evaluation of fundraising
evaluating programs III/241
looking at attitudes III/244
looking at results III/245
See also voluntary organizations – self-evaluation

Events
annual general meetings II/166
project launches II/167
recognition events II/169
inviting prominent people II/157
planning for success III/82
setting goals III/84
building audiences III/85, 86, 96
appealing programs III/85
leaders and helpers III/87
managing the finances III/88
attracting publicity III/91
follow-up and evaluation III/92
why events fail III/93
event ideas III/94

Fear of fundraising
overcoming fear of asking I/13
why the fear exists II/60, III/41
13 ways to overcome fear II/63
recognizing strengths and weaknesses II/65

Financial credibility
accountable fundraising management I/22
credible financial reports I/133
purposes of financial reports I/134
rules for budgeting I/138
sample budgets I/140-147
non-cash contributions I/143
cash flow projections I/145
guidelines for budget planning I/148
making the plan credible I/151
planning revenue and expenses I/152
what donors want to know I/154
monthly operating reports I/154
balance sheet I/159
importance of good records II/20

Fundraising
giving as a habit I/1
where to look for money I/2
developing many sources of support I/3
starting carefully I/4
getting team support I/4
getting people talking I/5
reasons for giving or not I/11, III/1, 4

Fundraising - beginning
giving as a habit I/1
where to look for money I/2
develop many sources of support I/3
start carefully I/4
get team support I/4
get people talking I/5
developing independence I/6
special satisfactions I/8
what donors want to know I/154
why people give II/1
how people can give II/5
what you need beforehand II/5

Fundraising management
managing donors I/47

goals in local fundraising II/2
studying current revenue II/3
costs of fundraising II/8
ratio of revenue to costs II/10
seeking seed money II/11
budgeting for fundraising II/14
personal contact at the office II/18
useful equipment II/19
need for good records II/20
memberships: pros and cons III/44
expanding overseas III/255
See also specific topics e.g. donation boxes

Governments
relationships with I/39
approaching for funds III/229
informing governments III/251

Grant applications
nature of granting agencies III/217
making the first contact III/219
preparing the proposal III/221
rules for clarity III/225
delivering the proposal III/226
waiting for the answer III/228
approaching governments III/229

Internet/e-mail
using e-mail II/172
using e-mail for fundraising II/199
effective e-mail messages II/174
making useful contacts by e-mail II/173, III/201
regular communications II/202
setting up a signature II/175
using the World Wide Web II/176, III/203
home pages/Web sites II/177
promoting a Web site II/180
financing a Web site II/181, III/204

Leadership
failures of leadership I/48
role of board of directors I/63
role of leader II/30
See also challenges in the future, credibility, fundraising management, vision/mission, voluntary organizations, businesses for fundraising

Media coverage
rules for interesting writing II/15
successful news releases: 25 rules II/158
effective writing II/160
surviving bad news II/164
dealing with reporters II/163
following up II/163
news conferences II/162

Newsletters
rules for interesting writing II/15
editorial boards II/149
effective newsletters: 7 paths II/146
starting a newsletter II/148
planning the design II/149
planning distribution II/151
first issue II/152

Personal solicitation
importance of donor research III/48
requesting the donation III/50, 56
rewarding the donor III/51
training canvassers III/52
making the case for support III/54
dealing with the donor's answers III/57
after the visit III/59
trying again III/60

Planning - long-range
what to include I/110
getting started I/111
the mission statement I/113
the right words I/115, 120
an attractive document I/117
planning components I/120
communicating the results I/130

Printed materials
analysis and planning II/124
capturing the readers attention II/129
effective design II/126
finding money II/128
good titles and openings II/129
business cards II/135
letterhead/envelopes II/136
symbols/logos II/134
poster planning II/138

poster design II/139
poster placement II/140
brochure design II/145
brochure planning II/141
brochures for fundraising III/20
degrees of impact III/20

Professional assistance
using consultants III/206
hiring consultants III/208
compensation for consultants III/209
hiring staff fundraisers III/211

Programs for fundraising
planning a project: an ad book III/23
approaching individual donors III/74
canvassing door-to-door III/75
street collections III/76

Service clubs and community organizations
researching the organization III/156
using your connections III/156
effective presentations III/157
putting forward a proposal III/158
following up on donations III/158

Speeches
rules for interesting writing II/15
finding opportunities to talk II/104
making a good impression II/99
preparing a presentation II/97
giving a speech II/100
holding the audience's attention II/101
when to stop talking II/103
using visual aids II/105

Sustainability/endowments
advantages III/234
disadvantages III/234
questions before starting III/235
making the plan III/236
community foundations III/237
advantages of community foundations III/239

Telephone campaign
is it a good idea? III/62
when is it effective? III/62

getting started III/63
effective conversations III/64
making the request III/66
completing the call III/67
follow-up III/68

Vision/mission
revising the vision I/40
keeping a sense of mission I/42
drafting a mission statement I/113
what is a vision statement? III/8
why have a vision statement? III/9
presenting the vision III/12
6 rules for good writing III/15
using images III/16

Voluntary organizations
stages of growth I/ix
finding new money I/x
future of small agencies I/xi
intelligence and determination I/18
record of accomplishment I/19
well documented projects I/19
necessary legal status I/20
good financial management I/22
good personal reputation I/24
the right name I/31
9 sources of strength I/34
18 areas to strengthen I/38
spotting trends I/46
reducing burnout I/46
personal contacts at office II/18
qualities of a senior manager II/28
role of the leader II/30
maintaining enthusiasm II/32

Voluntary organizations – self-evaluation
planning the research I/51
styles of research I/54
who to ask I/56
lists of questions I/56
good ideas from other organizations II/26
See also evaluation of fundraising

Volunteers
pros and cons of using I/75
why people volunteer I/76
find and enlisting I/77
questions for potential volunteers I/77
questions from potential volunteers I/80
assigning volunteers I/80
orientation and training I/81
13 rules for happy volunteers I/83
types of fundraising volunteers II/83
necessity of recognition I/86, II/75
company employees as volunteers III/167
See also programs for fundraising

Acknowledgements

Many thanks for their ideas, information, and time, all given generously, to Sunil Abraham, Prof. Ely Acosta, Fitri Aini, Dr. Duri Samin Akram, Owais Aslam Ali, Gavin Andersson, David Arnold, Rick Arnold, Eugenie Aw, Darlyn Baconguis, John Baguley, Alec Bamford, Hilary Bloom, Ann Bown, Tim Brodhead, Patricia Bryden, Eka Budianti, Anne Burnett, Gladys Calvo, Crouse Campbell, Hur Badilles Camporendondo, Sharon Capeling-Alakija, David and Dorothy Catling, Junko Chano, Chanida Chanyapate, P. Chatterjee, Sergio Chavez, Mathew Cherian, Florence Chirozwa, Rick Christ, Gayle Gifford, Murray and Indira Culshaw, Katalin Czippán, Jane de Sousa, Virginia de Souza, Bianti Djiwandono, Debora Dunn, Robert Dyck, Chakib El Hakmaoui, Federico Espiritu, Amin Fahim, Jaime Faustino, Richard Fehnel, Richard Fuller, Helen Fytche, Nancy George, David Gillies, Thisbe Glegg, Patrick Sanjov Lal Ghose, Oded Grajew, Ruth Groberman, Shelter Guni, John Gwynn, Anne Hamilton, Em. Haryadi, Mahmood Hasan, Gary Hawes, Charlene Hewat, Richard Holloway, Beverly Howell, Prof. Stephen Huddle, Komsan Hutaphat, Vandana Jain, Dra. Hira Jhamtani, Amelia Jones, Fred Musisi Kabuye, David Kalete, Judy Kamanyi, Elizabeth Kane, Zandisile Kanisa, Amita Kapur, George Kassis, Gurinder Kaur, Christopher Kedzie, Daniel Q. Kelley, Renata Kiss, Kim Klein, Wayne Klockner , Francis Kumbweya, Lee Hui Lin, Christina Lavalle, Rodrigo J. Llaguno, Melchora Logronio, James Gregory Lord, Ezra Mbogori, Malvika, Miklos Marschall, Livai Matarirano, Paula McEvoy, Stephanie Melemis, Chinwe Mezue, Louis Mitchell, Mokhethi Moshoeshoe, Horacio "Boy" Morales Jr., David Morley, Mohini Mubayi, Richard Mugisha, Robbie Muhumuza, Jane Nabunnya Mulumba, Leslie Ann Murray, Milton Murray, Kumi Naidoo, C. Shekhar Nambiar, Peter Nizak, Michael Norton, Paul Themba Nyathi, Ada Obi, Bridgette O'Connor, Silas Omanyo, Ir. Katarina Panji, Prasart Pasiri, Tommy Phillips, Kenneth Phillips, Richard Phinney, Jennifer Pittet, Dan Pizer, Tony Poderis, Prof. Amara Pongsapich, Mary Racelis, Douglas Ramage, Niresh Ramklass, Padma Ratnayake, Thabiso Ratsomo, Lance and Pen Reynolds, Neni Rochaeni, Oscar Rojas, Angela Rosati, Romeo Royandoyan, G. M Row, Eugene Saldanha, John R. Samuel, Vijay Sardana, Tamás Scsaurszki, Michael Seltzer, Margaret Sentamu, Hasan Sharif, Dr. Sudirendar Sharma, Bruce Shearer, Jennifer and Wesley Shields, Rosanne Shields, Dan Siegel and Jenny Yancey,

Professor Esperanza Simon, Brinda and Tejeshwar Singh, Victor Siburian, Ian Smillie, Barry Smith, Danilo Songco, Anne Speke, Per Stenbeck, Pushpa Sunder, Gary Suwannarat, Louis Tabing, Richard Tallontire, Martin Tanchuling, Senator Wanlop Tankananurak, Pam Tansanguanwong, Lawrence Taylor, Mattana Thanomphan, Jennie Thompson, Mark Vander Wees, Marianna Török, Sam Ugochukwu, Veerachai Veerachantachart, Richard Vokey, Goh Ruoh Wei, Rob Wells, David Wickert, Gordon Wilkinson, Ricardo Wilson-Grau, Judith Wright, Ken Wyman, Kikis Zavala, Wang Zhenjiang, the Mesoamerican partners of Horizons of Friendship.

Elizabeth W. Wilson
Port Hope, Canada
March, 2001

About the author

Elizabeth Westman Wilson is a Canadian consultant and writer with many years' experience in fundraising and communications, both overseas and in Canada. While living in the Philippines in the mid-1980s she acted as consultant in communications and fundraising to the president of the University of the Philippines, carried out fundraising studies, and gave workshops in communications in eight developing countries. From 1989 to 1996 she was executive director, Developing Countries Farm Radio Network, and from 1975 to 1984 director, information services at the University of Toronto. Ms Wilson is currently president, Horizons of Friendship, a Canadian agency supporting organizations in Central America and Mexico. She is also the author of two books on oriental ceramics.